MILITARY HISTORY OF THE WORLD

MILITARY HISTORY OF THE WORLD

A.K. Dixit

CYBER TECH PUBLICATIONS
4264/3, Ansari Road, Daryaganj, New Delhi-110002 (India)
Ph.: 011-23244078, 011-43559448 Fax: 011-23280028
E-Mail: cyberpublicationsdelhi@yahoo.com
Website: www.cybertechpublications.com

MILITARY HISTORY OF THE WORLD

A.K. Dixit

First Edition 2010

Published by :

G.S. Rawat for **Cyber Tech Publications**
4264/3, Ansari Road, Daryaganj, New Delhi-110002 (India)
Ph.: 011-23244078, 011-43559448 Fax: 011-23280028
E-Mail: cyberpublicationsdelhi@yahoo.com
Website: www.cybertechpublications.com

Printed at: Asian Offset Printers, Delhi-53

Preface

This book argues that the central factors determining whether a humanitarian war succeeds are the objectives of the intervention and the military strategy employed by the intervening states. Four types of humanitarian military intervention are offered: helping to deliver emergency aid, protecting aid operations, saving the victims of violence and defeating the perpetrators of violence. Military wars without a reasonable prospect of success is unjustifiable, especially when it is done in the name of humanity. Couched in the debate on the responsibility to protect civilians from violence and drawing on traditional 'just war' principles, the central premise of the present book is that humanitarian military intervention can be justified as a policy option only if decision makers can be reasonably sure that intervention will do more good than harm.

The focus on strategy within these four types allows an exploration of the political and military dimensions of humanitarian intervention and highlights the advantages and disadvantages of each of the four types. Yet it has become equally controversial not to intervene when a government subjects its citizens to massive violation of their basic human rights. Humanitarian military intervention is controversial. Scepticism is always in order about the need to use military force because the consequences can be so dire.

—Author

CONTENTS

1

Introduction

At the beginning of 1918, the prospects for the British Expeditionary Force (BEF) and its allies did not look promising. Russia had given up the war, the French army had suffered a serious mutiny and a considerable decline in morale in 1917, the Italian front had experienced a major setback at Caporetto in October 1917, while BEF morale was at a dangerously low level following the losses of the Passchendaele offensive.

This was reinforced by the shock of the German counter-attack after the Cambrai tank and artillery offensive in late 1917, when the German army was supposed to be in dire straits. Soon to come, in March 1918, was the German spring offensive and the precipitous retreat of the British Army's Fifth and Third Armies, with the loss of 40 square miles of territory. Yet in three or four short months, the tide turned and the BEF and allies went on to victory in 1918.

How did this happen? What changed in 1918 to enable victory to come about? There are a number of explanations, which, however, are not mutually exclusive.

For example, did new ideas make a difference? Did new tactics and strategy affect the outcome? Did new weapons and technology shift the balance, particularly tanks and aeroplanes? Or was success the result of using old technology, but much more of it? Was 1918 really a victory of attrition for the BEF, so that manpower was the key? Perhaps a revitalized GHQ leadership was crucial, with Douglas

Haig now coming into his own? Maybe the whole BEF had simply become more efficient, with army, corps and divisional commanders all improving?

Possibly the arrival of the Americans was decisive? Or did the Germans really defeat themselves through serious strategic mistakes and a subsequent loss of morale? Therefore, was the German offensive of March 1918 really the turning point of the war? Strangely enough, these questions have not been properly answered, and in most cases not even posed by those books that concern themselves with 1918. In fact, interpretations of what happened to the BEF on the Western Front in 1918 really fall into three categories. They are, first, the external or exogenous explanations, which attribute victory to German mistakes (particularly those of Ludendorff), or the American intervention, or the collapse of Germany's allies. Then secondly, there are the internal or indigenous explanations that focus on the decisive achievements of the BEF and the leadership of Douglas Haig, whether in 1918, or through the offensives of 1916 and 1917 which wore the Germans down and thus ultimately led to the collapse of German morale in 1918. Somewhat naturally, Haig himself, and his supporters, have espoused this explanation. Finally, thirdly, there is a variation of the latter (internal) explanation, which stresses the impact of new BEF technology in 1918, leading to improved BEF tactics and the wearing down of the German army. The present study will argue for a combination of all three explanations, but will emphasize German mistakes and the impact of the technology of the BEF.

Nevertheless, in attempting to answer the fundamental question of how the war was won, two themes emerged, plus a third subsidiary theme, and this book is really about these themes, and ultimately their relationship to the winning of the war. The first and most important theme, which runs as a central thread throughout, concerns the matter of command. Was 1918 really the triumph of Sir Douglas Haig and his GHQ? How did the BEF's overall command structure hold up from late 1917 to November 1918? Did the high command function well during the Passchendaele and Cambrai offensives? Then, in particular, did Haig and his GHQ organize the defence of the BEF against the German 1918 spring offensives in a sensible manner? Did the BEF's command structure conduct itself in an organized way during those spring offensives? Turning next to the midsummer Hamel and Amiens offensives, how did the command structure prepare for these Allied offensives? And during the necessary adaptations of the remaining months of the war, how relevant was GHQ and how did the rest of the command structure perform in mobile warfare?

The second theme relates to the innovation, acceptance and integration of technology into the BEF during this period. On the one hand, certain new or relatively new forms of technology became increasingly significant, particularly tanks and aeroplanes, but also Lewis guns, mobile trench mortars, smoke and gas, and this led, in fact, to the origins of mechanical warfare. How was this 'new' technology accepted, integrated and used in the BEF? What sort of new tactics were evolved for mechanical warfare, and did this entail a new strategy for winning the war? On the other hand, the BEF came to rely more and more on ever greater amounts of 'old' or traditional technology, especially the artillery, which was improved by increasing the number of heavy guns, and given greater range through streamlined shells; and the machine gun, which was turned into a corps, and given a wider variety of roles. How were tactics and strategy altered to fit the remarkable growth in the sheer numbers of this traditional technology, just as the supplies of manpower were dwindling in tragic fashion?

Finally, a third and subsidiary theme deals with the question of when the war was won. And here, it will be suggested that the war was 'over' much earlier than previous evaluations have concluded.

In late 1917 and 1918 certain images of war on the Western Front reflected some of the central issues of the period. There was, first, the most obvious aspect of war: death and burial, and what this implied in terms of manpower problems. Secondly, there was the image of an inadequate high command, and the question as to whether this was justified or not. And thirdly, there was the growing presence of the tank on the battlefield, and the relatively new experience of mechanical warfare. There was, first, therefore, the image of mass war and mass death. At the beginning of March 1918, the 1 Canadian Infantry Brigade defence scheme included an appendix outlining the procedure for the burial of soldiers killed in action. There were to be collection posts for accumulating the slain soldiers, and each battalion was responsible for bringing its dead to these collection posts. There, the bodies were to be taken charge of by the divisional burial party, who would send them by light railway to Aix Noulette cemetery for burial. No burials were to be made forward unless conditions were such that this was absolutely necessary, in which case statements must be forwarded to the division, giving reasons why this was done. Normally, however, each body at the collection post 'must be clearly marked showing name, number, rank, unit and date of death, also one ID disc is to be left on location of body'. Finally, the location of the divisional burial officer was noted, actually at 95 Grand Rue, Bully Grenay.

This was a sobering prospect, in which bodies were dealt with as the obverse of the living, with burial posts established just as collection posts were set up for the collection of stragglers during a battle. Or perhaps the dead were simply treated as the inanimate objects that they were, comparable in terms of transport to the artillery rounds carried on the very same light railway. Yet what these necessary arrangements really symbolize is not only the state of technical efficiency that the BEF had reached in 1918, but more important, that a crucial issue of early 1918 was the question of manpower—alive or dead. If dead, the men would be called 'liabilities', if alive, they would be seen as 'assets'. Either way, the problem was the rapidly declining numbers of men available in early1918, and the growing competition for these men between infantry, artillery, air, tank, machine gun and other corps, to say nothing of home demands for agriculture, transport, and industrial and war production. One important question, therefore, was: would the BEF have enough manpower for the forthcoming fighting in 1918?

A second scenario in 1918 concerns the capabilities of the high command. Would senior commanders and staff be equal to the decisive campaigns of 1918, or, failing that, 1919? One level of command that appeared to contain some officers of doubtful quality was the corps level, and one officer in question was the commander of VIII Corps, Lieutenant General Sir Aylmer Hunter-Weston. His senior officer in mid-1918 was Major General Bonham-Carter, who believed that although Hunter-Weston had a good brain, he lacked balance, perhaps because of sunstroke suffered in Gallipoli, so that his staff 'felt that he had never recovered completely'. According to another of Hunter-Weston's staff (his GSO 3, Major F.L. Freeman), the commander toured the front line one day in the summer of 1918, accompanied by a group of VIII Corps officers, taking notes. At one point, Hunter-Weston stopped the group and addressed them:

> 'Always T the T before T T T.' This, gentlemen, means 'Always teach the teacher before teacher teaches Tommy.' And a little later, when we arrived at a machine gun post, 'Notebooks, gentlemen please. Write this down.' 'The corollary of delegation of authority is intelligent supervision.' Every one of us was required afterwards to send in his notes.... They all, from the Divisional commander downwards, sent them to me so that I could vet them to see that they all told the same sort of story before they went in to the Corps Commander.

While Hunter-Weston was engaging in such mild eccentricities, his corps had not been idle in August 1918, a month of heavy fighting on the Western Front. VIII Corps was, in fact, preparing for its annual horse show on 24 August 1918:

> This was very exasperating to temporary officers like myself [wrote Freeman] because of course the last great advance had already begun, but the Corps Horse Show had to come first.... An enormous amount of work, time and money was being unnecessarily expended. The great Horse Show duly took place. The ground was a wonderful sight. There was a grandstand with bunting, there were marquees, there was lunch for about two hundred. The labour cost was at least £1,500 and the materials used amounted to as much. The lunch was most sumptuous.... [and] had caused much amusement beforehand. Turbot and grouse had been ordered from home, but the Food Controller had vetoed the latter. The former went bad, and the catering staff were busy fanning it and pouring lemon juice

on it to revive it. One of the aides went to Paris for salmon and ice. The salmon was unprocurable and the car broke down on the return journey, the bag in which the ice had been, arriving bone dry. However, everything went off with a flourish. The eccentricity of Hunter-Weston and the diversions of VIII Corps give pause for thought as to the quality of leadership of the BEF in 1918, especially as Bonham-Carter also remarked of another corps commander, Lieutenant General Sir William Pulteney (GOC III Corps), that he was 'the most completely ignorant general I served during the war and that is saying a lot'. It was no secret, either, that other BEF corps commanders in 1918, such as Lieutenant General Sir Herbert Watts (GOC XIX Corps) and Lieutenant General Sir George Harper (GOC IV Corps), were thought to be far from efficient. Indeed the then Lieutenant Colonel J.F. C.Fuller (GSO 2, Tank Corps and General Staff, War Office) recounted in 1918 a somewhat unkind story regarding Harper, which showed that particular corps commander to be backward in infantry tactics, just when it was essential to be open-minded in countering innovative German tactics. According to Fuller's informant, Brigadier General Hardress-Lloyd (GOC 3 Tank Brigade), in May 1918 Harper repudiated the new 'worm' infantry approach formation, which called for single file rather than the line formation, with a rather simple argument:

> 'Now,' exclaimed this old ass [Harper] 'If you were walking down the road with a girl how would you go?' 'Arm in arm,' answered H.L. [Hardress-Lloyd]. 'There you are', exclaimed old Harper.... 'Well General,' replied H.L., 'if you and the late Oscar Wilde were walking down a street together where do you think he would go?' Harper was very nearly taken out of the room in an ambulance.

Although these stories stress the less competent in order to make a point, yet there were sufficient numbers of these to raise the serious question as to whether the senior commanders in the BEF, from GHQ downwards, but especially at the important corps level, were good enough to win the war on the Western Front.

A third and final scene relates to the increasing importance of mechanical warfare, especially the role of the tank, and in particular whether the tank would be used in the best possible way. One vignette concerns the actions of the Tank Corps at Cambrai, in this case through the memoir of a tank driver in the 8th Tank Battalion, on the first day of the battle, 21 November 1917. The tank, named 'Hotspur', had crossed the Hindenburg Line successfully when we found ourselves in dire peril. A tank close on our right received a direct hit and burst into flames. I only saw one man roll out of the side door. The tank on our left also had a direct hit. I did not see anyone get out of that tank. All this time my officer and the side gunners were effectively using their Lewis guns.

Besides giving an interesting account of the experience of being inside a tank while it was actually hit by a shell, the memoir illustrates the very real vulnerability of the tank in late 1917 to artillery fire. However, Driver Brisco's story shows that his particular tank company was vulnerable just because it was obviously separated from the supporting infantry by a considerable margin, and thus there had been no proper tank-infantry cooperation in that particular action. Thus a central question was: would the tank be fully integrated and accepted in the BEF, and would mechanical warfare be the war-winning method of 1918 or 1919?

This prologue has focused on a number of key issues that faced the War Cabinet and the BEF in late 1917 and the first half of 1918, namely, manpower, leadership and mechanical warfare. These issues would be very important for the outcome of 1918, but they should be seen in conjunction with the efforts of the BEF in late 1917 and early 1918 to come to terms with how the war on the Western Front should be prosecuted, in other words, what strategies, tactics and methods might bring victory either in 1918 or 1919. Leaving aside the problem of whether to be on the offensive or defensive, the proposed methods of warfare (whether adopted consciously or unconsciously) really came down to four sometimes overlapping or exclusive choices, plus a fifth alternative, which really involved a question of fundamental attitudes toward warfare. There was, first, the infantry-artillery choice.

This approach emphasized manpower, the wearing down of the German army, and the general sense that more is better. More infantry and artillery was the key, but more of everything was bound to help. This might be termed the strategy of abundance, and by and large this was the choice of Douglas Haig and other senior members of GHQ such as Birch (Major General, Artillery adviser at GHQ); Lawrence (Chief of the General Staff at GHQ); Davidson (Major General, Director of Operations at GHQ); and Dawnay (Major General, Organization at GHQ). A second alternative was the mechanical choice. This stressed the introduction of mechanical warfare, primarily through the use of tanks and aeroplanes, but also a much greater use of the somewhat 'newer' weapons, namely, machine guns, Lewis guns, gas and mobile trench mortars. Some proponents of this attitude saw the tank as the war-winning weapon, around which other weapons should be combined. The members of this tank group thought of themselves as efficient prosecutors of war, countering the strategy of manpower abundance with one of scarcity—the saving of manpower by the efficient use of mechanical resources—and expected the fighting to conclude in 1919 with a massive tank attack. Somewhat naturally this group comprised tank enthusiasts such as Major General Sir J.E.Capper (Director General, Tank Corps), Hardress-Lloyd, Major General H.V.Elles, (GOC Tank Corps) and Fuller, but it also included others who were converted to this vision, such as Winston Churchill (Minister of Munitions), Henry Wilson (CIGS from 18 January 1918), Tim Harington (DCIGS), Aylmer Haldane (GOC VI Corps) and Major General William Furse (MGO).

The tank group was part of a wider set of supporters of mechanical warfare, who would include machine gun advocates such as Major C.R.Fay (GSO 3, Machine Gun Corps) and Lieutenant Colonel G.M.Lindsay (Machine Gun Officer, First Army), and the gas adviser at GHQ, Major General Harry Hartley. The mechanical warfare supporters might have termed their vision the strategy of mechanical efficiency. The third choice can be seen as a middle strategy, advocated by cautious progressives such as Lieutenant General Sir Henry Rawlinson (GOC Fourth Army) and Maxse (Inspector General, Training, GHQ). This group was in favour of mechanical warfare, but also considered the infantry to be the ultimate way of holding on to ground or achieving victory. Unlike the 'more is better' infantry school of abundance, they did believe in achieving results with a minimum of manpower, and unlike the mechanical war advocates, they still did see infantry and artillery as central, even if they were careful supporters of mechanical warfare. This strategy could be called that of the progressive traditionalists. A fourth choice lay with Lloyd George (British prime minister) and his supporters, who preferred to avoid the difficulties of the Western Front if possible, and instead either hoped for results elsewhere, such as in Turkey, or preferred to wait for the arrival of the Americans and a decision in 1919, using American manpower to a large extent. This attitude may be called the strategy of rational avoidance. Finally, and fifthly, there existed a basic division of opinion that was rarely articulated, but which tended to cut across all levels of thinking about strategy and tactics. On the one hand, there was the idea that the key to the future was the past. For example, the basic assumption of Haig and Lawrence at GHQ before the German March offensive was that it would resemble their own past offensives so that the BEF would be able to retreat slowly while inflicting heavy casualties on the German army.

On the other hand, there was the opposite perception, that the past was not a wholly reliable guide to the future and that it was possible to see warfare in different ways. This could be done through two main routes on the Western Front, either through tactical change, or through material innovation. On the whole, the German army made tactical changes, while the BEF preferred to make material alterations. For example, the BEF slowly allowed both old and newer weapons to find their own logic, and therefore separate out from the rest of the BEF as independent but concentrated arms or corps—this was true of the machine gun, the aeroplane and the tank—following the earlier example of the artillery. Tactically, these new weapons forced some changes, and were in fact the major means of BEF innovation in 1918, but it was the German army who produced new defensive and offensive infantry tactics, and who criticized the BEF for its 'stiff artillery creeping barrage', leading to the 'stiff, artificially conducted, material-breaching attack'.

One may therefore think of the followers of the past as adherents to the strategy of traditionalism, while in the BEF the supporters of innovation, chiefly through new weapons, can be seen as pursuing a strategy of flexible entrepreneurship. Another aspect of the past-oriented group at GHQ (the traditionalists) was their penchant for seeing things from the top down, leading to that artificial 'stiffness' so criticized by the German army, while the flexible entrepreneurs tended to design tactics from the bottom up. This contrast can be briefly illustrated through postwar German reflections on the differences between their offensive tactics and those of the BEF.

According to one German general, the structured and rigid offensives of the BEF denied the infantry any impetus of its own, did not lead to exploitation of tactical successes, and eliminated both the subordinate and higher leaders from exercising command. On the other hand, the new German offensive tactics were designed to allow subordinate leaders to exercise initiative, while the higher leaders were expected to economize their forces, to be careful about organizing immediately available reserves, and to be actually present on the battlefield.

This last injunction included divisional staff, corps commanders and even the army commander. In other words, flexibility was supposed to break down structure, and the past was not allowed to dominate the needs of the present. Such attitudes and ideas existed as an underlying conflict in the BEF throughout the remainder of the war and interrelated with the actual events of the war.

Meanwhile, the war on the Western Front had entered a critical phase in the second half of 1917, a crisis of inflexibility. Haig, Kiggell (CGS, GHQ until 24 January 1918) and Charteris (Brigadier General, Intelligence, GHQ until January 1918) at GHQ appeared inflexible in their running of the manpower-style operations on the Western Front and were supported in London by the CIGS, Robertson, and Lord Derby, the Secretary of State for War.

Lloyd George and his supporters felt the necessity of either breaking up this group by removal or outflanking them. Lloyd

George apparently feared what Robertson and the military might do, while Haig for his part was apprehensive as to the political intentions of Lloyd George. Tied to this political impasse was the crucial military question as to whether the war in late 1917 and early 1918 would be fought as primarily a mechanical-style war, or upon more traditional lines as a manpower war. This was the background for the fighting on the Western Front from Passchendaele to the end of the war.

PARALYSIS OF COMMAND: FROM PASSCHENDAELE TO CAMBRAI

The battle of Passchendaele revealed several fundamental planning and command errors as the campaign unfolded. Particularly obvious errors were the choice of the Passchendaele area as a battlefield; serious confusion over the objectives of the offensive, and the continuation of this confusion as the battle progressed; ambiguity over the type of offensive that was to be fought; the choice of Gough to command the offensive as GOC Fifth Army; and the continuation of the offensive in late 1917 when all hope of useful results had gone. In terms of the objectives of the Passchendaele offensive, it is worth pointing out that there were at least three aims expressed by Haig: reaching and clearing the Belgian coast; wearing down the enemy in preparation for a decisive offensive; and capturing the Passchendaele Ridge and the village of Passchendaele. (It is also worth noting that attrition—the killing of more enemy soldiers than BEF soldiers—was not one of Haig's specific aims.) By the time that the Cambrai offensive commenced in late November, the first aim had not been achieved, the second had been achieved only partially and the third was in the process of being achieved. Cambrai itself is well known as the first major tank offensive in the history of warfare, but after an initial remarkable success, the Cambrai attack also lost focus, realistic objectives were abandoned and, like Passchendaele, the offensive was carried on too long. Command failures then led to a reluctance to prepare for a German counter-attack, and subsequently the BEF high command failed to recognize the significance of the new German tactics used in the counter-attack, which would be employed on a larger scale in the spring of 1918.

The battle of Passchendaele, commencing on 31 July 1917, was flawed from the very beginning. One difficulty was that Haig, just as he was to do before the March 1918 German offensive, became overconfident and expected that the war could be won in 1917. It is true that there was some justification for this belief, since in 1916 the German Fifth Army had suffered some 572,855 casualties at Verdun between 21 February and 10 September 1916. Of these 75,000 eventually returned to the front from field hospitals, as did another 275,770 from temporary aid stations, but the casualty list was still formidable. In addition, there were approximately 500,000 German casualties at the Somme in mid- and late 1916. However, Haig overlooked the fact that in 1917 the German army had gone onto the defensive, and also planned to conserve manpower through new defensive tactics.

Thus Haig was mistaken when he told Robertson in early June 1917 that Germany was nearly at its 'last resources', and mistaken when he told the War Cabinet later in June that Germany was within six months of total exhaustion at the present rate of progress. By mid-July Haig was informing Rawlinson that all one had to do was press the Germans on all fronts, and the war could well be finished in 1917. Because of this confidence, Haig did not seem to be worried by some obvious problems that he actually admitted soon after the battle commenced; for example, that the front of the attack was too narrow; that the Germans had good artillery observation over Fifth Army positions, while his own guns were unavoidably exposed; and that the ground on the right was unfavourable for the attack.

Moreover, it is curious that Haig did not exploit the Messines success that had occurred earlier in June, and which his commanders Plumer (GOC Second Army) and Jacob (GOC II Corps) both wanted to pursue. Another major difficulty was that the objectives for the Passchendaele offensive went through several changes before Haig informed his army commanders on 5 July 1917 what the final plans were. Originally, in January, the idea had been to rush the offensive right through to clear the Belgian coast. This was modified, although mainly in order to reach the coast in stages, yet at the same time it was intended to capture the Passchendaele Ridge. Now there was some doubt as to which was the primary objective. In the end, Haig wanted to do both, and therefore neither objective was given the full attention it deserved. Haig's instructions on 5 July read that the Fifth Army would secure the Passchendaele Ridge, then after 'very hard fighting lasting perhaps for weeks' there would be more rapid progress northeast to gain the line Thourout-Couckelaere, where the offensive would continue north to join up eventually with a Fourth Army offensive along the coast from Nieuport to Ostend. There was also to be an amphibious landing, with tanks, on the coast, but this would take place only if the main Passchendaele offensive had already made the coast 'practically untenable' for the enemy. Haig also wrote that the first aim of the offensive was to drive the enemy off the ridge from Stirling Castle to Dixmude, which was puzzling since Dixmude was not part of the ridge, but was far to the north and could not have been part of the Fifth Army offensive, or even of the French participation on the north flank. However, the net result of these several objectives was that some of the key figures involved, including Haig, Plumer and Jacob, were more concerned with the immediate problem of capturing the Passchendaele Ridge, while others, such as Gough, Rawlinson, Davidson and Robertson, were more involved with what type of offensive 31 July would be—either a rush-through, or a step by step, limited objectives, advance.

In regard to the first problem—the emphasis on the ridge—one incident is of telling interest. This occurred when Haig told Rawlinson in early July 1917 that the key to Gough's attack was the Stirling Castle—Becelaere ridge (essentially the Passchendaele Ridge), and that this must be taken first before any other advance took place, and Rawlinson agreed but said that more important was the question of limiting Gough's objectives in the offensive. In fact, the problem of the ridge was directly related to the other problem, the breakthrough, or a step by step advance. Not only was the ridge a very formidable defensive obstacle, but there were particular problems on the right of the ridge, where not all of the high ground was included in the offensive, thus producing a vulnerable right flank. This was recognized by Davidson, who on 25 June 1917 bluntly told Major General Clive (British Liaison Officer at GQG, the French Army Headquarters) that Tactical difficulties of [the] Right flank make [the] idea of [a] big thrust hardly realisable.' This forthright appraisal either was not relayed to Gough, or did not make him alter his perception of the requirement for a breakthrough. Similarly, Haig either did not, or could not, impress on Gough the significance of the right of the ridge. Gough was simply not perceptive enough to take Haig's advice and see that the great weakness of his offensive was on the right flank. Even when the offensive was predictably held up on the right, Gough refused an offer from XIV Corps of an extra division for that flank, saying 'If you can't get on in one place, you must get on in another.' Unfortunately, this was just what could not be achieved and Fifth Army suffered heavy losses for the next month from problems on the right flank. Moreover, Haig further compounded the ambiguity of his offensive plans by his instructions to Gough, which were both to have a distant objective and to wear down the enemy. Not surprisingly, Gough was puzzled, but certainly still believed that he was meant to undertake a breakthrough.

Nevertheless, the basic choice for Passchendaele of a rush-through offensive (as Gough termed it), versus a limited series of advances, should have been a clear decision by Haig. It would seem that Haig was torn between his optimistic desire to achieve a striking success and, on the other hand, the limited objectives type of advance urged on him by a number of sources, including Davidson, Rawlinson (GOC Fourth Army), Robertson and the War Cabinet, which received backing from the forecasts of his chief of intelligence, Charteris. Yet Haig allowed Gough to go ahead with a rush-through style of attack, despite misgivings by other senior commanders. For example, Rawlinson's diary entries at this time are very instructive, starting with 25 June 1917 when Rawlinson learned for the first time of discussions at GHQ regarding an unlimited attack. On 29 June 1917, Rawlinson had a long talk with Robertson and advised him to 'hold on to Goughie's coat tails and ordering him [Gough] only to undertake the limited objectives and not going beyond the range of his guns'. Then on 3 July 1917, Rawlinson talked with Haig and urged him to make Goughie undertake deliberate offensives without the wild 'hurooch' he is so fond of and leads to so much disappointment. The rule is that they must not go beyond the range of their guns or they will be driven back by counter attacks. I am not sure that DH [Haig] will insist on this with sufficient strength and I fear that if he does not the attack may fail with very heavy losses. No doubt Rawlinson was remembering his own problems at the Somme, but his advice was ignored and on 21 July 1917 Gough declared that he was optimistic his Fifth Army would be able to get the (second) green line, and also, he hoped, the (third) red line, on the first day. (As it turned out, the red line was not obtained in the centre and south of the attack until 20 September 1917.) On 30 July, the eve of the offensive, Gough expressed great optimism that the attack would be a 'sitter' (that is, a sitting or easy target), but after the costly difficulties of the actual offensive of 31 July 1917, Rawlinson was able to report on 1 August 1917 that Haig had finally decreed limited objectives and 'no Huroosh! I am glad we have learned this at last.' Finally, on 5 August 1917, Rawlinson wrote that Gough was converted from his 'hurrush' style of attack to limited objectives, although on 9 August 1917, Rawlinson and his chief of staff, Montgomery, still felt it necessary to send a memo to GHQ outlining the utility of limited objective attacks, especially because of German defence in depth and counter-attack tactics.

Why couldn't Haig, as commander-in-chief, control his army commander, Gough, when setting objectives for the Passchendaele offensive of 31 July 1917? Partly because Haig himself evidently wanted to try a breakthrough offensive, which he had espoused as far back as January 1917, saying then that the 'whole essence is to attack with rapidity and push through quickly'; partly because Haig had accepted the advice of Plumer to try for a breakthrough; partly because Gough would not take advice; and partly because of Haig's belief that army commanders should be left to run their own battles.7 This last point is also illustrated by the possibility that the troublesome right flank of the offensive might be solved by attacking the area from the south and southwest. This plan was given to

Gough by Haig, but Gough refused to do it, and Haig again apparently did not insist. This 'hands-off approach was all the more curious in that Haig did not apparently fully trust Gough, since after one significant meeting on Passchendaele, Haig 'clearly hinted that whatever Gough said should be taken with more than a grain of salt.' This was a curious method of command in war, especially with a volatile, intolerant and unreceptive subordinate such as Gough. In fact, the whole decision- making process before Passchendaele was fatally flawed, with Gough being afraid to confront Haig over the plan, and at the same time an atmosphere of 'terror' operating in Gough's own army, so that 'none of his subordinates dared to tell him [Gough] the truth'.8 However, Haig was now stuck with a stalled offensive and a not very capable commander.

The solution was to bring in Plumer and his Second Army, and gradually phase out Gough, which occurred towards the end of August. Yet what were the aims of the Passchendaele campaign now to be? Originally, the Passchendaele offensive was supposed to aim for Roulers and the coast (Ostend), but this was clearly no longer obtainable. Instead the campaign now wavered between wearing out the enemy in preparation for a future decisive offensive—and capturing the Passchendaele Ridge and the village of Passchendaele as ends in themselves. Before the offensive began, the wearing-out option seemed feasible. Charteris had forecast that the German 1918 class of recruits had all been called up, and that the 1919 class of 450,000 men would start to appear in July 1917 and would be finished by about October, 'provided fighting is severe'. There was the expectation that German casualties of 190,000 in July, rising to 200,000 per month until October, would leave Germany with only 1,000 men available in depots by October.

In fact, in mid- to late August, Haig remained very confident, telling Major General Clive on 17 August that he was 'certain that by the end of September we shall win the battle, if we go on hard', and then at the end of August scornfully remarking that the new German defence in depth system, which utilized shell holes rather than trenches as protection for the forward zone, was 'simply the refuge of the destitute'. Haig was confident, therefore, of continuing to execute the original plan, which included the Fourth Army landing on the coast, but which would ultimately lead to his traditional concept of drawing in and using up the German reserves, and then launching 'the decisive attack', as he told the CIGS, Robertson, in late August.9 In fact the 'decisive offensive' did take place on 20 September 1917, and again on 12 and 26 October 1917, although without the results anticipated. Yet despite the image of mud and blood and inept leadership that the battle of Passchendaele evokes, it is well to remember that in September and October 1917, the BEF was successfully employing an unprecedented volume of artillery fire, as well as other forms of technology against the German army (on 24 August 1917, Charteris estimated that the BEF was using 5,496 guns against 2,557 German guns), and from the point of view of an involved but dispassionate commander such as Maxse (GOC XVIII Corps), the BEF was winning the battle. For example, Maxse reported that his corps' attack on 20 September 1917, using gas, tanks and a heavy creeping barrage, resulted in a gain of over a thousand yards, and great numbers of Germans killed and wounded. Maxse wrote that this proved

PARALYSIS OF COMMAND

'Haig was right and the croakers were wrong again as usual'. Then on 4 October 1917, Maxse wrote of a brilliant victory, with his corps gaining all objectives. On the other hand, there were certainly disastrous and bloody failures, as on 9 October 1917, when Lawrence's 66 Division arrived late at the starting line, because of the swamps. The troops were taking 12 hours to cover 2 1/2 miles, and they were therefore one hour behind the barrage, and so suffered 6,000 casualties.

As a means of attempting to come to some conclusions about the wearing-out option, casualty figures, however unpleasant, might provide some direction, although these figures are notoriously unreliable. One historian, using official figures, advances the estimate of 448,614 BEF casualties for the period of Passchendaele as against 270,170 German casualties. More recently another historian sees 200,000 German casualties, as against 250,000 British; and very recently a third historian includes contemporary figures for the whole of 1917, which result in estimates of 822,000 BEF casualties, and roughly 1,000,000 for the German army.

Although accuracy may be impossible, it seems that a reasonably close evaluation was that of the British official historian Edmonds, who estimated 271,031 BEF Passchendaele casualties, and 75,681 for Cambrai. It is at least possible that German casualties for the period July to December 1917 might have approached BEF casualty figures more closely than is generally acknowledged, except by Edmonds.11 If so, the bloody strategy of traditional wearing-out operations at Passchendaele may have given encouragement to some commanders such as Maxse, even if there were other, less costly options available to GHQ, such as Messines-type operations, or the future tank assault at Cambrai.

However, as the autumn of 1917 waned, Haig appeared to become less interested in wearing-out as a strategy, and instead became preoccupied with obtaining the Passchendaele Ridge and the village of Passchendaele as aims in themselves. As was reportedly said at GHQ: 'When we get the Ridge, we've won the war', while Brigadier General Tudor, commanding the artillery of 9 Division, wrote in his diary in late October 1917, that Haig was determined to capture the Passchendaele Ridge and that all else was forgotten. The ridge and the village of Passchendaele had become symbolic to Haig, who hated to change his objectives. Equally important, however, was the fact that he believed only in Flanders could decisive results be obtained, and indeed only in Flanders could the war be won.

Yet in discussing the capture of the village of Passchendaele, both Haig and Charteris could point only to its tactical significance, and both stressed that its capture had required only 700 casualties, as though this itself was a justification for the attack. However, a memo by Haig in mid-October 1917 points to another important reason for capturing the village and the ridge—it was that 'we shall have excellent artillery positions and complete cover behind our starting line'. In other words, the ridge was primarily useful as a jumping-off place for the next BEF offensive in 1918! Clearly, there was no other importance to the place, and indeed the strategic aims of the Passchendaele campaign, apart from wearing out the enemy, had long since disappeared in the slow progress of August and September 1917. In fact, a conversation between Haig and his liaison officer with the French, Major General Clive, in late September 1917, revealed a dichotomy in Haig's thinking. Haig told Clive that he believed the Germans would sue for peace over the winter, but that he hoped peace would 'not come' because Germany could be finished off next year.

This was because Haig did not want peace to arrive before the German army had been cleared from French and Belgian soil. Nevertheless, Haig's comment to Clive implied that he did not want the wearing-out option to succeed in 1917, which was presumably a major justification for continuing Passchendaele. But then Haig went on to say that Germany 'has lost all the high ground at Verdun, Morouvillers, Chemin des Dames, Vimy, Messines, and probably Ypres; her troops will be in the water'. This would seem to indicate that Haig was thinking of Passchendaele as a simple battle for gaining high ground—a traditional nineteenth-century army attitude. It is probable that in the later stages of Passchendaele Haig did not clearly know what he wanted.

Afterwards, Haig, Charteris and Davidson all attempted to argue that the Passchendaele offensive had been continued as late as November because of entreaties from General Pétain (French Commander-in-Chief), who pointed to the poor state of morale in the French army, which had earlier in 1917 suffered mutinies. However, it is crystal clear that Haig had always intended to continue the offensive in the hope that the Germans might crack; that already in mid-July Haig knew the French army was in better shape; and in fact far from protecting the French army, Haig was pressing hard for French offensives during the Passchendaele campaign. It may even be, according to Major General E.L.Spears, head of the British military mission to Paris in 1917, that it was Haig and not Pétain who thought the French army was capable only of minor operations! Finally, it is probably the case that Pétain would have preferred that the BEF take over more of the French line rather than continue the Passchendaele offensive. Ironically, it was less than a month after the end of the battle of Passchendaele in November 1917 that Haig was forced to tell his army commanders it was necessary to go on the defensive, move the guns back, and that there must be a defence in depth system, which 'avoids the present salient caused by our occupation of Passchendaele'. In other words, the ridge may or may not have been useful as an offensive starting point, but it was a definite liability for defensive purposes.

Even worse was the suggestion the next day, 10 December 1917, by Rawlinson, that because the sharp salient at Passchendaele allowed overwhelming German artillery fire upon it, therefore it was necessary actually to give it up in order to get a better defensive line. Rawlinson stated that such material considerations outweighed any 'sentimental' considerations. This was truly a very sad conclusion to the loss of life in acquiring the Passchendaele salient, purely as a result of an offensive that went on too long. However, it would appear that sentimental considerations did after all remain paramount, because Passchendaele was given up only in April 1918 when the German Lys offensive compelled its evacuation.

The seemingly meagre results, and the loss of life of the Passchendaele offensive, were strongly criticized by Lloyd George, who gave a powerful speech to that effect at the Inter-Allied War Council in Paris on 12 November 1917. Other leading politicians now also turned against Haig and GHQ, and their wearing-out option, including Lord Milner (Secretary of State for War), Smuts (South African Representative at the War Cabinet) and Bonar Law (Chancellor of the Exchequer), and it appeared that Haig's days were numbered. But Haig gained a surprising, if temporary, respite from criticism with the launching of the Cambrai tank offensive of 20 November 1917.

The idea of a surprise tank attack in 1917 was first suggested in a memo of the McMullen committee on 8 January 1917, as that committee struggled to fashion plans for the future Passchendaele offensive. But the suggestion was for an attack in the northern sector, in conjunction with clearing the Belgian coast. Then in early August Fuller and Elles put in tank raid schemes to GHQ, one for the Third Army Cambrai sector, and one toward Lille, in the First Army area. GHQ turned over the proposals to First Army, who liked the idea, but did not have enough divisions for either project, while Byng, GOC of Third Army, was also supportive. Third Army also received a combined tank and artillery attack scheme in the Cambrai area from Brigadier General Tudor, CRA 9 Division, on 23 August 1917.

However, these schemes were downgraded into an attack on Lens with the Canadian Corps and two battalions of tanks, and then came to nothing. Meanwhile, in early September, Major General Elles was proposing further tank raids to GHQ, but believed that if a big tank attack was planned in 1918, then tanks should be saved for that purpose, and Haig agreed on 10 September 1917. This was GHQ's opinion at this time, with the exception of possible tank raids in the Ypres and Lens areas. However, on 18 September 1917, Elles proposed a much more ambitious plan to GHQ, to take place on First Army front, utilizing a large number of tanks. This document was actually the key turning point in launching the battle of Cambrai.

Elles's plan, however, initially received short shrift at GHQ from Lieutenant Colonel Tandy (GS, GHQ) and Davidson, and the attack was shifted from the First to the Third Army front, probably due to Byng's visits to GHQ. However, Tandy believed that Elles's idea of 144 tanks 'was a much larger number than had hitherto been considered at GHQ as being likely to be needed'. Tandy also understood from Byng's chief of staff, Anderson, that Byng saw the tanks as subsidiary in the proposed attack, although this was no doubt a deliberate deceit in order to placate the backward-looking staff at GHQ. Hence, Davidson commented on the proposal that 'the maximum we will allot [of tanks] is probably 54, if less, so much the better'. However, Byng managed, with difficulty, to persuade Kiggell and Haig that the larger tank plan was feasible, although Kiggell now raised the major objection that since Passchendaele was in full swing, there were no troops available. Haig therefore called in Davidson's deputy, Tandy, in early October, as Davidson was absent, and asked for four or five specific infantry divisions for a tank operation at Cambrai. Tandy was forced to deny Haig the particular four or five divisions he had asked for, as they were not then fit for operations, but guaranteed 'two or three', and promised a further 'three or four more which he wanted'. This exchange seems to suggest that Haig always planned to use a limited number of divisions for the operation, and so the staff at GHQ were equally unwilling to supply more than a limited number of divisions, given the continuation of the Passchendaele offensive. At one point, Byng was promised the Canadian Corps, and with these troops felt he could take Cambrai. But again the needs of Passchendaele caused the Canadian Corps to be withdrawn from the Cambrai operation.20 In the end seven infantry divisions were used, with another two in reserve, plus five cavalry divisions and three tank brigades. Later, this lack of infantry strength in the attack, and particularly in the reserves, was to be a major point of criticism. And clearly, the Canadian Corps would have been better used at Cambrai than at Passchendaele.

The key to the Cambrai operation was surprise, and this was now possible due to three factors. First, large numbers of Mark IV tanks were available to crush lanes through the wire and overcome the immediate defences rather than rely on a lengthy preliminary artillery bombardment, which told the enemy exactly where the attack was to go in, and also churned up the ground and impeded the advance. Secondly, the artillery was now able to do counter-battery and suppression work, and fire a standing and lifting barrage, without previous registration, thanks to the development of field survey and calibration techniques over the autumn of 1917. And thirdly, some higher commanders such as Byng had grasped the fact that surprise was now essential to success. Indeed so committed was Byng to surprise that he himself was disguised as a Canadian when visiting front areas, while the tank experts, Elles and Fuller, wore trench coats and black goggles!

Nevertheless, Byng had some difficulties in persuading his own artillery to carry out the attack without previous registration. According to the GSO 1 of Third Army, this artillery plan was 'bitterly opposed by all artillery officers'. Moreover, Byng's own MGRA, Lecky, expressed doubt that the no registration plan could be carried out, but to his credit, Byng was determined to achieve surprise, and Lecky was forced to accede. Lecky's reservations were of some substance, because the delivery of accurate fire from a battery without previous registration depended on four factors: the accurate position of the battery and the target, the meteorological conditions of the moment, the calibration of the guns, and the supply of consistent ammunition. The accurate position of the battery had already been established at the Somme, Arras and Vimy attacks through the use of bearing pickets, and the location of enemy batteries had been solved to a considerable extent through the use of sound ranging techniques developed in 1917. Meteor telegrams had also made their appearance during and after the Somme, to give correct wind and temperature readings every four hours, so that it remained for accurate calibration of the guns to be achieved. This was done through sound ranging behind the lines, but this system was only perfected in Third and Fourth Armies in the autumn of 1917. Indeed Major General Birch, artillery adviser at GHQ, was not even aware in December 1917 that this system was fully operational. Finally, the supply of consistent ammunition could not be guaranteed, but a system of grouping shells by weight and date of manufacture was introduced at Cambrai, and proved beneficial.

The artillery survey teams worked feverishly to get the system in place for the offensive, and the last task was tackled at 2 a.m. on the morning of the assault, 20 November 1917, which was timed for 6.20 a.m. It is worth noting that the lack of previous artillery registration enabled the guns to be undetected, and thus moved much further forward than before, and this in turn enabled the artillery to conduct something of a 'blitzkrieg'style barrage on 20 November. The concept was to produce a swift attack, which required only the neutralization rather than the difficult destruction of both enemy guns and positions. Thus enemy batteries, assembly points, observation points, main routes, communications, command positions, villages, approaches and billets of reserve troops, were all targets in the early dawn of 20 November. Gas and high explosive shells were used, and the lifting and standing barrage in support of tanks and infantry was to fire one third smoke, one third shrapnel and one third high explosive. However, it must be said that the success of the initial advance was at least partly due to the fact that German artillery was not numerous. In fact the German 54 Division, occupying the greater part of the front to be attacked, had only 34 field artillery pieces in all, while the British artillery disposed of over 1,000 field and heavy pieces. This was amazingly one- sided, and the mismatch showed up in the relatively few BEF tank casualties as the offensive started. So, while approximately 360 tanks took part, only 65 received direct hits on the first day, for an 18 per cent loss rate. Even this would have been smaller had not some errors in tank-infantry cooperation been made.

Therefore, the other crucial aspect of the attack—the tanks—had considerable advantages built in to their offensive, namely, surprise and a very strong artillery barrage. But GHQ at this time thought of the tanks as simply an 'adjunct' to the attack of the other arms, and neither GHQ nor Byng insisted sufficiently strongly on the most careful cooperation between infantry, tanks and artillery. Thus when J.F.C.Fuller urged Byng to hold some tanks in reserve, Byng replied, 'I cannot go against the wishes of my Corps and Divisional commanders.' Fuller believed that Byng was 'far too soft to be a good general'. Despite two weeks of training in tank-infantry cooperation before the attack, there were instances of commanders who simply refused, or were unable, to comply with tactical rules. One well-known example was Major General Harper, GOC 51 Division, whose infantry followed the tanks in waves some 150 to 200 yards behind, instead of close up in 'worm' formation, leading to failure in front of Flesquières village. Harper was afraid that the 'worm' following the tank would be enfiladed by machine gun fire. (Harper's staff also turned down assistance from the two divisions next to them, 6 Division and 62 Division, which if accepted could well have resulted in the early capture of Flesquières.) But there were others with similar cooperation problems, such as Brigadier General Walker (GOC 16 Infantry Brigade, 6 Division), who admitted that training before the battle was poor, with tanks represented by flags only, while in the actual battle his men apparently had great fear of being crushed by a tank, and so did not stay close to the tanks either.

Then there was Brigadier General Berkeley Vincent (GOC 35 Brigade, 12 Division) who stated that only 9 of 36 tanks did well in his sector, because several ditched, so that 'Many platoons wandered about looking for tanks to follow'.

A good example of the problems of tank—infantry cooperation, despite success in that sector, was the report of the 7th Battalion, Tank Corps, whose 50 tanks accompanied 62 Division on 20 November, which attacked on the left of the offensive, towards Havrincourt and Graincourt. The initial attack was a success, but the infantry evidently fell behind as the assault reached a depth of 7,000 yards at Graincourt village, and six tanks were put out of action by two field guns in front of the village. There was obviously no artillery or infantry support for the tanks at this point, and the tanks themselves had to silence the two field guns with their 6-pounders. The story of Tank number G3, which caught fire in Havrincourt village, is another example of how tanks and infantry got separated. When the tank was alight, the crew was forced to abandon, but the tank commander went back to fight off German attacks on the tank:

> In a few moments a fresh party of the enemy made a rush and some of them got close up to the tank, one of them even attempting to get inside. This man and eight others the Tank Commander shot with his revolver. Another party then attacked the crew with hand grenades, and the Tank Commander opened fire with a Lewis gun, killing one and wounding four.... Two of the crew were missing and the rest were going back for them when a party of our infantry reached the village. The crew shouted warnings to them, but just then about a hundred Germans came out of their trenches with their hands up and a few minutes later others came out of dugouts in large numbers and surrendered. Apart from the successful conclusion of this operation, the most striking aspect of the story was the large gap in time and space that had obviously opened up between Tank G3 and its supporting infantry.

Up and down the line on 20 November, much the same had occurred. Although there were many problems in cooperation, as in the example of the 7th Tank Battalion, and in the stubbornness of Harper and his refusal to adapt 51 Division to the tanks, the initial attack had been a great success, due in equal measure to the tanks, surprise and the artillery. Yet cooperation between all the arms was not given top priority, and was not enforced, or perhaps was not even recognized as lacking by the higher command. This was particularly true of the cavalry, where the commander of the Cavalry Corps, Lieutenant General Kavanagh, did not seem sure of his objectives before the battle, and therefore was not likely to be able to exploit the success of the other arms. Major General Haldane was present at the only Cambrai conference before the offensive, and he recalled that Kavanagh 'was vague as regards his intentions. Next day Byng came to my HQ, and discussed his plan and prospects and when I hinted that Kavanagh did not seem decided as to what he would do he said that he would do all right on the day. Byng seemed hopeful of a great success, but was prepared either to gain some ground only or even not succeed'.

Quite apart from Kavanagh's vagueness, there was also the well-known problem that Kavanagh was far to the rear in his HQ at Fins, and was thus out of touch with the offensive. This is only too true, but even so there was also an inflexibility about the cavalry that made exploitation difficult. Thus, 5 Cavalry Division was told not to advance until the Masnières- Beaurevoir line was reached— and this was not reached partly because the leading battalion of 29 Division stopped to drink beer for half an hour at Marcoing and hence missed crossing the canal there. Similarly, Byng's ADC declared that the cavalry were imbued with the idea that they could not advance until Flesquières was taken.30 Kavanagh's absence from the front line was certainly a key factor in the cavalry's failure to exploit, but there was an Advanced Cavalry Corps Report Centre near La Vacquerie which could have filled Kavanagh's place. Yet even here, Major General Greenly (GOC 2 Cavalry Division), who might have sent the Cavalry Corps through, was told by J.K.McConnell (Brigade Major of 88 Infantry Brigade) not to proceed because only a lock crossed the Canal de l'Escaut in front of them. Perhaps because of this advice, in the late afternoon of 20 November Greenly told Brigadier General Seely (GOC Canadian Cavalry Brigade) that it was too late in the day to advance. Seely had also apparently failed to reconnoitre other crossings over the canal, and certainly there was a by-pass bridge available at Masnières that the Fort Garry Horse did cross on its own initiative. Probably the comments of two participants sum up the cavalry involvement in the exploitation phase of Cambrai. Berkeley Vincent (GOC 35 Infantry Brigade) argued that an infantry battle and a cavalry battle were superimposed on the same ground, but that they were not coordinated. Meanwhile, J. F.C.Fuller knew that Kavanagh was miles away from the battle, and was 'surely the worst Cavalry general in all history'. Thus 'Cambrai failed because it was rotten at the head.'

Fuller drew four tank lessons from the early stages of Cambrai, some of which refer to command decisions. First, that the narrow base of the attack at 10,000 yards was too small for a large tank operation. This was really GHQ's responsibility. Secondly, that a reserve of tanks should be held back, for exploitation. This was Byng's error. Thirdly, that the depth of penetration was really limited by the infantry man's endurance, of some eight to ten thousand yards. This should have been clear from previous offensives. Finally, that tanks had great difficulty in clearing villages. This was really a matter of experience only gained at Cambrai.

But all in all, the initial phases of Cambrai had been a considerable success. Yet it was at this point—the end of the first day—that the battle started to go wrong. And from the point of view of the future German March offensive in 1918, the German counter-attack of 30 November was actually the most significant aspect of the whole Cambrai battle, since the BEF could have recognized that the German army was using new offensive tactics.

On the evening of the first day at Cambrai, there was a basic decision to be made, as the GSO 1 of Third Army, Gervase Thorpe, recounts. When the cavalry failed to get across the canal at Marcoing or Masnières to exploit, the main objective of the battle had not been realized. Thorpe argued that when this situation was clear there was a vital decision to be made. This was:- 'Was the battle to continue as a frontal assault?' Or 'Were we to consolidate on a selected portion of the captured front and repeat the process elsewhere?' To us as Third Army Staff this was the problem in front of the C in C when he came to discuss future operations with the Army Commander. (I cannot remember exactly when this was, but it was about 6pm on the 20th). We, the Staff, strongly favoured the second selection. Douglas Haig, a determined man who hated to change his objective, selected the former. From then on the scale of casualties was progressively against us.

Later, in a letter to another member of Third Army staff, Thorpe was more decisive: 'Douglas Haig was quite obstinate and determined the battle should go on, when it should have been obvious that the failure to get a footing over the Marcoing canal made the main objective unobtainable. It was this decision of Douglas Haig's which made the setback later on inevitable.' Thorpe was not clear, however, whether Byng agreed with Haig, but if he had disagreed, Thorpe was clear that Byng would have been too loyal to say so. Byng's attitude toward Haig, as outlined by Thorpe, reveals a fundamental flaw in the command system of the BEF. Nevertheless, Thorpe's point of view about the continuation of the offensive may have gained in hindsight, since Haig had previously set a 48-hour time limit for reconsideration of the battle, and there was some justification for Haig deciding to proceed on the second day.

However, on the second day, when the offensive advanced on the two wings, one toward Bourlon Ridge and Wood, the other toward Masnières and Marcoing, the latter advance stalled, and so the thrust of the offensive shifted toward Bourlon Wood. It was at this point that the attack should have been halted, as was later admitted by Davidson, who conceded that the operation was based on a surprise breakthrough—'when that was out of the question it should have been called off. Davidson believed that the delays caused by the Flesquières ridge on the first and second days were serious enough 'to warrant the abandonment of the operation as soon as its effect was realised (ie., on the day when the C in C rode over the battlefield). I think it was about the third day of the battle; I was with him and remember it well.' And the reason the offensive should have been broken off was quite simple: 'we had not the requisite forces to persist in the operation after the first serious check.' In other words there were not sufficient reserves to pursue the battle. Why then did Haig order the offensive to continue? After all, he had ridden over the battlefield and knew the situation, and Davidson remembered that 'it was clear, after the first two or three days, that substantial German reinforcements were being brought up'.

Haig evidently continued partly because he hated to change his objectives, but partly because he saw himself as locked in a struggle with Lloyd George for control over direction of the war. Haig also feared for his job, and Lloyd George's 12 November speech to the Inter-Allied War Council had been a direct criticism of Haig. Now as he told his wife on 25 November, the success of Cambrai was the best reply to Lloyd George's criticisms 'and his attempts to set aside me and my views on military plans'. These feelings apparently interfered with Haig's thinking and persuaded him into the unwise decision to continue. Byng in turn felt the pressure, and equally forced unwise orders onto his unfortunate corps and division commanders, who were caught between front-line realities and their army commander. For example, Haldane (GOC 3 Division) was ordered on 24 November to attack along the trench line of the Hindenburg Line because the tanks no longer had fascines and could not cross the trenches, and so had to attack along the flanks. On learning of the plan, Haldane's GSO 1, Kearsley, leaned over to him and said in a whisper, 'You cannot carry out such an attack.' Similarly on 26 November, urged on by Haig, Byng sent out orders to 62 and Guards Divisions to take Bourlon (the ridge) and Fontaine. Feilding (GOC Guards Division) complained strongly to Woollcombe, his IV Corps commander, but neither Byng nor Woollcombe listened. As one of Feilding's brigade commanders later reported: 'It was criminal to have launched this attack—I know Feilding did his best to avoid doing so, but got little backing from the Corps Cdr.' After intense fighting and counter-attacks from fresh German troops, the 62 and Guards Divisions withdrew from Bourlon and Fontaine.

Thus far the Cambrai offensive was following the same depressing formula as the Somme and Passchendaele campaigns, if on a smaller scale—a battle carried on too long and with no clear objectives. And as at the Somme and Passchendaele, the command structure showed similar weaknesses in communication between the army commander, Byng, and his chief, Haig. Byng was unwilling to oppose Haig, and this must have played a key role in Third Army's reluctance to act on reports of a forthcoming large-scale German counter-attack. In fact the story of the German counter-offensive and subsequent breakthrough on 30 November 1917 anticipates March 1918 with each level of command blaming the other for what followed. It also seems to be the case that the further each level of command was away from the front line, the less urgency or apprehension there appeared to be over the forthcoming German attack. Thus Kiggell recalls the rather casual comment of the Third Army commander before the German counter-offensive: 'I remember Byng telling me, some days before it came, that he rather expected some move by the enemy on Jeudwine's [GOC 55 Division] front.'

Dealing only with the German counter-attack in the southern part of the Cambrai line, the chain of command stretched from Third Army to VII and III Corps, and from there to 29, 20, 55 and 12 Divisions. At the divisional level, there was much concern about the anticipated counterattack, but when it came at 7 a.m. with a fierce bombardment, followed an hour later by the infantry, there was something like panic. A staff officer of 6 Division, Standish Crawford, remembered that 'the whole of the high ground in our rear...was covered with men like Epsom Downs on Derby Day, and we realized some great disaster had taken place.

The men we saw were the 20th and 12th Divisions coming back from their front line in full retreat!' Later on, Crawford met the GOC of 29 Division, de Lisle, who asked him 'if I knew where his Division the 29th were' (de Lisle had managed to escape wearing only his pyjamas and great coat). And at about the same time, Crawford came across officers of the Heavy and Siege batteries supporting 12 Division, who were drunk and looting a brigade HQ of 6 Division. Crawford's observations were not unusual—for example, the GOC of 12 Division went back to Advanced Division HQ at the village of Fins during the battle, and stayed there until ordered back to his division.39 Overall it appeared that three divisions were in full retreat—20 and 12 in III Corps, and 55 in VII Corps. What had gone wrong?

The commander of 55 Division, Jeudwine, had apparently issued several warnings of a forthcoming counter-attack to his VII Corps superior, Snow, who had passed them on to the Third Army commander. For example, Jeudwine reported in January 1918 that

> On the evening of 28th November as a result of personal reconnaissance from the front line trenches, I made a report to the BGGS VII Corps [Burnett-Stuart] stating definitely that I considered an attack probable and giving full reasons. He said that the [VII] Corps commander [Snow] was thoroughly aware of the situation and that it had been reported to the Army. I asked whether I should send a report in writing. He said that it was unnecessary.

According to several sources, Byng did not seem unduly concerned with these warnings, and neither did III Corps under Pulteney. Furthermore, the Intelligence staff at Third Army, and those at GHQ, did not appear to have picked up indications of a German attack, and clearly underestimated German morale. Thus, Third Army refused to believe that the Germans were strong enough for an assault—a belief that was shared at GHQ.

If neither GHQ nor Third Army was listening, or they were perhaps too concerned with Bourlon Wood in the north, how did the two Corps commanders cooperate and react? This was of importance, because the place at which III and VII Corps adjoined was a steep valley called Banteux ravine, where troops could see the opposite side of the ravine, but little of their own side. Judging by Lieutenant General Pulteney's (GOC III Corps) own report, there does not seem to have been any anticipation of the German attack, and Third Army could not explain why one of III Corps' divisional commanders, de Lisle, had been taken by surprise. Even stranger was III Corps' refusal to use its heavy artillery to assist the neighbouring 55 division (in VII Corps), on the far side of Banteux ravine, with counter-preparation at 5 a.m. on 30 November. If this counter-preparation had taken place, it would have materially affected the German assault and might well have broken up the offensive before it began, but Pulteney would not agree. Jeudwine reported that During the 29th November, owing to my weakness in Field Artillery, and to the fact that the only Corps Heavy Artillery [in VII Corps] available to support the Division were four 6" hows., and as I was anxious to bring annihilating fire to bear at dawn on bridges and assembly places of the enemy, my CRA arranged with CRA 12th Division [the division adjoining 55 Division] that 5 Heavy Batteries of III Corps, which had been placed at disposal of 12th Division, should carry out this fire. Late the same evening the BGGS VII Corps [Burnett-Stuart] on the telephone personally informed me that the use of these guns could not be allowed. I represented strongly the importance of the action for which I wished to use them, but he informed me that the III Corps would not allow them to be used.

Subsequently, the GSO 1 at III Corps defended himself by arguing that Third Army paid too much attention to Bourlon Wood and neglected their sector, and that the brigadiers of 12 and 20 Divisions could not make their men dig defences because they were too tired. Both of these remarks were accurate, but still did not explain why III Corps did not allow its heavy artillery to fire the counter-preparation. According to Major General Scott (GOC 12 Division in III Corps) the staff at III Corps told him that the heavy artillery arrangements made between 12 and 55 Divisions were not his business, and could not be done. In other words, heavy artillery was the responsibility of corps and not division, which was true enough, but clearly III Corps simply did not take the situation seriously. According to Edmonds, 'Snow had full knowledge of the German counter attack coming, but Byng refused to credit it. Snow had asked Pulteney to concentrate his guns on the Crèvecoeur hollow [on 20 Division front] where the Germans were massing, but Pulteney would not'.

Thus far VII Corps has emerged as the more alert of the two adjoining Corps, but other evidence suggests that VII Corps was not without fault. Jeudwine of 55 Division hints in his reports that the BGGS of VII Corps (Burnett- Stuart) was not strong enough in supporting his requests for artillery support, and in a later discussion with Liddell Hart, Jeudwine remarked that the MGRA of VII Corps

(Major General Knapp) refused artillery action at Banteux ravine, despite Jeudwine's warning. Moreover, it appears that it was VII Corps as well as III Corps which actually refused to do counter-preparation on the morning of 30 November, because VII Corps did not want the 5 a.m. harassing fire programme to be carried out unless the SOS signals were sent up by the infantry for urgent and immediate artillery support. This was all the more critical as SOS signals were apparently not seen on 55 Division's front, perhaps because of mist and fog. In his report, Snow's defence was to blame III Corps, and to argue rather lamely that there were insufficient guns in VII Corps for the purpose.

It would seem, therefore, that a certain paralysis of command had seized the corps commanders and staff of III and VII Corps, as well as the Third Army commander and his staff, to say nothing of GHQ. As a result, Third Army lost 7,500 men (mostly as prisoners) and 162 guns, as well as much of the ground gained in the initial attack of 20 November. In order to explain this, a Cambrai court of inquiry was held in January 1918. Not surprisingly, the Third Army commander, Byng, avoided any personal blame, denied that the attack was a surprise and instead fixed the reverse, not on his corps commanders, but on the safer target of the lack of training of junior officers and NCOs.

Byng also blamed his machine gunners for the loss of two villages, Villers-Guislain and Gonnelieu, but was later forced to withdraw his comments about this as incorrect. It was soon very clear that the Cambrai court of inquiry was going to avoid asking awkward questions and was not going to search very thoroughly for any command failures. Indeed, one of the two corps commanders involved, Pulteney, was on leave, and neither he nor his staff were required to contribute any remarks on the reports of his three divisions, including 12 and 20 Divisions. Still more remarkable was the fact that neither Byng nor his chief of staff were called as witnesses. Instead, the proceedings of the court soon focused on the question of lack of training of the troops, especially the machine gunners, and on the lack of doctrine for the defence in depth, and in fact on the lack of doctrine generally.

The actual causes of the success of the German counter-attack are not hard to find, and they principally relate to command failures on the part of GHQ and Third Army, who did not anticipate the attack, believing the Germans not to be capable of a major effort. If GHQ and Third Army did have an area of concern, it was not in the south, but in the northern Bourlon Wood area. Of the two corps commanders, Pulteney was sceptical of a German attack and only Snow took the German threat more seriously, due to warnings from Jeudwine, his 55 Division commander. But even Snow did not do his job, which was to coordinate the defences where III and VII Corps joined, and to force his MGRA to coordinate properly their heavy artillery defences with III Corps. It may also be the case that Snow was simply too old to command with vigour—he was nearly 60—and as the future victor of Alamein was to say of Snow in regard to the battle of Arras in April 1917: 'Snow was of course quite useless; he was an old man and ought to have been sent home long before.'

Finally, it was left to the unfortunate divisional commanders to try to save the situation, but their divisions were to a large extent left unprotected. Although there were other contributory factors for the Cambrai reverse—the thinness of the line, the lack of artillery and reserves, the tiredness of the troops, the poor join of the two corps at Banteux ravine, the German surprise, the lack of defence in depth—the final judgement must be that it was a command failure. And ultimately this command failure resulted from an inflexible system, which operated as a totally 'top-down' system of decision-making, rather than a combined 'top-down' and 'bottom-up' structure. Thus when the warnings of the attack came from 55 Division, these warnings ran into greater and greater resistance the higher they went. Hence the divisional level was caught in the inability of the corps and army structures to communicate with each other.

From the point of view of the future, there was perhaps an even more important omission in the results of the Cambrai court of inquiry than the command failure. The court of inquiry was not going to search out specifically German reasons for the success of the counter-attack. In other words, there was little appreciation that the German army was trying something new in its attack methods. There was a report from a GHQ interrogation of German prisoners that stressed the intense artillery bombardment, surprise and weight of the attack. However, this interrogation evidently was looking for the causes of the retreat of specific BEF units. And there were divisional reports that emphasized the short but powerful artillery barrage, the use of gas, smoke and low-flying aircraft, and the successive lines of German infantry using 'Artillery formation'. Again, however, these reports somewhat naturally focused on the operations of BEF units. Therefore, it was not surprising that the lessons learned from Cambrai did not recognize the new German stormtroop tactics, but the BEF instead focused on tactical training—learning defence in depth, and improving cooperation between tanks, air, artillery and infantry. These were worthy aims, but only a few such as Rawlinson and General Smuts recognized at the beginning of January 1918 that with the BEF now on the defensive, the German army might again try the same tactics as were so successful in its Cambrai counterattack. On 13 January 1918, Rawlinson urged Haig to send around the 'Lessons of Cambrai counter attack' report because the anticipated German offensive in 1918 would model itself on that attack. Haig said he would so so, although up to that time he had curiously neglected to circulate the document. Then in a memo to the War Cabinet on 3 January, Smuts wrote that 'the enemy may have been encouraged to expect a repetition on a larger scale of what has happened at Cambrai. It remained to be seen whether GHQ would pay attention to such advice.

2

Traditional and Mechanical Warfare

At the beginning of 1918 a struggle took place for control over the conduct of the war on the Western Front between Haig and his supporters on the one hand, and the British prime minister, Lloyd George and his supporters, on the other hand. One way for Lloyd George and the War Cabinet to exert control over the Western Front was to regulate the flow of manpower, and this was attempted. Another method was to change key personnel at GHQ in France, as well as the CIGS, and this was done. Finally, there was an attempt on the part of certain individuals, particularly Winston Churchill as Minister of Munitions, to change the way the war was actually fought on the Western Front. This took the form of a concerted effort to replace the traditional infantry-artillery form of warfare with a manpower-saving mechanical form of warfare, employing such weapons as tanks, aeroplanes, machine guns, mobile mortars and gas. This potential shift in the conduct of the war generated a stiff debate through the first half of 1918 and beyond, between the mechanical and traditional warfare supporters, particularly over the role of the tank.

Neither Robertson nor Douglas Haig recognized in late 1917 and early 1918 that the Cambrai tank-artillery operation and the German counterattack meant that warfare was changing. In fact, Haig's comment to his wife on the German counter-offensive of 30 November was that it would be good for the BEF officers who were 'getting careless by reason of our uninterrupted successes all this year'. Nor was Haig willing to accept that Russia's leaving the war had altered the balance on the Western Front, so that as late as mid-December 1917, Haig did not expect a German offensive in spring 1918 because of their losses in 1917 of 'nearly a million men against the British alone'. Instead Haig aimed to continue his wearing-down offensive policies of 1917 on the Western Front, although Robertson was less confident about sticking to such a policy. But Haig's point of view really provoked a crisis of inflexibility, in which the past- oriented Commander-in-Chief clearly did not mean to change his structured concept of the wearing-out battle, leading to the decisive offensive at the decisive point on the Western Front.

Haig's inflexibility ran into contrary ideas expressed by Lloyd George and the majority of the War Cabinet, who had had enough of BEF casualty figures at Passchendaele and Cambrai (a total of 346,712 according to Edmonds, the official historian), and who decided to gain control of operations on the Western Front. This was all the more necessary because of Haig's deliberate refusal to face the facts—perhaps a psychological defence mechanism; for example, on 2 August 1917, Haig calculated BEF casualties on the first day of the Passchendaele offensive and remarked that they compared 'most favourably' with the attacks at Vimy and Arras. Although Haig himself wrote down the figures of casualties per division employed, he simply ignored the results, which were that the Passchendaele offensive of 31 July 1917 had cost 1,258 casualties per division, as compared to 1,003 for Vimy and 1,170 at Arras. It was not surprising, therefore, that Lloyd George and the War Cabinet decided that one way of gaining control, or at least improving efficiency at GHQ, was to change the staff, and a host of new appointments were made in late 1917 and early 1918—Lawrence as the new chief of staff; Dawnay as Major General Organization; Maxse as Inspector General Training; Cox as chief of Intelligence, replacing Charteris; Hartley to take charge of gas warfare; Wace to organize the disregarded area of Labour; Crookshank to control Transport; Heath as new chief engineer; Dill, Fuller and Nethersole to do liaison and make the staff at GHQ more efficient, and so on. As one member of the GHQ staff later acknowledged with a note of resentment: 'Over a curiously wide range of subjects swept a wave of reform and retrenchment.'

Lloyd George and the War Cabinet also decided to firmly control manpower; to go on the defensive and wait for the arrival of the Americans; to send troops to Italy; to order Haig to take over more of the French line; to form a general reserve; and to unify the Allied command either under a Supreme War Council or under one supreme commander. Haig reluctantly accepted the staff changes at GHQ, but fought against all the other decisions (apart from the arrival of the Americans), regardless of their value and regardless of whether they would enhance the war effort of the Allies, for two reasons only. These were that he wished to retain his overall command of the BEF without outside interference, and he wanted to maintain his idea of an offensive in 1918, preferably in Flanders.

Haig's reaction to just one of these War Cabinet policies is worth pursuing. On the question of taking over more line from the French, Haig mounted a two-pronged defence. On the one hand, he argued that the decision to extend the British line beyond Barisis was really a question of whether he or the Inter-Allied War Council at Versailles was responsible to the government for 'his army'—in other words, whether Haig enjoyed full powers of command or not. On the other hand, Haig argued forcefully with the French that he could not agree to the defensive exercise of extending the BEF's line, when instead he should be going on the offensive. It was better to go on the offensive, and therefore attract double the number of German divisions, than to extend the line and stand on the defensive, which would hold only the same number of German divisions as before. In fact, it was essential to go on the offensive in 1918 on the Flanders front in order to clear the coast as the great strategical objective. Thus Haig's primary objection to the BEF taking over more of the front was because of his projected offensive.

Haig's attitude toward the offensive and his position as Commander-in- Chief also applied to other areas. This was particularly true over the question of his authority. For example, the real reason that Haig did not want a general reserve formed was apparently because this would place a greater authority than his own over his actions, so that Lloyd George could force his views onto Haig. He (Haig) also told Lloyd George that no one could give him orders except for the Army Council and a field marshal senior to him. Thus, as he wrote to his wife in November 1917, Lloyd George would not be able to modify the way 'I carry out my duties here', despite the attempts of the Prime Minister to 'set aside me and my views on military plans'. Similarly, Haig would not hear of the possibility of an Allied Commander-in-Chief, who would of course diminish Haig's authority.

The conflict between Haig and Lloyd George escalated with Lloyd George's speech on 12 November to the Inter-Allied War Council in Paris; with the German counter-attack at Cambrai on 30 November; plus the decision to send divisions to Italy; the creation of the Supreme War Council at Versailles; and the organization of a cabinet committee to take control of manpower in December 1917. So much so, that Haig began to have apocalyptic visions of what was happening. According to Haig's letters to Lady Haig, in late 1917 and early 1918, Lloyd George was afraid of Haig because he had the army at his back, while Lloyd George wanted to discredit him and then break up the army into factions. Haig believed, correctly, that Lloyd George also wanted to get rid of Haig, but was afraid to do so. A little later, Haig thought that Lloyd George wanted to turn Britain into a republic, but to do this he had to get rid of the army first. The only way to do this, considered Haig, was for Lloyd George to discredit the army leaders and put in civilians instead (which he believed had been tried at the earlier Calais conference). Then in. early March 1918, Haig told his wife that if he could have a go at reorganizing the House of Commons with the army at his back, with his own audience, and with the press well in hand, he would be popular!

All of this reflected Haig's shaky position at the end of 1917 and the beginning of 1918, and his curious lack of introspection or self-reflection —he simply could not imagine that any criticism directed against his army leadership and ideas might have any merit. (The closest Haig came to admitting responsibility for reverses was to threaten to resign, but perhaps he never actually intended to do so.) Although Haig may have been only half serious in his political suggestions to Lady Haig, his political solutions probably did reflect his real wishes. Strangely enough, Lloyd George may have had the same illusions about the army leadership as Haig had about Lloyd George. According to Lord Beaverbrook, (owner of the Daily Express and Minister of Information), at the end of 1917 'Lloyd George, convinced that Robertson and his military colleagues now aimed at over-throwing the Government and setting up a new administration under Army control, determined that he must get rid of both Robertson...and Haig'. Lloyd George succeeded only in regard to Robertson, who was forced to resign over the creation of a competing military executive in Versailles. Then Lloyd George sent out General Smuts to the Western Front in January 1918 ostensibly because 'he [Lloyd George] did not know many of the various generals at the front', but really with the intention of finding a better commanderin-chief than Haig.

The names of Jacob, Plumer and Rawlinson were suggested as possible replacements for Haig, but the plan came to nothing. This was partly because no one could be found who was significantly better than Haig, partly because enough of the army still had faith in Haig, partly because of the uproar that would be created by Haig's resignation, and partly because Haig was already being neutralized via Military Representatives in Versailles and the forthcoming appointment of Wilson as CIGS, who would act as the 'real' Commanderin- Chief.

So with Haig temporarily secure in early 1918, but with Lloyd George and the War Cabinet exercising greater control over GHQ, especially regarding the question of manpower, what were the alternative strategies for Haig and the War Cabinet on the Western Front? It is roughly at this point in time that an important division of opinion in the army and in London occurs regarding the direction of the war. Although there was general agreement to go on the defensive on the Western Front, and wait for the Americans to arrive, there was also the question of how the rest of the war was to be fought, and how the manpower shortage was to be dealt with. It appears that two basic alternatives emerged, which might be termed the mechanical means of warfare, versus the traditional means of warfare. On the one hand the mechanical supporters advocated the use of 'new' technology (particularly tanks and aeroplanes, but also innovations such as mobile trench mortars, gas and smoke) which would be more efficient and would replace manpower, while the other school of thought stressed the use of manpower (infantry) in the traditional manner, and advocated using more of the 'traditional' technology, such as rifles, machine guns and artillery, but did see the 'new' technology as a useful auxiliary tool.

The underlying causes of this debate were the decisions of the Cabinet and Supreme War Council committees in late 1917 and in January and February 1918 to deny manpower to the Western Front, and the ordering of priorities so that shipbuilding, aeroplanes, tanks and food production came ahead of men for France. Originally, on 24 November 1917, GHQ had estimated that infantry manpower would be 250,000 below establishment on 31 March 1918. One suggestion to deal with this difficulty was simply to maintain 31 divisions at full strength and break up the remaining divisions to supply the original 31 with men. The Army Council rejected this plan, and instead decided on 10 January 1918 to reduce battalions in the BEF from 12 to 9 in each division. GHQ responded by requesting 615,000 men for the Western Front in early 1918, but they received only 100,000 'A' men. Nevertheless, according to one source, a comparison of manpower on 1 January 1917 and 1 January 1918 showed that there were actually only 70,000 fewer fighting men on the Western Front in 1918 than in 1917. This may have been reasonably accurate, since postwar figures prepared by Lieutenant General Sir Herbert Lawrence, chief of staff at GHQ in 1918, revealed that the total of all BEF personnel in France, both combatant and non-combatant, was 1,365,394 on 1 January 1917 and 1,949,100 on 1 January 1918. However, much of the 1918 advantage was due to a large increase in labour from 87,832 in 1917 to 354,577 in 1918. (This, in passing, tends to refute GHQ's claim that it was short of labour before the German offensive of March 1918.) However, looking only at fighting troops of all kinds, Lawrence's figures show 1,077,343 on 1 January 1917 and 983,399 on 1 January 1918, for a decrease of 93,944 between January 1917 and January 1918. Since Lawrence's figures did not include the Royal Engineers for 1917, and since technical troops tended to increase markedly through the war, the original number of 70,000 fewer combatant men at the beginning of 1918 than in 1917 probably was reasonably accurate. In an army of around a million men, however, this represented only a relatively small difference of some 7 per cent. And it was certainly possible to achieve the same efficiency as before by maintaining the same number of divisions with fewer men, but with greater firepower, as in the German army, and as suggested by Foch. This option was rejected by Haig and by others at GHQ. But the key point is that the past-oriented emphasis at GHQ and elsewhere on manpower and wearing down produced the strong impression that the BEF was short of men, and this set the stage for the discussion between the two schools of thought represented by the manpower and mechanical warfare advocates.

The 'new' technology advocates were led by Winston Churchill, who set out his proposals in a paper on munitions prospects, dated 21 October 1917. In this paper, Churchill concluded that the way to inflict a decisive defeat on the enemy on the Western Front was by mechanical means and not by manpower: 'If, therefore, we could by organized mechanical processes and equipment impart this faculty to our armies in 1918 or 1919 [of advancing continuously], it would be an effective substitute for a great numerical preponderance.' The means by which this would be done involved a further emphasis on artillery, but particularly a development of the air weapon, trench mortars, tanks, gas and railway or mechanical mobility. Churchill also advised applying these mechanical means to what he called the battle of Surprise rather than the 1916 and 1917 battles of Exhaustion.

On 23 November 1917, on behalf of the 'traditional' school, Haig replied to Churchill's document with caution, but argued that the true use of guns, mortars, gas, aeroplanes and tanks, 'is as an aid to infantry. Without sufficient and efficient infantry machinery can neither win victory in offence, nor save us from defeat in defence.' Curiously enough, given that the successful tank offensive at Cambrai had occurred only three days earlier, Haig went on to state that 'Tanks under conditions suitable to their use are of great value and to some extent, for certain purposes, are capable of replacing numbers of guns and economizing infantry. But suitable conditions for their employment cannot always or even often be found.' Haig's conclusion was that 'an insufficiency of infantry cannot be compensated for by a development of machinery beyond a certain point'.

Churchill's paper and Haig's reply were sufficiently significant for a conference to be held on the subject, on 5 December 1917. However, the report of the conference shows that Haig and his supporters in GHQ, as advocates of the 'traditional' school, emerged victorious from this debate. For example, the conference downplayed the importance of tanks and argued that for a large tank attack to succeed, 'Favourable weather, that is misty conditions, seem necessary'. The report conceded that tanks had certain advantages, for example, surprise, but that 'to exploit the Tank to the prejudice of rifle and manpower would be bad policy, and would end in exalting the servant above the arm it exists to assist and serve'. The recommendation was that in future the Tank Corps should be limited to 27 battalions of 60 tanks (1,620 tanks) and an establishment of 22,500 men (as opposed to the then establishment of 18 battalions). The conference concluded by stating that the infantry establishment should first be placed on a footing satisfactory to Sir Douglas [Haig], and that only then should manpower be applied, in sequence, to aircraft, artillery, transport, locomotives, tanks and rope railways.

The argument between the two schools of thought was complicated by a number of factors. Focusing only on tanks as the central feature of mechanical warfare, it was the case that there were several tank designs, with the Mark V, first used at Hamel on 4 July 1918, being considerably advanced over the Mark IV, which was used at Cambrai. The Mark V was particularly improved in the area of steering, so that now one man could control the tank rather than the four men required for the Mark IV.

Therefore, attitudes toward tanks tended to change over time, as the tanks became more reliable. Nevertheless, Haig and the senior staff at GHQ clearly saw the role of tanks as simply existing to assist the infantry, but for two reasons. First, tanks were obviously machines, and being inanimate objects, therefore by definition could not gain or hold ground. And second, stemming from earlier experiences in 1916 and early 1917, tanks were not seen as mechanically reliable and therefore could not be given a major role. These two sentiments were expressed in Haig's November 1917 reply to Churchill, quoted above, and in the GHQ tank policy statement of August 1918, which argued that tanks could only assist the infantry, because infantry 'is the only arm which can seize and hold a position, and upon its skill and endurance depends the security of the defence'. The memo agreed that tanks could materially assist the advance of the infantry, but 'it is unwise to place too much reliance upon mechanical contrivances'. This document really reflected the way in which the tank, as a piece of technology, tended to retain its original characteristics of adjunct to infantry, and as mechanically unreliable, thereby delaying more favourable views of its potential, just as the evolution of the machine gun was delayed because of its own original mechanical flaws. The GHQ document therefore imagined a past-oriented and manpower-centred battlefield in stressing the need for tanks to cooperate with other arms in assisting the infantry, but contained a hint of uneasiness in admitting that 'As the speed of tanks is developed and their machinery perfected, it is possible that their tactical employment may develop and that their role may become more independent'. But this goal was evidently thought by GHQ to be some way in the future, for in July 1918 the VI Corps commander, Haldane, went to a tank demonstration and remarked that the GHQ staff were anti-tanks and were preventing Haig from seeing them. This may have been partly because there was a push on by the Tank Corps to break up cavalry units and put them in tanks, since there was little manpower available for the tanks.

GHQ's negative but apprehensive view of the growing power of the tanks was further reflected in its ambiguous approach to the Tank Corps. After initially conceiving of the Tank Corps as similar in structure to the Royal Flying Corps, an analogy which Elles approved of (although the War Office did not), GHQ settled down to a contradictory policy of either depreciating the value of the Tank Corps, and thus not issuing a policy on tanks at all until August 1918, or of attempting to take over the tank weapon. There were many complaints in early 1918 of the attitude of GHQ (and the War Office) toward tanks. J.F.C.Fuller told Churchill in March 1918 that 'GHQ is inert and will lay down no policy', and in June 1918 he reported that GHQ acted as a post office concerning tanks, because it did not know them and therefore could not formulate policy. Fuller believed that both the War Office and GHQ were devoid of the means of acquiring and sorting tank knowledge and experience. Soon after, Elles declared that the General Staff at GHQ simply 'won't function on Tanks and this has its effect throughout the Army' because 'Armies get no guidance from above except by suggestion'. As late as July 1918, the Deputy CIGS remarked that the tanks 'have never had a policy' from the General Staff. GHQ finally issued a tank policy in August 1918, but it was apparent to both Elles and Major General Sir J.E.Capper (Director General Tank Corps) that the real problem lay in not having a senior tank adviser at GHQ, like the artillery, and in not having tank advisers in each army, again like the artillery. A Supreme War Council document in May 1918 declared that 'the Tank Corps should be represented on the General Staff [GHQ] in the same way as is the Artillery, otherwise there must be misuse of tanks through a lack of understanding of their powers and limitations'. Similarly, a War Office conference in late June 1918 advised the appointment of a Tank General Staff officer at GHQ, and the acceptance of GOC Tanks as tank adviser to GHQ.

Eventually, the War Office itself was reorganized with a tank staff, but at GHQ there was no change. Essentially the Tank Corps was commencing the same long-drawn-out process as occurred earlier with the artillery in fighting for, and eventually being granted, staff advisers at the highest levels. But Haig and GHQ were simply unwilling to grant higher status to a new arm which did not accord with their vision of the battlefield.

If one GHQ attitude was scepticism regarding the tanks, the other alternative envisioned at GHQ was to try to take over the tank weapon in some way. Even in the early days of 1916, Butler and Wigram at GHQ were apparently lukewarm about the tanks, but had their own plans for taking them over. However, the appointment of Lieutenant Colonel Elles to command the Tank Corps in 1916 prevented their ideas from working out. Thereafter, the Tank Corps developed its own staff, tactics and defenders. Meanwhile Haig's attitude to the Tank Corps was simply that it join the army—in other words that it maintain its role as adjunct to the infantry—and thus come under the orders of army and corps commanders. This in turn meant that the Tank Corps would not exist as an arm, but come under the direct control of GHQ. In fact, by the end of August 1918, Haig was writing that ' "Tanks must join the Army" and manoeuvre on similar lines to Infantry, ie. in accordance with FSR [the prewar Field Service Regulations] volume 1'. He went on to order a leaflet saying that the GOC of the attacking force should be in control of how tanks were to be used. It was not surprising, therefore, that the General Staff at GHQ were puzzled as to what to do about the tanks, and why, with no Tank Corps staff officer at GHQ, and little knowledge of tanks, they should have trouble coming up with a tank manual.

Under some pressure, GHQ made an attempt to produce a tank manual in June 1918, but it was delegated by Major General Dawnay to Major Headlam (GSO 2 at GHQ), who, according to Fuller, 'knows nothing about either Tanks or Tactics'. Then when Elles looked in at GHQ in early June 1918, he found Dawnay attempting to answer a paper on tank organization written by General Capper. According to Fuller, Dawnay was working off notes supplied by Lieutenant General Butler, who was now III Corps commander, but who had never seen a tank off the parade ground. 'Though Elles is nominally the tank expert', wrote Fuller, 'this answer [to Capper] was not going to be referred to him. Butler's suggestions were what one might expect from an intensely stupid man.' Subsequently, Tim Harington, the Deputy CIGS, assured Fuller he had spoken to Lawrence at GHQ about these problems and that things would now get a move on.6 However, GHQ did not really improve on the subject of tanks, instead the tank attacks of July and August 1918 were proposed and organized by Fourth Army, and the general BEF advance of the remaining months produced a negative attitude toward the tanks. A different and opposing view to that of GHQ was expressed by Major General W.T.Furse, Master General of the Ordnance (MGO), who in his notes on the report of the conference of 5 December 1917, declared that the conference had shown insufficient appreciation of the value of the tank. 'I know no soldier who suggests that tanks can win victories unaided by infantry and artillery. It would certainly be "bad policy" to "exploit the tank to the prejudice of rifle and manpower", but to fail to make sufficient use of the tank as a means of gaining victories in combination with a reduced number of infantry would be an even worse policy.' Furse went on to criticize the excessive use of infantry in the attack: 'It is here that in my opinion our tactical methods are at fault—We have been far too conservative in our preconceived ideas of the necessity of using our infantry in what may practically be called "massed" formations. One or 2 Divl. Comdrs. & Corps Cdrs. have to my knowledge broken away from this.' Furse suggested instead using tanks, smoke and artillery with fewer infantry. Clearly, Furse was attacking the past-oriented option of manpower and wearing down, and the inflexibility that went along with it. He also recommended an establishment of 2,160 tanks and 35,000 tank personnel. To obtain the manpower for this, Furse suggested the cavalry be reduced, or if this be vetoed, even an infantry division might be broken up. A similar approach was taken by the tank commander in France, Elles, who wrote to the then CGS, Kiggell, in early 1918. Since manpower was the key, 'every effort should be made to supplement the manpower at our disposal by machine power'. Elles suggested tanks and aeroplanes as a 'new method of warfare', but Kiggell was very doubtful.

The difference between the advocates of mechanical warfare and the advocates of traditional infantry methods, was in fact quite evident. Haig and GHQ were perfectly willing, and in fact, eager, to use aeroplanes, tanks, trench mortars and so on, but thought of mechanical means as strictly auxiliary to the use of infantry, and did not think through the use of new weapons. On the other hand, the mechanical advocates thought of the 'new' technology (particularly tanks and aeroplanes) as of equal or greater importance than the infantry, and argued their case by starting with the technology first, and then visualizing the battlefield, rather than starting with a preconceived, manpower battlefield. A good example of this was a paper by Lieutenant Colonel Ollivant, liaison officer with the French Tenth Army. In May 1918, Ollivant believed that an equilibrium had been reached, and suggested breaking the stalemate by using the Allies' superiority in aircraft and especially tanks. But his primary principle was that it was necessary to visualize the weapon and its role first (the battle), and then work backwards to organization and manufacture.

In discussing mechanical warfare, it will now be useful to focus on the tank as the centrepiece of mechanical warfare. Although other weapons were involved, such as aeroplanes, gas and machine guns, nevertheless the BEF itself thought of the tank as the touchstone or benchmark of mechanical warfare. The debate over mechanical warfare versus traditional (infantry) warfare continued through 1918, with a growing number of converts to the mechanical thesis. For example, there was the new Inspector General of Training, Maxse, who on 13 March 1918 was reported as wanting to win with Lewis guns, Maxims and tanks. The day before, on 12 March 1918, Rawlinson had read Churchill's munitions proposals, which he interpreted as wanting to win with mechanical devices, especially tanks and machine guns. Even though in February 1918 Rawlinson had had little time for the tanks, he now wrote in his diary that with command of the air, and plenty of tanks, it could be done.9 Then, on 13 March 1918, the Inter-Allied War Council at Versailles, under the signature of Rawlinson, produced a memo entitled 'Notes on economy of manpower by mechanical means'. This anticipated that the Allies would be on the defensive in 1918 and so advocated a series of very large raids, utilizing plenty of tanks and low- flying aircraft, which would thus economize on manpower: 'it is suggested that tanks, escorted by low-flying armoured aeroplanes, should be the chief weapon to clear the way for the infantry'. This saving of casualties through mechanical means would be even more the case because ground was not to be held, rather the raiders would withdraw to their original lines. Apart from the withdrawal suggestion, this mechanical scenario was in fact the basis for Rawlinson's future attacks at Hamel in July and at Amiens in August. By the end of April, therefore, Elles believed 'we [the Tank Corps] now have a firm backer in Sir Henry Rawlinson', and this was correct, although Rawlinson's support was based primarily on the principle of saving infantry casualties. Rawlinson was in fact one of the moderate supporters of the tanks, and after the war confirmed this view by expressing the contention that the tank enthusiasts spoilt their case by overdoing it—but they were on the right lines. This debate between the supporters of mechanical warfare and those of infantry-based warfare, was in fact a critical argument, and would set the scene for much of the fighting to come—would it be primarily traditional or would it be primarily mechanical warfare? Chances were that the traditionalists would win out in the short run, partly because of problems in weapons production, partly because mechanical innovation met with opposition from deeply held theories as to what warfare was all about, partly because of lack of direction at GHQ, partly because it was simpler, and partly because of uncertainty over whether to seek a decision in 1918 or 1919 (the traditionalists such as Haig and some at GHQ favoured 1918, while the mechanical warfare supporters looked toward 1919). All of this created too much confusion or 'noise' for a clear-cut decision in favour of mechanical warfare.22 Thus the preamble to a tank report from the Inter-Allied War Council at Versailles in May 1918 postulated that the introduction of the tank created two violently antagonistic schools of thought—the enthusiasts and the ultra conservatives. But the report went on to place the tank within a wider context:

> The aspirations of the most advanced school of thought are not confined to the ordinary use of tanks as a help to Infantry. They go much further. The enthusiasts hope to win the war rather by mechanical than by muscular means; that is by a wholesale use of aeroplanes, machine guns, tanks, gas, and motor transport.... It has

even been suggested that aeroplanes, machine guns, tanks, and gas should be combined in a Mechanical Warfare Section, with its own representatives on the General Staff. We may regard the acceptance of any such idea as very improbable.

This report was correct in stating that a basic decision had to be made as to whether the war was to be won with mechanical means, or by traditional means. But it was wrong in dividing the army into two such widely separated schools of thought, for Haig and GHQ did accept and welcome mechanical forms of warfare as auxiliary resources. Indeed Elles pointed out later that while the army had originally been divided into only two groups—those who believed in the tanks, and those who disbelieved—by about the middle of 1918 there was a considerable body of opinion in the middle that was prepared to weigh the advantages and disadvantages of the new weapon. Therefore, Elles's argument, the attitudes of Haig and GHQ, and the conversion of Maxse and Rawlinson as moderate supporters of the tanks in 1918, lead to the question of how senior officers did relate to the tank weapon after Cambrai. Four broad categories can be identified. First, there were the obvious enthusiasts such as Fuller, Elles, Capper, Churchill, Furse and those in the Tank Corps, who saw the tank as the primary war-winning weapon. Second, there were the moderate to strong supporters such as Maxse, Monash (GOC Australian Corps), Rawlinson, Wilson, Harington, Haldane and some divisional and corps commanders, who believed that mechanical warfare could win the war in 1918 or 1919, and who often saw the tank (and the aeroplane) as key weapons, but who at other times thought of the tank as only one of various arms that had to cooperate together to gain victory. Third, there were the traditional manpower supporters at GHQ such as Haig, Lawrence, Butler, Wigram (GS Operations, GHQ) and Dawnay; some conservative senior staff and commanders such as Harper and Montgomery (Chief of Staff, Fourth Army); and some senior artillery officers such as Birch and Major C.N.F Broad (Artillery Staff, Fifth Army), who all thought of the tanks as purely auxiliary to the traditional infantry and artillery. This traditional group was composed of those who either frankly opposed the tanks, or placed little value on them, or saw them in a purely limited and auxiliary role. Finally, there was the category of the indifferent or undecided, often cautious or conservative divisional commanders such as Deverell (GOC 3 Division), who had to be won over to tank-infantry cooperation.

The most important reactions were obviously those of Haig and GHQ. For his part, Haig clearly still continued to believe in the classical, manpower-oriented, wearing-out battle, as he wrote in his diary on 21 August 1918: 'We are engaged in a "wearing out" battle and are outlasting and beating the enemy. If we allow the enemy a period of quiet, he will recover, and the "wearing out" process must be recommenced.' In this scenario, mechanical means of warfare such as tanks need not be given a decisive role, and here Haig's reaction to Fuller's Plan 1919 (proposing a massive tank attack in 1919) is of interest. Initially Haig argued that in the plan, the proportion of tanks to infantry was faulty, there being too many tanks and too few infantry!

However, he agreed that 'a large force of tanks is likely to prove an invaluable adjunct to...a general offensive'. Then in a more detailed examination of the plan, Haig reluctantly accepted the need for such a tank assault, although he added that 'If the time and the opportunity were available to train sufficient divisions to the standard of the original Expeditionary Force it would be another matter, but as matters stand at present the above hypotheses can be accepted in principle'. In other words, infantry were still better than tanks, but given manpower and time constraints infantry could not take their rightful place as before. Haig was also backward-looking in assuming that a breakthrough required a massive 50-mile front, and therefore geography would preclude tanks from operating on more than 50 per cent of the front, so that it was necessary to cut back the number of tanks involved. It was also necessary to increase the corps and divisional cavalry, and to place the tanks firmly under the orders of corps and divisions. For Haig, the touchstone regarding traditional or mechanical warfare was manpower. Thus in March 1918, Haig read Churchill's proposal to produce 4,000 tanks, and his comment was that Churchill had not considered the problem of manpower, namely, where to find the crews to put in them. Haig simply could not conceive of manpower being used except in traditional ways, and he could not conceive of manpower being saved by using tanks. And this was because he basically understood warfare to be the movement of masses of men over a battlefield.

From the point of view of GHQ, the clearest and most authoritative statement concerning mechanical warfare came from Major General Dawnay (MGGS Operations, GHQ), who was in charge of issuing the official GHQ 'Notes on recent fighting'. In August 1918 Dawnay drafted a statement, which was then issued in September as no. 20 in his 'Notes on recent fighting'. In the draft, Dawnay argued against the 'over-mechanical attack theory.... The Infantry isn't there to be put from place to place behind barrages or tanks; it is there to fight.'

He went on: 'The over- driven barrage theory is a little out of favour in view of the success of the hurricane bombardment and surprise—But the tank theory is becoming a slight danger.' Dawnay concluded by writing that the 'war of machinery' was a lot of nonsense, because machinery was a good servant but a bad master. Mechanical warfare might be useful to 'help the human element, and to conserve man-power—up to a point—But in the last resort it is our men (especially Infantry) against the enemy's men (especially Infantry); and there is no mechanical "royal road" to victory.'

There was some merit in Dawnay's observations, but the conscious or unconscious decision taken by Haig, Lawrence, Dawnay and others at GHQ in mid1918, was not to embrace mechanical warfare in the second half of 1918, except as an auxiliary, but to continue the traditional manpower forms of war, even if 1919 would bring an enforced change.

The opposition of GHQ to mechanical warfare was emphasized when GHQ attempted in February 1918 and again in April to cut back the Tank Corps, and to stop the dispatch to France of the new Mark V tanks, although tank supporters fought off these moves. Predictably, this opposition earned GHQ the contempt of Lieutenant Colonel J.F.C. Fuller (GSO 2, Tank Corps), who in typical overemphasis labelled Douglas Haig as 'Dunder Headed', or the

'Military Trappist', Kiggell as Ethelred the Unready, and General Wigram (OB, or Operations Branch, GHQ) as the 'Obsolete One'.

Then in June 1918, when Fuller asked Dawnay if GHQ intended to win the war by old methods (infantry and guns) or by mechanical methods (infantry and guns, but emphasizing tanks and aeroplanes), Dawnay said he did not know; 'Have you no idea?' asked Fuller; 'None,' replied Dawnay, 'General Foch is now in command. We do not deal with these things' (Foch became Generalissimo of the Allied Forces, France, at the end of March 1918, following the hasty retreat of the BEF after the German offensive of 21 March 1918). It was during this conversation with Dawnay that Fuller learnt that many important subjects, including tanks, were still being referred by GHQ to General Butler, who had been removed from GHQ and appointed as III Corps commander. Fuller was shocked: 'What a monstrous state of affairs. The wooden-headed Haig still using the wooden-headed Butler, also the sycophant, as if he was still at GHQ. Personally I feel perfectly confident that no change for the better will take place in the British Army until it is given new brains in a new C in C.'

It is not surprising, therefore, that despite the successful tank battles of Cambrai and then Amiens (August 1918), tanks were often used by GHQ in an ad hoc manner during the second half of 1918, and even Edmonds, the British official historian, in a rare moment of specific criticism, wrote 'it is to be greatly regretted that no massed tank attack was made [after Amiens], not even planned'.

However, matters would probably, although not certainly, have been different in 1919. Already by May 1918 the War Office had been converted to the tank idea, and it was also in May that Fuller wrote out his ideas for a future massive tank attack, to be called Plan 1919. Then in July 1918, the CIGS, Henry Wilson, set out his plans for 1919, based on Fuller's Plan 1919. These called for man-killing equipment, particularly machine guns, tanks and aeroplanes. The plan called especially for 3,000 tanks and 7,300 tractors. Reinforcing Wilson's orders was a letter from the Army Council in August 1918 outlining the expansion of the Tank Corps, disbanding 1 Cavalry Corps HQ and 1 Cavalry division—'despite what you say'—and maintaining battalion strengths at 900 men rather than the 999 requested. With this plan and the Army Council letter, it may be said that the mechanical vision of war had officially arrived and the option of manpower and wearing-down had been devalued. Thus mechanical warfare had received the highest sanction at the War Office and the War Council, even if it was aimed at 1919 rather than 1918, which as it turned out was to prove a crucial difference.

Starting with the perceived manpower shortage in late 1917 and early 1918, and stimulated by efforts from Lloyd George and the War Cabinet to gain control over strategy on the Western Front, there took place a serious, in fact, critical, debate in the BEF and the War Office over what form of warfare to pursue on the Western Front. The main argument centred on whether to shift to mechanical warfare—meaning a primary emphasis on tanks and aeroplanes, but also mobile trench mortars, gas, Lewis guns and new machine gun tactics, to break open the stalemate for the infantry and artillery. The alternative was for the infantry, artillery and cavalry to retain their traditional manpower-oriented predominance. The debate was intensified by the German spring offensives, which produced approximately 300,000 BEF casualties by the end of April 1918, and so reemphasized the manpower problem. Thereafter the conflict between the two schools of thought accelerated, in the period May to July 1918, and involved GHQ and most senior commanders, even if only in the form of such things as a simple letter from Lord Home (GOC First Army) to GHQ in mid-June arguing for 'machine power' to cover the shortage of manpower.

The debate was resolved in favour of mechanical warfare, because Haig and GHQ were defeated by a combination of factors: the conversion of several key senior officers; the arguments of the Tank Corps; the conversion of Wilson and Harington at the War Office; and political support from the War Cabinet. Yet full-scale mechanical warfare could actually only take place in 1919, partly because of problems with tank and aeroplane production, and this left Haig and GHQ with considerable control over the strategy and tactics of the BEF for the remainder of 1918. The results of this situation were to have consequences into the postwar period.

Within the centre of the mechanical warfare debate lay the discussion of the role of the tank. Officers and staff tended to divide over whether tanks or infantry would dominate in an offensive. Of course neither operated alone, and both had to cooperate with each other and with other arms, but ultimately officers were either converted to a mechanical warfare paradigm, or remained traditionalists, usually because of temperament, training, or arm jealousy. The tank proved a difficult weapon to ignore, despite its very real technical shortcomings, because it could not be easily assimilated into any other arm, and thus accommodated into a traditional image or role.

After Cambrai, senior officers had either to support the tank as a primary concept, or relegate it to an auxiliary role. The latter was the easy option taken by several senior officers such as Haig, who basically failed to think about the weapon at all. (It is curious how Haig's diary entries relating to his visits to tank units in 1918 are often simple descriptions of their technical abilities or problems without comments on their potential as an independent weapon.)

From the point of view of staff and command, therefore, the question was how significant, and thus how independent, an arm the tank was, and hence how much of a voice the Tank Corps should have at GHQ and the War Office in the form of senior staff and decision- making. As it turned out, events overtook the evolution of tank predominance in 1918, and prevented the Tank Corps from emerging with a strong voice at GHQ, which would have been the case had the 1919 tank offensive actually taken place. Consequently, as Fuller told Liddell Hart after the war, the tanks had a greater evolution from 1916 to 1918 than from 1918 to 1922.

The role of the tank in mechanical warfare was mirrored by the evolution of the machine gun in some respects. As the machine gun became recognized as a more significant weapon in offence as well as defence in 1917, because of its collective action on a large scale, there was pressure on GHQ to pool machine guns in divisions and corps and to appoint divisional and corps machine gun staff officers. These positions were agreed to in mid-1917, but then in July GHQ changed its mind and the corps MGO (machine gun officer) was abolished! The fight over this position continued throughout 1918, with Byng and Home demanding such an officer to coordinate machine gun action at the corps level, and to give the machine gun organization a staff liaison between GHQ and the rest of the army.

There was also a request for a machine gun officer on Maxse's staff at GHQ. In February and March 1918, GHQ seems to have acceded to all requests, including corps MGOs and a BGGS Machine Guns at GHQ. However, matters were apparently not yet settled, for Lindsay (First Army Machine Gun Officer) was fighting to save the corps MGOs in June against what he thought of as GHQ reactionaries, and at the beginning of November 1918, Dawnay at GHQ was still rejecting the concept of a corps MGO, only to have the War Office approve the retention of corps MGOs on 10 November 1918! In other words, as with the tank, GHQ accepted the weapon, but dragged its feet in acknowledging the importance of the weapon, and then resisted appointing higher level staff to reflect the contribution of the weapon. Only in the progressive Canadian Corps did the matter work out well, with the Corps MGO acting in the same way as the GOCRA for the Corps artillery. As Haldane noted earlier in 1917, having secretly appointed his own divisional machine gun officers, 'A Divisional Machine Gun officer is badly wanted, but GHQ are behind the times as regards the question of machine guns and terribly conservative. They still think in terms of the time when we had two guns per Battalion.' Ironically, however, when the machine gun battalions were formed in early 1918, and they were put under the control of Divisional HQ as a form of centralized fire power, it was the brigade and battalion commanders who initially resented this removal of the gun from their control, although their attitudes did soon change.

A similar story occurred in regard to machine gun supply and policy. In April 1918, Brutinel (Canadian Corps Machine Gun Officer) worked out the ratio of machine guns to rifles in the French, British and German armies and sent it to his superior in First Army, Lord Home. Haig had proposed a ratio of 1 to 90 in the BEF, compared to 1 to 52 in the French army, and 1 to 70 in the German army.

Suspecting therefore that GHQ would not push the matter, Home took the matter straight to the CIGS, hoping for assistance from the top. Only the Canadian Corps benefited by another 90 machine guns, since the War Council in August could not authorize any increase in the number of machine gun battalions. On another occasion in April-May 1918, C.R Fay (GS Machine Gun Corps) went directly to Smuts to help machine gun development. In just the same way, the Tank Corps method of operation was to bypass GHQ and go direct to Wilson and Harington at the War Office, or appeal to Churchill, on matters of importance. Then in regard to policy, the Machine Gun Corps found there was considerable drift and lack of direction from both the War Office and GHQ at the beginning of 1918. As Inspector General of Training, Maxse at GHQ finally issued a leaflet on machine guns at the end of the war, and there were comments on machine guns by Dawnay in his 'Notes on recent fighting' through the second half of 1918. Yet according to Lindsay, it would appear that the First Army machine gun policy of May 1918 was the only official doctrine to have come out of the BEF during 1918.

Finally, GHQ had earlier resisted the creation of a Machine Gun Corps, realizing that this meant recognition of the corps as a separate entity, and therefore a further diminution of the role of infantry. However, such a corps was created in 1916, although disbanded in 1919. An amusing poem was composed to celebrate this partial victory, one verse of which details the efforts of Lieutenant Colonel George Lindsay to establish a Machine Gun Corps: So off he went to GHQ to reason with the Staff, He argued first then flattered them, and then went on to chaff, But neither method helped at all the Staff refused to see Their notions had got crystallised 10,000 years B.C. He tried again and many times but it was all no use, The Chesterfieldian Staff were near descending to abuse And posted up all round Montreuil [GHQ], George very plainly saw, Machine Guns shall be infantry, they shall not be a Corps.

Thus, the tank and the machine gun appear to have gone through several similar stages: first, recognition of significant impact on operations on the Western Front; second, development of enthusiasts to promote the weapon; third, an important stage: the separation out of the weapon from other arms and weapons into a distinctive arm with tactics of its own; fourth, resistance at GHQ and the War Office to the recognition of the arm as a separate entity with tactics and needs of its own; fifth, eventual recognition of this separation through the creation of a separate corps; sixth, fight to have the significance of the weapon/corps recognized at GHQ through appropriate organization and staff appointments; seventh, bypass GHQ and obtain results through other channels, such as the War Office, supporters, politicians; eighth, slow integration of the weapon/ corps into mechanical warfare operations, usually over the objections of competing arms, and some army, corps and division commanders. Lastly, in the case of these two weapons, the eighth stage was overtaken by 1918 events, and by the end of the war.

This process might have been easier and quicker but for the traditionalists in the BEF, especially the senior staff at GHQ. One may have some sympathy for the General Staff at GHQ who were busy fighting a war and trying to integrate competing weapons and interest groups into the BEF at the same time. However, two factors seem to have prevented swifter innovation in the BEF in regard to mechanical warfare: first the lack of an independent group at GHQ or the War Office, or both, to think through changes and make doctrine and tactical policy, separately from the immediate business of fighting the war; and second, the necessary open-mindedness by senior commanders to accept such doctrine and tactics. The first could have been achieved, but the second was harder both because of the 'top-down' structure of the BEF, and because of the traditional manpower image of war retained so strongly by Haig and his senior staff at GHQ.

But while the strategy and tactics of mechanical versus traditional manpower warfare were thus being argued out in early and mid-1918, events on the ground were radically transforming the situation.

3

USE OF GERMAN TECHNOLOGY IN WARS

The massive German 'Michael' offensive of 21 March 1918 was expected by the BEF, but the nature of the German offensive caught the BEF by surprise. In a matter of hours the command structure of the BEF began to break down, and continued to do so for the next six or seven days. But the underlying reason for the rapid retreat of the BEF's Fifth and Third Armies was the failure to understand and properly apply the new three-zone, defence in depth system, copied from the German army. As a result, Fifth and Third Armies separated, and more seriously, Fifth Army separated from the neighbouring French army, leading to a hitherto misunderstood disagreement between Haig and Pétain. During the BEF's retreat, three major events help explain how GHQ and the BEF command structure lost control: the initial German breakthroughs of 21 and 22 March (which will be followed through the fortunes of just two divisions, 16 and 47); the tardy evacuation of the Flesquières or Cambrai salient by Third Army on 22 and 23 March; and the hasty retirement of Fifth Army behind the line of the Somme from 22 to 25 March. Further problems also occurred with the BEF's artillery and air arms. But the innovative German stormtroop tactics were not sufficiently maintained either, and German casualties mounted when traditional mass tactics were used. All in all, however, the keynote of the BEF retreat was the collapse of the command structure, and the inability of the army to comprehend, build and properly employ, the new defence in depth system.

This conclusion is at variance with the explanations given by Haig and his supporters, who argued that external factors were responsible for the retreat. More recently, Martin Middlebrook has advanced various reasons for the retreat of the BEF, including the defence system, but also referring to the shortage of men, the weather and the low morale of the BEF.

The latest explanation, by J.M.Bourne, alludes to various problems with the defensive strategy, but seems to lay responsibility primarily on the leadership of Douglas Haig. Nevertheless, it does appear that the German offensive of 21 March 1918 had taken GHQ by surprise—not so much the timing of the offensive, nor exactly the place, but the nature of the offensive—and consequently GHQ had not thought through the necessary defences against the onslaught.

Plate 1 Panaromic view of the battlefield on Passchendaele Ridge, showing state of country over which the troops had to advance. Canadian Division area 14 November 1917. This was the result of the poor choice of battlefield, and shows how difficult it was to mount deliberate offensives.

Plate 2 Panoramic view of the battlefield on Passchendaele Ridge, showing state of country over which the troops had to advance. 2 Canadian Division area, 14 November 1917. This was the result of the poor choice of battlefield, and shows how difficult it was to mount deliberate offensives.

Plate 3 Cambrai offensive, 20 November 1917. Mark IV tanks standing at a station before the offensive, waiting despatch to the battlefield. Note the individual tank names (they begin with 'C' and 'D', thus indicating that they belong to 3rd and 4th battalions respectively). Note also fascines for crossing trenches.

Plate 4 Before the German March offensive. A 60-pounder battery sergeant copying down instructions for S.O.S lines. Note camouflage netting. Monchy-le-Preux, 18 March 1918. This picture reveals the sophistication of artillery methods by 1918.

Plate 5 The German March offensive. British artillery preparing to pull out of Omiecourt on 24 March 1918, having first set fire to stores and huts. There is a certain amount of bustle, but no panic.

Plate 6 German prisoners waiting to be interrogated on 22 March 1918. Near Bapauma. The prisoners look sullen and determind, in contrast with those captured later in the offensive.

Plate 7 Prisoners taken during the German offensive in a Prisoners' Cage. Near Albert, 31 March 1918. The strain of the offensive shows on their faces, and compares with the determination shown by those captured early in the offensive in Plate 6.

Plate 8 The Amiens offensive. 1 Australian Division moving past a line of machine gun emplacements which have just been cleaned up by a tank. The action is taking place near. Harbonniers on 9 August 1918. Dead Germans in foreground and a Whippet in the background. The picture shows how mobile the war had become, and that the German trench was a poor affair.

Plate 9 German barbed wire defences, the Hindenburg Line. At Quéant, 1918. Although the wire had sagged, the defences were still formidable, requiring tanks or other means to make a path through th wire.

Plate 10 Battle of the Canal du Nord. The canal was empty, bull still an obstacle. showing tanks of A Company, 7th Battalion, parked after capturing Bourlon village. They carry undiching beams. In the foreground, prisoners carry British wounded. Near Moeuvres, 27 September 1918.

Plate 11 Canadian troops advancing through the ruins of Cambrai, 9 October 1918. This was an area of fierce fighting. Parts of Cambrai were burning, possibly the German demolition teams set the city on fire.

In regard to the timing of the attack, by 17 March Lawrence believed that the German offensive would commence on 21 or 22 March, although Cox, the new Intelligence chief at GHQ, considered the attack was not imminent. Nevertheless, there was a general perception in mid- March that a major German offensive was due in a few days. Concerning the area to be attacked, there was uncertainty over whether the French or British armies would be attacked first, in fact in February GHQ expected the French would suffer the main assault. There was also a serious miscalculation caused by Haig's preoccupation with the Flanders area and the Channel ports, so that GHQ focused too much attention and too many reserves in the north. Hence, on 6 February 1918, Haig told Rawlinson that after the Germans had failed in Picardy and Champagne, 'he [the Germans] might put in a big attack in Flanders with a view to gaining the Channel ports later on in the year when all our troops were tired and he had still some fresh Divisions available'. And as late as April, according to Rawlinson, Haig was still shouting for divisions to go up north. However, although on 17 March GHQ still did not expect an attack south of the Bapaume-Cambrai road, just before the March offensive GHQ did move its estimate of the area to be attacked further south, to the Arras-St Quentin sector, and this was a correct assumption. Yet Haig himself still found it difficult to shift to a more southerly perspective, and his preoccupation was with the junction of First and Third Armies at Arras (which turned out to be the northern limit of the German attack), rather than with the junction of Third and Fifth Armies, or the Franco-British junction, both of which were actually more vulnerable. Even after the attack commenced, Haig still expected an attack toward Arras. The liaison officer with the French, Major General Clive, was surprised at Haig's ignoring Fifth Army's lack of reserves, but realized that Haig 'keeps his eyes turned towards Arras, where he expects the attack to extend'. Strangely enough, even after the war was over, Haig apparently still was certain he had been correct in thickening the centre of the line, as opposed to the right flank.

It was not surprising, therefore, that GHQ did not include the crucial Oise sector in its estimate of the assault area. This sector was even further to the south of St Quentin, at the junction of the Franco-British armies, where there was soon to be a major German breakthrough. Interestingly enough, the reason that GHQ overlooked the Oise sector stemmed back to the government decision to take over more line from the French in late 1917. Before Haig would agree, in a personal arrangement with Pétain, how much line he would take over in this sector, he sent Rawlinson to scout the area. Rawlinson reported that the Oise front could be held as far south as the Barisis railway with only four infantry divisions and one cavalry division because there was good observation, and it was a very quiet front. It was also the case that the area was wet and marshy and contained the Oise River. Rawlinson's initial perceptions carried over into GHQ planning, so that in February 1918, GHQ considered the southernmost 20,000 yards to be an inactive front because it was river and marsh, and strongly defended. GHQ even expected to use the divisions in this area as reserves for the rest of Fifth Army. However, a mistake had been made because III Corps, which held this southernmost sector, found that the river, presumably the Oise, which was supposed to protect much of the sector, 'was almost dry and afforded a very slight obstacle to the passage of troops'.

Nevertheless, apart from problems with the Oise sector, and the northern emphasis, GHQ was not far out in its evaluation of the location of the German attack on the eve of 21 March, expecting it to include Third and Fifth Army fronts, roughly from Arras to St Quentin. There was, however, a decisive error in GHQ's estimation of the nature of the German offensive. This was that GHQ obviously expected the German offensive to follow the 1917 BEF model of a major manpower and wearing-down campaign. As Lawrence put it, the Germans would follow 'sound principles' and would first wear out and use up reserves, and then throw in their major effort at a later period, when the occasion was favourable. Haig thought the same, writing in March 1918 that the modern battle was now a prolonged 'bataille d'usure', a wearing-down battle. This was strange since Rawlinson had already urged Haig in January 1918 to send around the 'Lessons of Cambrai counter attack' document, saying that the German 1918 attack would model itself on that rapid action.

However, Haig was not to be persuaded and 'pointed to our long drawn out offensives as an indication of what was to be expected'. And since this kind of attack required a much higher ratio of offensive to defensive divisions, Lawrence at GHQ was not particularly worried by the larger number of German divisions facing them. In fact, while at Passchendaele the BEF had a 7 to 4 offensive advantage, in March 1918, the German army had a lesser 6 to 4 advantage. Thus Lawrence thought in mid-January 1918 that there were not enough German divisions for a 'decisive victory'. Lawrence was correct, but he had forgotten that there were results short of total victory that could be very damaging.

Because the senior staff at GHQ expected the German army to mount a BEF-style prolonged offensive, there was confidence that the attack would not succeed. And in a curious parallel to the BEF Somme and Passchendaele offensives of 1916 and 1917, confidence at GHQ increased as the attack drew near, only this time the BEF would be on the defensive! According to Major General Bernard, GS at GHQ, there was 'overwhelming confidence of most of the people in the Ops. Branch [at GHQ]. He remembered only too well the way they welcomed the first news of the German attack, and how they chortled at the lesson they were about to give the Germans.' There was also much confidence at lower levels; for example, XVIII Corps had done a lot of work on their defences, and one officer believed they were 'impregnable'. Haig himself confidently wrote in his diary in early and mid-March, before the offensive, that he was only afraid the enemy would not attack, and that he believed he could smash any attack.

And on the day before the attack he wrote to Lady Haig that 'Everyone is in good spirits and only anxious that the Enemy should attack'. He also told Lady Haig that it was not even necessary for him to be in France at the moment of the attack, but that on general principles, he should be there. Even on the day of the attack, Haig thought that The Enemy's attacks seem to be coming exactly against the points on our front which we expected and where we are prepared to meet him'. And still on the second day of the attack, Haig declared that the men were in great heart, that the BEF had done very well, and that it was 'Kill, Kill, all day long'. Only on the third day of the battle did Haig realize that the situation was serious, and by this time panic had set in at GHQ, with Davidson, Dawnay and Lawrence apparently losing their nerve. The problem at GHQ, which caused so much over-confidence before 21 March, and then deep alarm after, was that the nature and methods of the German attack had not been foreseen. This seems to have been particularly the case with the initial German bombardment on 21 March which accurately destroyed communications, and thereby paralysed command structures. For example, an officer of the 12th Royal Irish Rifles described the bombardment of his regimental position with high explosive shells, trench mortars and gas, and then, as though this was a logical conclusion, recorded that 'With this intense Bombardment all Telephone wires were almost immediately cut & only one Company Runner got back to forward Battn. Head Quarters…and he was very badly wounded'. An officer of the 2/6 Battalion, the Sherwood Foresters, recalled the same problem, in the same matter-of-fact tone:

Exactly at 5 a.m. the enemy bombardment began, the bulk of the shells going over us on to the back areas. Soon afterwards however, our Reserve line was heavily shelled by guns of all calibres, & the forward Companies were heavily trench mortared. All our communications were severed at the commencement, with the exception of the line to Brigade, which held for a short time. Not long after, there was gas shelling, and then a conventional bombardment of the 'greatest severity' so that communication with the forward companies was cut off, even by runner, and 'nothing further was heard from them'. Even with proper precautions, little could be done, as an officer of 14 Division remembered: 'We had in the Division area deep cable trenches to a very large degree. These were a snare and a delusion. They had been photographed from the air by the Germans with the result that they fired at the junctions (with armour piercing shell) and everyone was disconnected in a few minutes.'

The destruction of communications resulted in the almost complete disintegration of the command structures of the Third and Fifth Armies. Thus an officer of 61 Brigade, in 36 Division, recalled a fairly common situation:

On the evening of the 21st. [March] I saw the 36th. Division commander at Ollezy. I never saw him again during these operations, nor did I ever see one of his Staff Officers, nor did I receive any assistance of any kind from Divisional Headquarters. Also I did not see a Staff Officer of any other formation. Mine was, I regret to say, not an isolated experience. As soon as telegraphic & telephone communications with Brigades ceased to exist, Divisional Headquarters in many cases became paralysed. They had become so welded to a set piece type of warfare, that, when open warfare occurred, they failed to appreciate the situation, and were unable to function independent of a fixed headquarters. They glued themselves to a housed headquarters miles to the rear, and were not in any kind of communication with their fighting Commanders.

Many were satisfied by saying 'It is impossible to keep touch with my Brigade Commanders, and in such a situation the fighting is best left in their hands etc.' It is impossible to understand this attitude, in view of the number of Staff Officers (12) Motor Cars (6) horses (30) and despatch riders (12) at the disposal of Divisional Headquarters. These provided ample facilities for finding out the situation at the front, and it gave freedom of movement to keep close touch with Commanders. At the end of each day Divisional Commanders should have gone and seen their Brigade Commanders, and arranged for some kind of concerted plan for the next day. As it was, Brigade Commanders were left in many cases entirely unassisted, and at the end of the day were too exhausted to do any more. They had not adequate means of finding out the situation on their flanks.—There was no improvement in this state of affairs, from my experience during the whole of these operations up till March 30th., when I was relieved.

J.F.C.Fuller found the same situation, in which lack of information led to confusion. On 25 March, he asked rhetorically, 'Who is fighting this battle? No one. GHQ and Armies know next to nothing of what is going on. Each Brigade and Battalion is attempting to carry out a dozen orders and counter orders at the same time. As the Corps move their headquarters back so do the Divisions. Then the fighting troops follow suit and position after position is abandoned.' Brigadier General Ironside had the same overall comment, that with corps and divisional headquarters and their large staffs continually on the run, they ceased to command through lack of communication. According to Ironside, these commanders should have used horses and cars and resumed command in that fashion, particularly because there were plenty of staff officers available.8 What clearly happened was that with the loss of communications, corps and divisional headquarters were unable to function as long as the battle continued to be moving warfare.

Besides communications, another problem was the ineffectiveness of the outpost zone or line. The general idea was to have outposts which would hold up the enemy attack, and would then retire to the main defensive or battle zone. What tended to happen, however, was that the outposts were either bypassed, infiltrated, or easily captured. Hence, an officer defending in the Fricourt area of Fifth Army reported that 'When the barrage fell these posts had orders to fall back to the main body of the company. Unfortunately, only one Post succeeding in doing this intact, a second came back with half its numbers, of the other two posts we only saw one man.' In the same way, the previously mentioned officer from the 12th Royal Irish Rifles, wrote that with the mist early on 21 March 'it was a comparatively easy matter to get through unseen between the outposts, which at this particular part of the line were from 150 to 200 yards apart'. The German idea was to 'contain the outposts...and to push through all troops as far as possible, & eventually to capture the outposts later'. This was done on that sector by about 11.30 a.m on 21 March.

Again in 14 Division, the German attack simply cut off the forward positions by advancing at an angle, and by using fog to infiltrate and attack them from the rear.

The disappearance of the outpost zone in many areas underscored what was undoubtedly the greatest weakness of the whole BEF defence in March 1918, and which was responsible, more than any other factor, for the disorganized retreat of the BEF. This was the failure of GHQ and senior commanders to thoroughly understand, coordinate and apply the three-zone, defence in depth, defensive scheme. This scheme had been copied from the German defence in depth regulations issued in March and August 1917, and basically outlined a forward zone, a battle zone and a rear zone. The main resistance was supposed to develop in the battle zone, on ground favourable to the defenders, and sufficiently distant from the offensive artillery to leave the attackers vulnerable. However, two aspects of the German plan obviously puzzled GHQ.

First, what was really supposed to happen in what was variously called either the advanced zone, the forward zone, the front system, or the outpost zone? Was there to be serious fighting in this zone, or did it exist merely to delay the major attack?

For example, the Brigade Major of 140 Infantry Brigade, in 47 Division, of Third Army, was told to fight for the front line and hold it at all costs. But on their immediate right 26 Brigade was told that in the event of a serious attack, they were to fight for the battle zone and not for the forward zone. On the other hand, Gough, commanding Fifth Army, tried to have it both ways, according to an officer in 2 Cavalry Division:

By the 5th Army defence scheme there was no intention of fighting on the outpost line, the real line of defence was the battle zone, the outposts however were told there was to be no question of retirement they were to hold on to their posts at all costs and die there if necessary, the object being to break up the enemy attack.... How our artillery were expected to act under these circumstances it is difficult to make out, as once the enemy penetrated the outpost line they would either have to cease fire or shoot friend and foe alike. I walked every yard of the III Corps front a few days before the attack and the thing which struck one most was the thinness of the troops, and the great distance between the various advanced posts. All hopes were built on a very well thought out system of machine gun defence from positions in rear [of the outpost zone], but this as we know broke down entirely due to the fog.

When in fact the enemy did penetrate the outpost zone, and Fifth Army next day (22 March) gave orders for a retirement, 'brigadiers and COs... were rabid at the idea of having to desert those of their forward posts whom they knew to be still holding out. They had personally given them the order that they were on no account to retire and now they had to go away and leave them without being able to communicate with them.' As in Gough's example, and in the other accounts mentioned above, the outpost zone did not actually work, and commanders did not know what to do with it. In fact, according to Major van Straubenzee, Fifth Army artillery, the failure of their advanced zone system on 21 March, when the men were mostly captured, meant that in succeeding days troops in the advanced zone did not wait to be captured, but simply retreated.

Then, secondly, the key to the success of the German defensive system was not just depth, but flexibility. In other words, there was an emphasis on defended localities, such as machine gun nests, rather than trenches; and on the all-important counter-attack system. Defended localities were foreign to the BEF which had spent three years defending parallel lines of trenches and holding onto ground as an end in itself, and so the BEF found great difficulty in trying to adapt to a different concept. Thus, one officer in Third Army claimed that the retreat began in January 1918 with the introduction of the defence in depth system, and his own division simply refused to follow GHQ's policy of defended localities. However, of greater importance was the German counter-attack system, which anticipated that counter-attacks would take place either from the back of the battle zone, or, in the case of a major counter-attack, from the back of the rear zone. This system gave considerable leeway and initiative to commanders on the spot. Yet GHQ's instructions on counter-attacks were vague, except that the spirit of the counter-attack was to be 'inculcated'.

And instructions for the main battle zone were contradictory, since at one point Kiggell told the War Cabinet that this zone was to be held at all costs, thus negating the flexibility built into the system, while at another point GHQ saw the main counter-attack going in on the battle zone. This confusion continued in February 1918, when Lawrence told Gough, commanding Fifth Army, that he might not need to fight in the battle zone, but instead fall back on his rear defences of Péronne and the Somme, and prepare a counter-attack there.

Not only were the German concepts hard to grasp and put into practice, but the 'top-down' hierarchical system of the BEF basically ruled out the flexible German counter-attack system. Senior and junior officers alike were unwilling to use their initiative in rapidly changing situations and their constant complaint was that orders were not received from relevant HQs, or that senior staff or corps or divisional headquarters left them to their own devices. Consequently, with higher commanders frequently out of touch, counter-attacks did not materialize. Instead units waited for reliefs or reinforcements, or retired, but felt unable to use their own initiative. A typical case is that of III Corps, where the GSO 1 complained that 'after the first day or so we were practically cut off from the 5th Army Headquarters, and in the absence of orders to the contrary, we could only adhere to the original plan'. When reinforcements did arrive at III Corps for defence or a possible counter-attack, they were debussed too far in the rear, 'as all the bussing arrangements were worked from GHQ, and no latitude was allowed to the Commander on the spot'. Conversely, when direct orders did come from higher commands, these were often inappropriate because GHQ, army and corps were out of touch with what was going on, and counter-attack chances were missed. A good example is the case of 20 Division, which was released from GHQ reserve on 21 March to Fifth Army, and then sent to XVIII Corps. According to a member of XVIII Corps staff,

> What was the result? Was the 20th. Division used for the counter attack? Not a bit of it. One brigade was put in to help the 36th Div. &: the other two were strung out all along the rear zone to act as a net on to which, and through which, the Corps was to retire. The 20th Division as an offensive unit ceased to exist.... In my view this was the turning point between the active offensive-defensive visualised in the Corps scheme and the passive defence which so quickly deteriorated into a disorganised retirement.

Later on, the lack of contact between front-line troops and staff showed up in counter-attacks that were not feasible, so that on 25 March when 24 Division was supposed to attack, the brigades were really too tired to manage the assault.

One of the crucial elements of the German defence in depth system— the counter-attack—therefore did not operate in Third and Fifth Armies, largely because the BEF system of command could not adapt to the more flexible German plan. For the same reason, other actions that should have been taken by the BEF were not, because of the hierarchical system. This was the case with the blowing up of bridges behind the retreat. The bridges in front of III and XVIII Corps over the Crozat canal and the Somme River were either not destroyed or not sufficiently blown up. Generally speaking, the bridges were the responsibility of the relevent corps, although the major bridges were under the control of army HQs. However, when the retreat took place, corps staff were unable to cope. Thus Brigadier General Harvey, GOC 109 Brigade, found that on 22 March, 'nothing was being done to prepare it [the railway bridge at Pithon] for destruction. I remembered reading in XVIII Corps Instructions that the Corps was responsible for this—so I got into telephonic communication with Corps & told them about the bridge.' Later, he found French engineers working on the bridge, but they had not advanced very far in their labours. A more strident criticism came from an officer of 61 Brigade, who complained that the rout of III Corps on 24 March was largely the result of failure to destroy the bridges efficiently on 22 March: 'This was one of the greatest blunders committed during the war.... The responsibility rested with the III Corps Commander. He should have satisfied himself that the arrangements were satisfactory.... Neglect to take such precautions had the most disastrous results and nearly lost us the war.' Similarly, XIX Corps failed to blow up the bridges at Brie, and there were hot words over this at XIX Corps headquarters, according to an officer of the 9th Manchester Regiment.

It was apparent that corps staff were not able to adapt to moving warfare, nor could junior officers in the Royal Engineers reasonably take the initiative in blowing bridges themselves. Meanwhile, Corps itself was hamstrung in regard to the main bridges by army orders. A member of XVIII Corps staff reported later that

'One of the difficulties in the destruction of the Main Bridges lay in the Army reserving to itself authority for their destruction. This was one of the causes why some of the main Somme Bridges and those over the Aisne in June 1918, remained intact— The smaller and less important bridges were in most cases destroyed.' This officer made the comment that 'Events move too quickly for Army Headquarters to make a decision of this nature and in our present Field Service Regulations [1927] it is laid down that authority must be delegated to Subordinate Commanders'. The same muddle took place in Fifth Army, where Gough was reportedly over-confident and did not blow the causeways, perhaps also because GHQ did not give him definite orders.

And the railway bridges at Péronne were not destroyed because that was left up to the Railway Branch. This need for flexibility was one of the hard lessons learnt from the war, but in March 1918 the BEF command structure was not capable of incorporating it from the German defensive system.

If flexibility was the second of the two aspects of the German plan that the BEF found hard to put into practice (the first being the outpost zone), there was also the fundamental problem of actually constructing the three zones, and then making sure that all units adhered to the same plan for the three zones. GHQ had set up a committee of Jeudwine, McMullen and Edmonds to advise on defence in early 1918, and this committee pointed out that it would take months to get the three defence lines in good shape. The difficulty therefore was labour, yet there were 354,577 men specifically available for this task on 1 January 1918 (including 104,739 coloured labourers, and 71,000 prisoners of war), and of course the infantry divisions themselves were also available.5 With this amount of labour power, it might be expected that reasonable defences could be ready for the anticipated attack in the spring. However, GHQ only asserted itself over the allotment of labour for special work on defences on 3 March 1918 (perhaps again showing over-confidence), and thus there were complaints of lack of labour, especially in Fifth Army. Despite this, Gough did rashly tell Haig on 13 February that in another month his front would be very strong. This was clearly over-optimistic, because only two days later he told Haig that he had no labour, which Haig found to be a serious cause for concern, given that he expected the Germans might penetrate Fifth Army defences. Curiously, on 8 March, Gough again told Haig that he had no defences and no labour. Yet Haig apparently made no special effort to redress the problem, simply remarking that Gough's reserve lines needed more work.

Haig's attitude toward Fifth Army's defences and lack of labour appeared to be the result of the previously mentioned optimism and overconfidence at GHQ. This lack of urgency seemed to permeate Third Army and Fifth Army. Hence, of the three zones in Third and Fifth Armies, only the outpost zone (the old front lines) was guaranteed to be ready, while most but not all units had wired and dug the battle zone (the old corps and army sketch lines). Some, such as Deverell's 3 Division in Haldane's VI Corps, completed their battle zone only on 13 March 1918, while others, such as the divisions in XVIII Corps, had done a lot of work on their defences and had largely completed them before 21 March.

Indeed, there appeared to be a tendency for the staff to be satisfied with 'pen and ink' defences (just as Ludendorff was later accused of running a pen and ink offensive). Therefore, an officer from 36 Division reflected that the battle zone in his area was not occupied in most places, and had no artillery or machine gun defences. Yet a spirit of unjustified optimism prevailed amongst the Higher Commanders. These showed elaborate trench systems protected by strong barbed wire entanglements. To these were added arcs of fire of machine guns and artillery barrages, that not only did not exist, but in all probability, and as it turned out, would never exist. In trench warfare, these Commanders and their staff had so little to do that they indulged in a form of map warfare from which they were unable to divorce themselves when operations away from a set piece occurred.

Others remarked on the same 'pen and ink' style of defence, for example, an officer in 2 Division succinctly remarked that the 'Green line [rear zone] did not exist except on the map'. Then an officer in 14 Division stated that the Crozat canal line 'was a purely paper one, and about as bad as possible'. He also argued that even genuine strong points 'were such only in name. They were absolutely untenable and troops left them and held ground between them.'

Probably there was a wide variation between the illusory 'pen and ink' type of defence, and the stronger defences in units that had been longer in the area. The problem here tended to be, not the outpost zone, or in many cases, the battle zone, but the rear zone. So when III Corps took over its line from the French, it found that there was nothing behind the well- prepared French front-line defence. III Corps' solution to building a rear zone therefore was simply to make posts at the rear of the battle zone, which apparently did delay the German offensive as it broke through the other zones. This probably accounts for the fact that XVIII Corps, with time to build its well-constructed defence system, could afford to hold the line in depth, while III Corps felt obliged to hold its front line in strength.

According to Lieutenant Colonel Lindsay, the machine gun adviser of First Army, 'Only on one or two Corps fronts on March 20 was the rearward zone system anything more than a name or a novelty. Only on one or two Corps fronts was there any visible sign that we had taken to heart the meaning of the German provision for "at least one rearward defensive zone, behind the battle zone".' There was also the natural tendency to construct the rear zone last, and so this was the least well-prepared defence.

Therefore, when Edmonds visited Gough's Fifth Army defences just before the battle, he found the rear zone was like a long Great Wall of China trace, only 3 feet wide and a few inches deep. Gough had ridden along the rear zone with a cavalry unit, instructing them where to stick in lances to mark the line for future construction.

Fifth Army's poor rear zone, which Haig significantly called the Reserve Line (implying therefore not so much a defensive line as an area to hold reserves), and which he constantly drew Gough's attention to, did pose a considerable problem. This was partly because it was not completed. But more serious was the fact that GHQ evidently felt that Fifth Army might have to retreat and fight in its rear defences, on the line of the River Somme and the town of Péronne. And this reveals a deep-seated flaw in GHQ's plan, namely, that from the outset GHQ anticipated Fifth Army falling back, rather than fighting in the battle zone as the defence in depth system required. Such an action would automatically create strains between Fifth Army and Third Army to its left, and very probably open up gaps between the two armies. This result was even more likely because Third Army, in contrast to Fifth Army, was supposed to hold on to its front and battle zones and not fall back. This inbuilt problem was definitely compounded by Gough's decision to hold his front zone in strength, particularly with his machine guns and Lewis guns. If this front zone was lost, then Fifth Army was going to be in very considerable difficulties. Fifth Army therefore did not adhere to the three-zone defence scheme, and the whole defence in depth concept of GHQ was in trouble at the very start.

Before the battle, Gough was ordered to take 50 per cent of his machine guns and put them behind his front line. However, according to Brigadier General Ironside, he did not do this, 'and derided the idea of not fighting for the front line'. Ironside was sent up to the front as Inspector of machine guns (being the commander of the Small Arms School) and verified Gough's dispositions of his machine guns in the front line two days before the German offensive. A qualified confirmation of Ironside's point comes from a staff officer of 14 Division, in Fifth Army, who recalled that his division placed 30 machine guns and 2 brigades of field artillery in the front zone, as opposed to 34 machine guns, a number of trench mortars and 2 brigades of field artillery in the battle zone. This was not as much strength in the forward zone as Ironside indicated, but it was more than should have been there. In contrast, Third Army had thinned its forward zones more than Fifth Army. Ironside recalled that Gough was supercritical of orders from above, and sneered at GHQ, and so ignored GHQ's orders. The result was predictable, as described by the GSO 1 of III Corps, who wrote in understated fashion: 'The German attack in swamping the forward troops, captured or destroyed a large proportion of our Machine and Lewis Guns, and our lack of these was very much felt during the subsequent days of the fighting.' This officer tended to blame his divisions rather than Fifth Army for these dispositions, saying that 'The Corps difficulty was to prevent Divisions putting all their men in the front line, and although we thinned them out and kept a Brigade in Reserve, we should have done better, if we had thinned them out still more.'

On the other hand, a staff officer in 36 Division of XVIII Corps indicated that the problem of the defence lay between the corps within Fifth Army. About a week before the attack this officer realized that while his corps was going to hold the line in depth— the three-zone system— the next corps to his right, III Corps, was going to hold the front zone in strength, and not in depth. Consequently, the Fifth Army staff was appealed to, but the reply was that the two corps would have to settle the matter between them. In the end, the matter was not resolved (and obviously could not be, given Gough's point of view, and the differing state of the defences in the two corps). The 36 Division staff officer feared that because of the different policies, the flank of his XVIII Corps would be turned when and if III Corps' front line was overwhelmed. When this did happen, he believed that 'to my mind this was the cause of the disaster [to 36 Division] on the first day'. However, the general impression before the battle was that Fifth and Third Armies had different policies, the former to retire and the latter to hold fast. This was, of course, correct, and it had a poor effect, since as an officer of 2 Division remembered 'it seemed to me wrong at the time, however, that it should be known by everyone down to private soldiers that the troops on their flank were intending to retire when the attack came.... I do know that even before the 21st March, and afterwards during the Retreat, there was so much talk of retiring that whenever an attack came everyone was asking "when are we to retire".'

The three-zone defence in depth system was evidently almost unworkable before the German offensive. It simply did not fully exist on the ground, nor did it operate as an integrated system. A good example of the latter problem lies in the machine gun defensive arrangements. Lieutenant Colonel Lindsay observed that even in those few divisions where the machine gun defences spanned the forward system from the rear of that system, there was little relationship between the forward system and the battle zone, or between the battle zone and the usually non-existent rear zone. Even in the battle zone, there was normally a linear machine gun defence, reflecting the idiosyncrasies of infantry commanders and CREs, and which showed up only too well to aerial reconnaissance. Lindsay also pointed to improper chains of command, poor communications, and the continued use of the unworkable belt filling machines, rather than the web belts, available in England, for loading machine guns. Finally, Lindsay deprecated the lack of a key element of the German defence scheme, namely, the mobile machine gun reserve. In this latter statement, Lindsay was supported by several corps commanders, who called for the formation of mobile corps machine gun reserves. Lindsay believed that only on the VI Corps front, and on the front of 56 Division, First Army, was there a proper machine gun defence in place before the German March offensive, and it was just in those areas that the defence was most successful.

One does not therefore have to look far to explain the German success in March 1918. This was not primarily due to German superiority in divisions, nor to the mist, nor to the French line taken over by the BEF, nor to the lack of manpower, nor to the reduction of infantry battalions in the BEF, nor to the divisions sent to Italy. Rather it was due to a defensive system that was not understood, did not work and did not properly exist at all. This was primarily the fault of GHQ, which lacked a sense of urgency in preparing defences, which advocated different policies in Fifth and Third armies, and which did not ensure the BEF's comprehension, coordination and compliance with its defensive concept. One may have some sympathy with GHQ, for as Lieutenant Colonel Lindsay observed, there were plenty of corps, division and brigade staff who 'either mistrusted this doctrine [defence in depth] or insisted on the exact opposite'.24 In this regard, the failure of the system was also the fault of Gough, GOC of Fifth Army, who placed too much emphasis on defending the front line or outpost zone, and who as always (as before Passchendaele) refused to listen to advice. Finally, corps commanders and staff must bear some responsibility for not ensuring that there was good coordination in applying this defence system between adjoining divisions in their corps, which was exactly the same problem as occurred at Cambrai when the German counter-offensive took place.

One other aspect of the defensive preparations may be noted, and this was the cooperation with the French. With the initial failure of the attempt to create a General Reserve, except on paper, there was an effort to coordinate a plan for mutual assistance when the enemy offensive took place. The BEF plan to assist the French Sixth Army was organized by Lieutenant General Hamilton Gordon, GOC IX Corps, in February and March. On 6 March, the French anticipated an attack on the BEF's Third and Fifth Armies and considered the line of the Oise a dangerous area. The French also expected an assault on the French line at Rheims in the south, and this was to slow down their assistance to the BEF. (On 21 March, Haig believed that the German attack had extended to Rheims and beyond.) However, the BEF IX Corps plan for helping the French did not reach GHQ until around 22 March, and it was only on 17 March that Davidson began to form the nucleus of an intervention staff at GHQ. Due to the late timing of these intervention plans, had the German army first attacked the French, it is unlikely that the BEF would have acted any more swiftly in aiding the French than the French did in assisting the BEF.

From the French point of view, the arrangements made on 7 March were that the French would either intervene in Fifth Army's rear zone and counter-attack if the offensive was serious, or relieve Fifth Army in the battle zone. On 20 March, General Humbert (GOC French Third Army) promised six divisions, either in six days, or in two days if detrained from Amiens. On the second day of the German offensive, 22 March, Haig chose the more significant of the two assistance plans and requested French intervention. So two French infantry divisions and one French cavalry division were immediately ordered to form in the rear of Fifth Army to secure the line of the Crozat canal. By 26 March, Pétain said that 9 French divisions were engaged, and 15 more were on their way up. Afterwards,

Davidson argued that the mutual reinforcement plan had failed, because the French anticipated an attack on their front, and Haig complained of the slowness of French help. But on the whole, French asistance had been as prompt as could reasonably be expected, given their fears of an attack, the late date of the arrangements, and the confusing situation with Fifth Army.

Subsequently, relations between the French and the BEF took a turn for the worse at a meeting between Pétain and Haig on 24 March. In a celebrated incident at the meeting, Haig understood that Pétain intended that the French divisions around Montdidier would retreat to the southwest, in order to cover Paris, and thus cause a break between the French army and the BEF. At this disastrous news, Haig asked the CIGS, Wilson, to come over to France from London, and on 26 March, at the Allied conference at Doullens, Foch was named as the overall Allied commander on the Western Front. Foch's appointment was intended to overrule Pétain, in order to ensure that no break occurred between the two armies, and that the retreat be halted. However, the matter is not as clear as Haig makes out, for on 23 March, the day before the critical meeting, Pétain and Haig had also met, and at this meeting Pétain had emphasized very strongly to Haig the need for the British Fifth Army and General Pellé's French V Corps to keep in touch. Pétain also said that in order to make sure the enemy did not cause a break between the BEF and the French forces, he would place two armies under Fayolle (commanding the French Reserve armies) in the Somme valley to stem the retreat and keep the two countries' armies in touch. He could not meet Haig's request, however, to place 20 French divisions around Amiens because of a possible German attack in the Champagne area.

Since at the meeting of 23 March Pétain had stressed above all the need to maintain contact between the French and British armies, it does not seem likely that Pétain would so radically change his mind by the next day, at the meeting of 24 March. In fact, on 24 March, at the crucial meeting between Pétain and Haig, it is apparent that it was Pétain who was afraid that the BEF would break with the French army and attempt to retire on the Channel ports, and not the other way around. In fact, in order to support his case for the necessity of continued contact between the two armies, Pétain pointed out to Haig that while the French army had all of France to retire in, the BEF would not be so well situated if they tried to break with the French. To back up this argument, Pétain also said that in that case, if the BEF retreated northwest to the Channel ports, then, if necessary, the Montdidier divisions would fall back south-westwards toward Beauvais, to cover Paris. However, Pétain obviously felt that he had persuaded Haig to maintain touch between the two armies, since another participant at the 24 March meeting, Major General Clive, reported that Pétain came away from the meeting satisfied with Haig's plans, saying that he would sleep better that night than for many nights. Again, the sense is that it was Pétain who was more seriously worried about Haig's plans than Haig was worried about Pétain's ideas. Nevertheless, it was as a result of that meeting that Haig immediately ordered Lawrence to send a wire to Wilson to come to France.

However, Wilson's diary does not conform to Haig's account. According to Wilson's entry for 24 March, although he was not satisfied with the plans of Haig and Pétain for mutual assistance, nevertheless it was at about 7 or 8 p.m. that night that Haig telephoned to say the BEF's Third Army was retreating and that Wilson should come over. This telephone call took place some three hours before Haig met Pétain at 11 p.m. on the evening of the same day, 24 March. Thus Haig's request for Wilson to come to France could not have related to the meeting with Pétain, which had not yet taken place. Instead Haig's telephone call to Wilson actually related to his visit to Third Army on that evening, 24 March, when a critical gap had opened up between Third and Fifth Armies. Haig obviously did not hold out much hope for Fifth Army, since his instructions were for Third Army to cling, not to Fifth Army, but to the right of First Army at Arras at all costs. This indicates a break with Fifth Army and the French, and so Haig was already contemplating the BEF swinging back to the northwest toward the Channel ports, breaking with the French and abandoning Fifth Army. Certainly this was sufficient cause to summon Wilson to France, but it was not because

Pétain proposed a break with the BEF. In fact, the whole situation was the reverse of what Haig actually believed or afterwards stated. Instead of Haig facing a crisis because of Pétain's proposed actions, in reality it was Haig who had created a crisis for Pétain in suggesting a break with the French. Moreover, the real reason that Haig summoned Wilson to France was because Haig was seriously worried that the BEF was in danger of collapse. No doubt the meeting with Pétain late on 24 March accentuated Haig's worries, especially as to whether Pétain would bring up French divisions to hold the area around Amiens. This interpretation is supported by the entry next day, 25 March, in Wilson's diary, which otherwise makes little sense. On this next day, Wilson reported that Haig was cowed, saying that unless the whole French army came up, the BEF was beaten, 'and it would be better to make peace on any terms we could'. Then Haig and Wilson discussed the possibility of an Allied supreme commander, and Haig suggested Pétain. It was hardly likely that Haig would have nominated Pétain for this post if he had been deeply concerned with Pétain's plans for breaking with the BEF and retreating to cover Paris. Wilson writes that he brushed aside Haig's preference for Pétain and suggested Foch, to whom Haig objected, but 'in the end Haig agreed'. With Foch as supreme commander, Wilson recorded that on the following day, 26 March, Haig was '10 years younger tonight than he was yesterday afternoon'.

It would seem, therefore, that Haig had understandably been considerably shaken by the retreat of his own BEF from 23 to 25 March. It is possible, then, that Haig used the Pétain 'incident' to conceal the fact that on 24 March he thought the BEF was in a desperate position, and really called Wilson over to France because he thought the BEF was near to disaster. This argument is supported by the fact that from 23 to 25 March Haig's primary objective seemed to be to obtain reinforcements of 20 French divisions from Pétain in order to save Amiens and the BEF, rather than concern over any break with the French. Hence, the central consideration of his talk with Wilson on 25 March was not Pétain's possible break with the BEF, but whether the French would at once provide 20 divisions north of the Somme, to cover Amiens. These French forces, being north of the Somme, would not have acted to keep Fifth Army in touch with the French army, although they could have been used as a counter-attack force.

One other piece of evidence suggests that Lawrence, the other participant in the critical Dury conference on 24 March between Haig and Pétain, was also not fully convinced of Haig's version of events. There exists a postwar correspondence between Lawrence and Haig in regard to the Dury conference, which includes a letter from Pétain to Haig. In Pétain's letter, the future leader of Vichy France denied that he issued orders to his forces to 'replier l'Armée Françise sur PARIS', and also denied that he told Haig this. Instead, Pétain claimed that he said to Haig 'de ne pas lâcher la main que je vous tendais'. Despite Pétain's letter, Haig maintained to Lawrence that his own version of events was correct. Lawrence evidently made a contrary argument in his reply to Haig, for in Haig's second letter to Lawrence he agreed to accept amendments to his version of events. Nevertheless, Haig remained convinced that Pétain had warned his divisions around Montdidier that they should retreat southwest if the German advance on Amiens continued. Haig concluded that he therefore felt Pétain was not sound in his ideas. One final aspect reinforces the obscurity of the Pétain 'incident', namely the fact that Haig asked Lady Haig on 19 April 1918 to type up notes of various meetings which he had with Pétain and Foch after 21 March, since GHQ wanted these notes and 'none have been kept by them of what took place'.

In other words, the version of events of 24 March and surrounding days would be based on what Haig had written in his diary and sent home to his wife. Thus the final version of the incident, which was prepared by Lawrence and Davidson, and used in the British Official History, was apparently based on Haig's recollections of Pétain's verbal statements as amended by Davidson. And even here, Pétain was reported as only providing possible future alternatives at the meeting on 24 March, rather than explicit statements as to what he would do. For example, Pétain thought that the main German attack was yet to come and would be in Champagne. In that event, Pétain said he might be obliged to cover Paris, and should the Germans continue to advance on Amiens, the southwest retreat could take place.

From Pétain's point of view, the meetings of 23 and 24 March with Haig really revolved around the question of whether the BEF would maintain contact with the French or not. As has been argued, this was a justified concern, and there was evidence to support Pétain's suspicions. According to Brigadier General Charles Grant, British liaison officer at the French GQG, Gough's Fifth Army had received conditional orders, 24 hours before the German offensive, that his primary concern was to cover the Channel ports, thus discounting the importance of contact with the French. In fact, it was general knowledge in the BEF before the German offensive that retirement to the Channel ports was a distinct option. So, for example, Lieutenant General Fanshawe, GOC V Corps, Third Army, told Edmonds soon after the war that on 23 March, Byng, GOC Third Army, informed his corps commanders that it had not yet been settled whether to retire northwest on the Channel ports or due west in order to keep in touch with the French. In fact, according to the Official History, Haig visited Byng at 8 p.m. on 24 March and told him to cling to First Army near Arras, to his north, rather than to Fifth Army or to the French to the south. Similarly, Brigadier General Currie, GOC Canadian Corps, recalled several discussions with Brigadier General Dyer, GOC 7 Canadian Brigade, over the winter of 1917–18: 'You will remember how often we debated the advisability of our separating from the French and retiring on the Channel ports—or of our keeping in contact with the French and leaving the Channel to take care of itself.'

Then, when the offensive did arrive, Edmonds recalled that Dill at GHQ could not tell him at an early stage of the retreat whether the BEF would keep connection with the French, or go into a defensive 'island'. Certainly by 25 March, Haig's plan was to retreat northwest, toward the Channel ports, as he told Weygand on that date, and more specifically he told Byng, also on 25 March, 'that the BEF had now to safeguard itself and that no help could be expected from the South [i.e. the French]. He [Haig] made it quite clear that any further withdrawal must be in a North West direction and the Third Army must safeguard the right flank of the BEF by swinging its own right back [that is, breaking with the French]. Sir Douglas also took it for granted that no help was to be expected from the remains of the Fifth Army.' Thus in a prefiguring of a future date, 1940, and a future war, the French had considerable reason to worry that it was the BEF that was going to abandon them, and not the other way around. Consequently, even on 26 March, after Foch had been agreed upon as Allied commander, the French were still afraid that the BEF would leave the road to Amiens open and retire on the Channel ports. Finally, this interpretation is also supported by Liddell Hart, who argued later that GHQ and Byng were thinking of covering the Channel ports before they were thinking of maintaining links with the French.

The inside story of the 24 March meeting between Haig and Pétain, and the arrival of Wilson (and Milner) in France, is therefore a reversal of the normal interpretation. Haig desperately sought help from the War Office, not because of Pétain, but because of the severe problems of Fifth and Third Armies. This reason for Haig's appeal to the War Office was hidden as the blame was laid on Pétain, who was accused of aiming to separate the French forces from the BEF. However, on the contrary, it was Pétain, and the French GQG generally, who were afraid that the BEF would desert the French. It is also true that Haig did not trust the French, or their intentions, and the meeting with Pétain late on 24 March must have increased his already considerable anxiety. However, that was not Haig's primary concern during the period 23 to 26 March. Instead, this was, not surprisingly, the survival of the BEF, to such an extent that he was willing to serve under Foch, whom he disliked. However, the end result of these events was the creation of a supreme Allied commander, a new spirit of confidence in Haig and GHQ, and a turning point both in the defensive battles of spring 1918, and in the war as a whole.

With this understanding of the background of the BEF defensive battle in March 1918, it is now possible to turn to certain central events of the defensive battle of the BEF. Other books have discussed this battle in some detail, and so it is intended to focus only on the key elements of the retreat.30 There were really three major events that will be discussed: first, the initial German breakthroughs on 21 and 22 March; second, the belated evacuation of the Flesquières or Cambrai salient by Third Army on 22 and 23 March; and third, the retirement of Fifth Army behind the line of the Somme between 22 and 25 March. Some of the reasons for the initial German breakthroughs have already been addressed, namely, overconfidence at GHQ, the early loss of communications, problems with the outpost zone and, most important, the difficulty of the BEF in comprehending, adapting to and actually constructing, the three-zone defence in depth system.

It may be useful therefore, first, to follow the fortunes of just two divisions—16 and 47 Divisions—in order to understand the reasons for the initial German breathrough. In discussing the actions of 47 Division, it will also be possible to use this division's story to explain the tardy withdrawal of V Corps from the Cambrai or Flesquières salient.

Commencing with 16 Division, it is of interest that the commander of VII Corps, in which 16 Division served, Lieutenant General Sir Walter Congreve, was less than complimentary about this division: 'the real truth is that their reserve Brigade did not fight at all and their right Brigade very indifferently, but there are excuses to be made for them in length of time they had been in the line and in a late reorganisation of units'.31 Congreve may well have been correct, yet a review of personal accounts of the battle shows that one of the most difficult aspects of command in retreat was the coordination of adjoining units, whether they be brigades, divisions, corps, or armies. Almost every description of events contains direct or indirect references to lines of command passing vertically downwards from various headquarters, but with very little horizontal contact between units that shared a geographical area, yet could not coordinate their defences. Another and more understandable feature of personal accounts is constant surprise at German tactics in avoiding frontal assaults, and thus getting around to the flanks and rear of defending units. A final aspect of these personal accounts is the wide range of reactions by units, some fighting fiercely, others being content simply to retreat. Colonel Ramsay (48 Brigade, 16 Division) later remarked that on 21 March, 'the enemy made no frontal attack on the 16th Division front, except on the extreme flanks.... On both flanks the enemy advanced in column formation up the valleys and under cover of the smoke wheeled round and on the south [or right] side came in behind the 49th and 48th Brigades.' On the other hand, on the north or left side, the withdrawal of an advanced post of 21 Division left 48 Brigade (2 battalions of the Munsters) holding a salient. Another account by a captain of the 2nd Royal Munster Fusiliers reports that outposts of his battalion held out in this salient, with parts of the neighbouring 21 Division, until 22 March, and thus prevented withdrawal of the right flank of 21 Division for 24 hours. Another officer from 16 Division, Colonel Goodland, this time in the 1st Royal Munster Fusiliers of the reserve brigade, simply recalled a steady retreat throughout 21 March, thereby supporting Congreve's critical comments mentioned above. But on the evening of 21 March, when the reserve brigade fell back to the rear zone, they found no defences, 'it was only an imaginary line marked out by cut turf, and no wire'. This brigade continued to fall back until 26 March when it reached the village of Proyart. There 'after watching the enemy infiltrate, in the most extraordinary and efficient manner, into the cover of the dead ground,

[the enemy] attacked in force, and the rest of the history of the 16th Division, after that evening is shrouded in mystery'. In other words, the division had disintegrated, and Goodland 'spent all that night commanding a company composed of individuals of every Regiment in the Division'. By 28 or 29 March, Goodland had been wounded, and he found himself and his runner alone in Moreuil Wood, with no living soul in the village of Moreuil, and the Germans ten minutes behind him. He escaped by getting into a railway hand car and being pushed by his runner along the railway line to Boves!

What had caused the collapse of 16 Division? This unit was unfortunate in being the extreme right-hand division of VII Corps, adjoining XIX Corps, and those divisions which bordered other divisions in different corps almost all had severe problems during the retreat. For example, on 23 March at a critical stage of the retreat, 16 Division never knew which division from the adjoining XIX Corps was actually on its flank, and in fact tried to keep contact with the wrong unit, 50 Division, when in reality the division next to them was 66 Division. The GSO 1 of 16 Division also remembered that late at night on 22 March he had been expecting to fight on the green or reserve line, when to his great surprise he discovered that his neighbouring divisions were already retiring behind the green line: Gen. Malcolm [GOC 66 Division]…came in to see us at Doingt [16 Division HQ] during the night. I cannot now remember the exact time, but I had been asleep, and it seemed very late.

General Hull [GOC 16 Division] was also asleep, and we did not wake him. Gen. Malcolm told me that his division was already on its way back to the left bank of the Somme, and I gathered from him that 50/ Div. was also retiring. My recollection is that I told Gen. Malcolm that we had been expecting to fight on the Green Line on the 23rd, and that as soon as he left I rang up VII Corps to find out whether they knew of this change.

Soon after, VII Corps replied and issued a warning order to 16 Division that if a further withdrawal was necessary it was to retreat to a position astride, and then behind, the Somme: 'Our actual orders to move were issued on receipt of their [VII Corps] 5 am message [on 23 March].' This seemingly independent decision by the two XIX Corps divisions, 66 and 50, to retire, is explained by the GSO 2 of VII Corps, who wrote that at 4 am on 23rd [March] Gen. Watts GOC XIX Corps rang me… up to say that he had issued orders for a withdrawal behind the Somme. The VII Corps at that time was fairly secure and reorganised on the rear (Green) line and I told him the withdrawal of the XIX Corps would leave our right [that is, 16 Division] at Tincourt in the air, that it was a very serious matter and would he speak to Gen. Congreve. He said he was sorry but it was a matter of necessity and I got him to speak to my general. We always thought that this withdrawal and our consequent retirement in day-light from a good position on the Green line was the cause of our subsequent troubles.

Why had XIX Corps forced VII Corps to withdraw, thereby of course requiring 16 Division, as part of VII Corps, to follow suit? A staff officer of 8 Division in XIX Corps was an eye-witness to events in the early morning hours of 23 March at XIX Corps headquarters at Villers- Carbonel, where he had gone to seek orders. He described a scene of considerable chaos:

> The BGGS was up the line trying to find out the situation, the Corps HQ were trying to pack up and move back quickly, an operation for which a Corps HQ at that time were singularly unsuited. To add to the general chaos a bomb had just dropped in the middle of the GS building killing or wounding nearly everyone in it. The Q Branch were very helpful, but being quite in ignorance of the situation they could not well issue fresh orders.

The impression is of a corps HQ under considerable pressure, and issuing retirement orders as it retired itself.

With the retirement behind the green or reserve line on 23 March, ultimately due to XIX Corps' troubles, 16 Division was basically in a constant state of retreat until relieved that night by 39 Division. Then on 24 March 16 Division went into reserve at Cappy, but by this time had lost a very considerable number of men, either killed or wounded, or as prisoners and stragglers, so that brigades were down to perhaps sixty to one hundred men each. However, the German advance continued, and on 26 March, due to a series of counter-orders from a mentally and physically worn-out VII Corps commander, Congreve, the division retired rapidly, and simply ceased to exist. Congreve was sent home in May 1918, ostensibly for health reasons, although he was in fact perfectly healthy. Thus the story of 16 Division comes full circle back to the corps commander, despite his original criticisms of 16 Division. However, 16 Division was not the only unit that essentially disappeared, the same was true of its neighbour, 66 Division, in XIX Corps, whose HQ also ceased to function on 26 March, and then the next day disappeared.

So far, therefore, it would seem that the root cause of divisional problems tended to lie with corps commanders and staff, who did not coordinate or cooperate with adjoining corps, and who were, perhaps, too quick to retire themselves. The story of another division, 47 Division, may help to confirm or refute these ideas. This division was on the extreme right of V Corps, which itself was on the right of Third Army. As 47 Division and V Corps occupied the right of the Cambrai or Flesquières salient, so the adjoining division on the right of 47 Division was not in V Corps, but was 9 Division, which was the extreme left of VII Corps, within Fifth Army. At a lower level, Captain Dawes of the 1st Surrey Rifles (21st London Regiment), in 47 Division, tells the story of 21 and 22 March. Although the 1st Surrey Rifles suffered little on 21 March, its neighbours, the 17th London Regiment, were heavily attacked and its front zone occupied, largely, it seems, because of the severity of the artillery and gas bombardment.

About 5 p.m. on 21 March, the 1st Surrey Rifles lost contact with 9 Division on its right, and probably because of this the CO of the 1st Surrey Rifles asked for reinforcements and assurances as to his right flank. These were denied, and he was told to retire the regiment the following morning. This was done early on 22 March, with no interference from the enemy. Attacks were later beaten off, but that evening a further retirement took place, which on 23 March turned into a retreat to Equancourt around midday. The warning order for this retreat was issued between 9 and 9.30 a.m. on 23 March, but the confirming order was never received. Instead men of the neighbouring battalion (23rd) were seen retiring, and they told the 1st Surrey Rifles Battalion HQ that they and their entire brigade was on the move back. Indeed the commanding officer of the 23rd Battalion announced rather brazenly 'that he was leaving shortly with his HQ and asked O.C. 21st to cover the withdrawal of his right Coy (Captain Brett)'. It is at this point that 47 Division obviously starts to unravel.

According to Captain Dawes, their battalion commander then issued orders to the 1st Surrey Rifles to retire around 1 p.m. on 23 March, because the brigade on its left was withdrawing, although 47 Division had not been heard from with a confirming order. Soon after, while the commanding officer of the 1st Surrey Rifles was reconnoitring, 'troops were seen coming over the hill, and on their near approach proved to be Germans so O.C. 21st [1st Surrey Rifles] retired rapidly in the direction of Equancourt'. Unfortunately, Equancourt was also occupied by the Germans, so a makeshift headquarters was established by 140 Brigade (under whom the 1st Surrey Rifles served) where 'details of all units of the brigade' were established. In other words, units of this brigade of 47 Division, including the 1st Surrey Rifles, were all mixed up. Under enemy artillery fire, this ad hoc defensive line came back to the outskirts of the village of Bus, where they found troops of 63 Division consolidating, which had originally been on the left of 47 Division. Eventually, the scattered units of 140 Brigade, including the 1st Surrey Rifles, were reunited at Rocquigny.

What is clear from this low-level account is that 47 Division lost touch with its brigades, and therefore with its battalions and regiments, some time on the morning of 23 March. This is confirmed by the brigade major of 140 Brigade, who reported that we also suffered through losing complete touch with our divisional HQ (47th Division), and after getting the orders for the withdrawal which took place on the morning of the 23rd, received no further orders till the middle of the 24th when we were ordered to retire on Combles, (these orders were received when we were holding a line near Le Transloy and knew the Germans were already in Les-Bouefs and approaching Flers!).

In other words, 47 Division had got back into touch, but was a long way behind events. The problem seemed to be that V Corps itself had lost contact with 47 Division, as recalled by a staff officer, who wrote that in the early morning of 24 March, V Corps did not know where 47 Division was. (This was especially critical because 47 Division was supposed to be covering the gap between V Corps and VII Corps, the boundary of Third Army and Fifth Army.) 'The point I want to make is that it was the task of 47th Division to fill the gap, that this Div. failed to do so…17 Div. could not get in touch with 47th Division all day 24 March. The latter Div. seemed to have disintegrated and many elements of it dribbled in during the day and joined Bde. of 17th Div.' On 24 March, 47 Division was lost, in fact it had disappeared, and 'I had many talks on the telephone with Gen. Boyd (BGGS V Corps) from dawn onwards and it was very definitely understood between us that 47th Div. was non-est [not operating] and that 17th Div. had automatically become right Div. V Corps'.

Essentially, then, 47 Division had become disorganized by the hesitant retirement of V Corps from the Cambrai or Flesquières salient, which was supposed to be held as a false front, and the division had then disappeared. So, turning secondly to the evacuation of the Flesquières salient, it seems that the fault lay partly with Byng, Third Army commander, under whom Fanshawe, as V Corps commander, served. Byng later told Edmonds that he decided not to evacuate the salient on the evening of 21 March because the report from Fifth Army to the south was more optimistic than the situation later turned out to be. But obviously more important in Byng's mind was the visit that he made to his V Corps commander, Fanshawe, on the afternoon of 21 March. This was before Byng had heard from Fifth Army, and in this visit he and Fanshawe had already decided that they could re-establish their line of defence in the salient, and so V Corps should do no more than retreat to the intermediate line. Byng was apparently unwilling to give up the salient he had gained in the Cambrai battle, and his delay in ordering the retirement to the base of the salient meant that V Corps was caught in a German pincer operation designed to pinch out the salient. It is amusing to learn that shortly afterwards Byng told Haig that the March retreat had been a corps commanders battle!

Byng's delay in ordering a withdrawal was supported by Fanshawe, since another source indicates that V Corps, and at least 63 Divisional Headquarters, were thinking of a counter-attack on the night of 21 March. No doubt therefore Fanshawe cooperated with Byng in delaying their retirement from the salient. Some of the fault must lie therefore with Fanshawe, who also admitted that his V Corps headquarters was delinquent in being too far back, and thus poor in communicating with his divisions. As a result, V Corps HQ was always behind the battle, and out of touch. The combination of leaving the salient too late and of the poor contact between V

Corps and its divisions meant a series of hasty retirements, as illustrated by 47 Division, in which the division had 'very little rest', and was 'kept constantly on the move, by frequent withdrawals, or movements to support a flank, throughout the three nights and three days 21st, 22nd, 23rd'. Hence, the problems at the lowest level of the 1st Surrey Rifles really reflected a series of unwise decisions at division, corps and army level.

The experience of 47 Division had unusual results, because the division was, as previously mentioned, at the junction of V and VII Corps, and also therefore at the junction of Third and Fifth Armies. When 47 Division retired, however, it was northwest, away from 9 Division of VII Corps, Fifth Army. Curiously, even before the German offensive, 9 Division had been assigned a certain amount of Third Army frontage, and perhaps even half of 9 Division's front was actually in the Third Army area. An officer of 9 Division wrote:

> In vain we begged them [47 Division] to take over down to the boundary. It was when our line was stretched to 12,000 yards, at least half of which was in Third Army area, that it was broken for the first time. From the first day, 21st, we (9th Div.) saw that the right of the Third Army, not being attacked, was holding on too long and dreaded their being driven north-westwards. On 23rd the inevitable happened and a wide gap was left by 47th Div. being driven in that direction. All the ground in the gap was in Third Army area, and the left flank of 9th Div. was completely exposed.

In fact, by the morning of 23 March, there was not much of 9 Division left. Why did 47 Division retire away from 9 Division, and thus cause the critical gap that impelled Haig to summon Wilson to France? Judging by the accounts of 47 Division and the 1st Surrey Rifles, it was because they were forced to by German efforts to cut off the salient, and perhaps also because of problems with the terrain.

The experience of these two divisions—16 and 47—over the first days of the German offensive, really shows that once the retreat started the command structure lost control of the battle, starting with the corps level and filtering down to the division level fairly quickly. In some ways, Byng's comment that the March retreat was a corps commanders battle, has merit. On the other hand, Byng's initial decision at the army level on 21 March to defend the salient did set in train a sequence of events which basically unravelled V Corps, and then the adjoining VII Corps.

Finally, thirdly, what was the cause of Fifth Army's rapid retreat behind the Somme River line of defence? Later accounts of the battle include the usual recriminations between corps commanders in Fifth Army as to whose divisions either caused a gap, or forced other divisions to retire. Hence, the GSO 1 of III Corps said that 36 Division of XVIII Corps was not forced back by the retirement of 14 Division in his own Corps, but by the presence of the enemy 5 1/2 miles to his rear, due to XVIII Corps' mistake at the canal defence at Ham! On the other hand, the corps commander of III Corps, Butler, admitted 'that the role of the III Corps was to cover the French left, i.e. Compiègne, and that this came before keeping touch with the Corps on my left [XVIII Corps] i.e. it was essential that the break through should not be between the English & French'. However, according to an officer of 36 Division, the state of III Corps was not good on either flank: the French were called upon to intervene on the 23rd when the whole of the III Corps was in a state of confusion. There was no definite line to take over, or units to relieve. The ground was unfamiliar to the French. They had indifferent maps, and they were not provided with proper guides to their new positions. Every village was full of disorganised troops. The so-called relief by the French on the night of 23/24th was a purely paper one. A relief under such conditions was doomed to failure. The result was that on March 24 when the Germans renewed their attack, the whole left wing of the III Corps collapsed. The retreat soon developed into a rout. The admixture of British units was so general that all command had ceased to exist.

If the flanks of III Corps were porous, so was the join between XVIII Corps and XIX Corps to the north. A staff officer of 25 Brigade, the extreme right unit of XIX Corps adjoining XVIII Corps, was afterwards accused by Maxse (GOC XVIII Corps) who 'said I let him in by not protecting his left flank & this is true but the fault was bad arrangements at the junction of the two Corps when officers and men were tired and it was pitch dark'. This officer actually blamed 1 Cavalry Division, who had previously held the join between the two corps before his 25 Brigade took over on the night of 23–4 March, but the cavalry 'either did not join up with Maxse's Corps or did not hand over to my 25 Brigade properly during the night'. As a result the Germans came through the gap, crossed the Somme River at Bethencourt, and moved south to menace the flank of Maxse's XVIII Corps.

Another example is on 23 March between XIX and XVIII Corps, where 24 Division (XIX Corps) and 20 Division (XVIII Corps) allowed a gap to appear. In this case, the gap was apparently created by the orders of XVIII Corps to 20 Division to retire behind the Somme, rather than by enemy action. A final example concerns IV and V Corps, who managed to create a large gap between them as they retreated, to the point where V Corps was withdrawing across IV Corps' line of retreat! The truth of the matter is that, just as in Third Army, once the retreat began in earnest, it was largely controlled by corps commanders, but the 'top-down' corps line of command in structured warfare was not designed for moving warfare, and so these lines of command simply did not cross over and link one corps with another. It was for this reason that the junctures between corps (and therefore armies) proved particularly vulnerable to the enemy's advance.

Corps commanders clearly had the utmost difficulty dealing with their flank divisions and brigades, but in XVIII Corps there were also special problems. One specific difficulty concerned the bridge at the village of Ham, a major crossing point of the Somme River. On the afternoon of 22 March, orders were issued by the XVIII Corps commander, Maxse, to retire behind the line of the Somme River, but the bridges were to be guarded while this retirement went on, and then blown up. According to Maxse, troops of 89 Brigade of 61 Division were allotted to hold Ham and its bridge, but owing to some mistake, they withdrew behind them, and uncovered Ham at a critical moment. However, an eye-witness account by Brigadier General Duncan (GOC 60 Brigade, 20 Division), explains what actually happened. Apparently, on the night of 22 March, Duncan left an officer and a lance corporal to stand at the entrance to Ham bridge until dawn on the 23rd, but they saw no sign of either British or German troops. (Ham, being on the right side of the Somme River, was more or less under German control, but the bridge was not.) To illustrate the haphazard nature of events at that moment, Duncan related the story of a battalion officer and his adjutant of 60 Brigade 'who had lost their regiment', but who ran into a German sentry in the village of Ham at about 9 p.m. on the night of 22 March. 'The Sentry claimed to take them prisoner, and the Officer made a counter claim. After some discussion, the Colonel asked the German "what the Devil he meant by talking like that to an Officer" whereupon the Sentry allowed him and his Adjutant to pass on unmolested!!!'

Meanwhile, Duncan himself stood at the entrance to Ham village until 2 a.m. on 23 March collecting all the men he could find, having sent what was left of his own brigade on to defend the line of the Somme. Duncan here was obviously functioning as a straggler post, but around 9 a.m. on the morning of 23 March, he received a strange order from General Gough via telegram (strange because Maxse should have issued the order, rather than Gough). The message read: 'Brigadier-General Duncan, 60th. You will counter attack Ham Bridge immediately.' Duncan did not believe he could move his few men of 60 Brigade from their positions, but he found a few men of 61 Division close beside him, behind a wall, lent them his brigade major, wrote out orders for a counter-attack, and sent them off to Ham bridge. These men must have been the remnants of 89 Brigade of 61 Division that Maxse had referred to, but they were not successful: 'They were able to hold the Germans for some time, but had to fall back and I collected them in the afternoon. I gathered from the German officer afterwards, whom we had taken prisoner, that Ham Bridge had not been completely blown up by our Engineers'.49 This story shows how intermingled units had become in XVIII Corps after only two days of the retreat, and also how the lines of command had become fractured—with the army commander Gough issuing direct orders to a brigade, and a brigade commander giving orders to men in a different division. On the other hand, this also displays a useful flexibility in reacting to a crisis. The action of Gough in issuing direct orders to a brigade raises the question of the relationship of Fifth Army to XVIII Corps. Here it is apparent that Gough and Maxse tended to misunderstand each other. Perhaps because of Lawrence's orders to Gough in February 1918 that Fifth Army could fall back on the rear defences of Péronne and the Somme, although maintaining the line of the Somme at all costs, Gough was already prepared to retreat before the battle began. According to an officer of 2 Cavalry Division, Gough had also informed Haig before the offensive started, that 'in the event of a heavy attack he did not expect to be able to hold the line with the troops at his disposal but that he would fight a rear guard action and maintain the line while retiring. He therefore presumably envisaged moving warfare.'

In fact, according to Major General Tudor, CRA of 9 Division, in Fifth Army, Gough's basic plan for Fifth Army was to bend, but not break. So by the evening of 21 March, Gough had issued a conditional order: a retreat to the line of the Somme was permitted, but only if necessary. On the morning of 22 March, XVIII Corps had lost the outpost zone, but was firmly established in the battle zone. Then at about 11 a.m. Gough visited XVIII Corps headquarters at Ham where Maxse explained the situation, but said that his flanks were being turned. According to a staff officer of XVIII Corps, Maxse then asked permission to move his Headquarters forward and fight his Battle on the line of their battle Zone, forming Defensive Flanks— the Army Commander refused this request on the grounds that, whereas the XVIII Corps would no doubt inflict some casualties on their front on the enemy, the German advance would continue, and having no Reserves at his disposal a gap would occur which he had no means of filling.

Gough had evidently decided to maintain his concept of a rearguard action, and so he issued orders to his corps to retire to the rear zone, in the early afternoon of 22 March. Meanwhile, GHQ was obviously lagging behind Fifth Army in its control of the battle, because on the same day, but at 8 p.m., Gough telephoned Haig to say that German parties were through his reserve line, and Haig told him to fall back on the Somme and Péronne bridgehead. Yet at 11.30 p.m., Davidson officially told Fifth Army to hold the Péronne bridgehead, but if forced back, to hold the line of the Somme (which was the rear zone line). Fifth Army itself seems also to have underestimated the resolve of its troops, for one of XVIII Corps staff officers, Major Ling, was disgusted by the order to retire. He had gone along the battle zone at midday on 22 March, and found strong positions and resolution all along the line, except on the right flank. But everywhere else 'I found wonderful spirit & optimism and a determination & assurance that they could stay there for ever.... Then shortly after came the order from the [Fifth] Army & passed on by the Corps to retire to the rear zone along the whole Corps front.'

Major Ling complained that the corps had too easily and 'slavishly' passed along Fifth Army's order, although in fairness it is hard to see Maxse disobeying a direct order. Major Ling states that after the retirement order, he saw 61 Division of XVIII Corps 'marching sullenly back—it was obvious that their spirit was gone—broken by the order to retire for which they saw no reason whatever'. However, XVIII Corps staff apparently had a much more pessimistic view of the corps than did Major Ling, for while Ling found the divisions to be in 'wonderful spirit' at midday on 22 March, in contrast the XVIII Corps narrative says that it was obvious that the divisions were tired, their line was extended, and they would have to withdraw. Soon after, at 2.30 p.m., XVIII Corps headquarters shifted back from Ham to Nesle (a distance of some 10 kilometres), and around this same time XVIII Corps issued orders for the corps to retire behind the left bank of the Somme.

The conclusion is that, following the conditional Fifth Army order to withdraw, at about midday on 22 March, XVIII Corps headquarters became pessimistic, and instead of defending the line of the Somme as ordered, the corps went behind the Somme. Along the way, episodes such as the defence of Ham and its bridge on 23 March showed that XVIII Corps, like so many other corps, had lost contact with its divisions, and thus Fifth Army had to attempt to intervene. Yet the story of XVIII Corps and Fifth Army is curiously similar to that of V Corps and Third Army, in that an initial decision by the army commander set in train a series of events, which the corps commander on the spot was thereafter unable to control. Put simply, the articulation of the BEF was not able to meet the challenge of moving warfare—perhaps not surprisingly given three years of largely static warfare—and the whole chain of command from army downwards became unravelled.

A good example of this unravelling concerned 63 Division in V Corps, when on the morning of 24 March the division commander called up V Corps, and reported, ' "The BOCHE is through the Green [Battle zone] Line—what are your future plans?" The reply was "There are no future plans—you must fight it out as a unit." ' GHQ certainly contributed to this process with its initial over-confidence, expectation of a long-drawn-out battle, and subsequent confusion and slowness to react. So, for example, two of the reserve divisions behind Fifth Army, 20 and 39, were not released from GHQ reserve until 12.30 p.m. on 22 March, although Gough did apparently order them forward before then: 'It is indeed fortunate that the Fifth Army did not wait for GHQ for these divisions.' The delay in providing these reserve divisions also meant that a counter-attack was going to be difficult to mount with them, and in fact this never took place. The net result of all such command and communication problems was a German breakthrough in Fifth Army, which was not really halted until the end of March. As Major Ling put it, 'Once the backward movement had commenced the virus spread & it became almost impossible to prevent it'.

It is extraordinary how many accounts of the March retreat come back to the idea that this was really a battle of headquarters (whether army, corps, division, or brigade), and of how these headquarters set the pace of the retirement. Thus an officer of the 9th Royal Sussex Regiment accused his brigade commander of simply leaving them on 21 March: A brigade commander left his HQ at Hervilly at 6 pm—sending a message forward to O.C. 9th Roy Sx [Royal Sussex] at Hesbecourt that a Brigade commander (cavalry) would come and take over at midnight, which was never done. It was this retiring by H.Q.'s, leaving the Battle Zones uncommanded, that caused such confusion and loss. Had this infantry brigade commander come forward to Hesbecourt and reorganised this area...a great deal could have been done.

This account went on to argue that instead of brigadier generals staying close to the firing line, they left, and so 'What the men did hear was that Brigade, Div. & everybody behind them were packing up, had packed up & gone'. Whereas at Ypres in 1914, commanders went to the front lines, 'on the Somme 1918 they kept packing up.... All through this retreat many brigade & probably all divisional commanders could have been much nearer their troops than they were.'

Moving up to the divisional level, a strange story unfolded regarding the command of 150 Brigade of 50 Division, XIX Corps. During the afternoon of 22 March, 150 Brigade was out of touch with the divisional commander. This was because the Divisional Commander was actually, I believe, in search of the Corps commander [Maxse] who moved that afternoon. Divisional Headquarters moved that afternoon with the result that the Brigade Commander of the 150th Brigade who was the senior Brigade Commander, visited the other two Brigade Headquarters and decided what line was to be held that night. This line was afterwards confirmed by the Divisional Commander.

What this meant was that because XIX Corps moved, so did 50 Division, and because of this, 50 Division GOC could not find his Corps GOC, while 150 Brigade GOC could not find his 50 Division GOC! Therefore, the brigade commander of 150 Brigade had to take the place of his divisional commander and arrange the defence of the division.

The example of 150 Brigade precisely illustrates the 'filter down' chain reaction of corps decisions. Perhaps because of their distance from the front line, corps headquarters and corps commanders gave the impression of believing the worst of rumours and situations. One case in point was Haldane, GOC VI Corps, on the left of the area attacked in Third Army. According to the next-door Corps, VI Corps was not as badly beaten as it thought it was. The 3 Division GOC, Deverell, in VI Corps, proposed to Haldane to hold a new line south of Monchy on 22 March, but Haldane would not listen, probably because of his concern over IV Corps to his right. Then on 26 March when rumours of a German tank breakthrough (which turned out to be false) reached VI Corps headquarters, there was a hasty retirement by the corps commander, who departed an hour after his return to corps headquarters, and ahead of his staff. In his autobiography Haldane recalled that 'an hour after my return to the chateau the road had been cleared and a start could be made…I drove slowly through the village'. Haldane actually went to Noyelle Vion, and 'there when my staff later joined me', he heard that the rumour had come from Third Army and was false!

What seemed to happen in the BEF was that the army HQ level gave the conditional orders for a retreat if necessary, then corps HQs became pessimistic first, and withdrew quickly, thus setting the pace for the respective HQs and staff officers beneath them to follow suit. Currie, the Canadian Corps GOC, whose corps was in the north and not involved in the German attack, reported on 25 March 'Nurses and staff of hospital running away. Everything very windy down there, gale increasing the further back you went.' A similar story concerns a staff officer and the King's Own Yorkshire Light Infantry [KOYLI], near Bucquoy, as told in the memoir of Guy Chapman:

'You can't trust anyone,' said the adjutant bitterly. 'Two days ago we were in a magnificent position, place we could have held until the end of the world. Then we suddenly found the companies coming back. Some blasted brass hat had come along and given the order to retire. By the time we had stopped the retreat the Boche had nipped into our old line and the brass hat had disappeared. So here we are in the blue again about a hundred times worse off. Well, it's yours for keeps now. Take my tip; if you see any brass hats knocking around, shoot 'em.'

If the infantry were having problems with communications, lack of information, an inflexible command system, and very little understanding of the defence in depth concept, what of the artillery? Was the artillery, both heavy and field, supporting the infantry, or was it facing problems of its own?

Retirements of headquarters and consequent loss of of communications particularly affected the heavy artillery under corps HQ control, and this is reflected in the experiences of VII Corps on 21 March. Here the brigade major of VII Corps' heavy artillery reported that by 10 a.m.: practically all Artillery communications had been broken. The consequence was that no definite news was ever received at Heavy Artillery Headquarters as to when the German Infantry actually attacked, and similarly many batteries, which should at 9.15 a.m. have been firing on their S.O.S. lines, had no news, and were silent or only firing slowly. The first intimation many batteries had of any infantry action was when our own men retired through or near the Batteries.

The VII Corps heavy artillery HQ followed VII Corps HQ as it retreated, and a certain number of heavy guns and stores were lost as a result of lack of transport as the retreat became general. Moreover, 'it was found impossible for the GOC, Heavy Artillery to maintain touch with [heavy artillery] Brigades'. However, the artillery staff were equal to their task, and on 22 and 23 March, they largely broke up the VII Corps heavy artillery into a series of mobile horsed brigades, which were transferred to the CRAs of 9, 21 and 16 Divisions, and this flexible plan proved successful in overcoming the inertia of a corps-controlled heavy artillery in a moving battle.

In contrast to the frequently rather ponderous control of heavy artillery at corps headquarters (although not in VII Corps), the impression gained in regard to the field artillery is of an arm that was capable of looking after itself, and showing flexibility in the retreat. This did not necessarily mean keeping in touch with the infantry, who in the person of General Sir John Coleridge (GOC 188 Brigade) stated later that The idea of close support artillery was non-existent in those days, and much artillery was taken out of action prematurely which might well have stayed with the infantry to a much later period'. On the other hand, the artillery frequently felt let down by the infantry, who sometimes retired, leaving gun positions unprotected. So one brigade major, having lost four forward gun positions on 21 March, composed this poem on the same day:

The Boche commenced attacking us

So we began to run

And as we ran away we said

Ha! Ha! the Boche is done

And this was curious because

You might have thought he'd won!

Nevertheless, battery accounts of March 1918 reveal a fairly resourceful field artillery, although often out of touch with the infantry, and very tired after both firing and moving day and night for several days in retreat. One small but sad story illustrates this, for on 27 March, Major Gordon, CO of the 12th Heavy Battery, was killed when he fell off his horse through falling asleep, while riding beside his battery, and a 60-pound gun wheel went over his neck. As might be expected, the artillery also found ammunition resupply difficult on the move, and it was bothered, too, by the German system of using low-flying aircraft to machine gun the batteries. One other aspect of the first three or four days of the German offensive proved difficult.

This was that until the early morning fog or mist lifted, there could be no observation, and without observation, there could be no artillery support during mobile warfare, except for shooting off the map. On the other hand, previously prepared SOS or 'counterpreparation' shoots were planned for prepared defensive positions in static warfare, even in the fog, and must have been what occurred on the Fifth Army front, where on the morning of 21 March, the artillery supporting the Royal West Kent Regiment was accurate, despite the fog: 'A message calling for artillery barrage sent by runner was replied to very effectively by heavy guns and although the actual position of the enemy could not be seen, the flashes of the bursts could be seen through the fog and indicated they were just about on the line where they had been called for.' An example of an artillery brigade that seemed to be in touch with the division that it was supporting, was the Royal Canadian Horse Artillery Brigade, covering 24 Division. This brigade fired 'counter-preparation' and SOS as required on 21 March, and in subsequent days maintained targets through air reports, infantry reports and forward observation officers, such as Lieutenant Forbes, RCHA. This officer, at 4 p.m. on 21 March went forward with a telephone into the battle zone, where he remained until dark, 'sending in most valuable information; although the enemy had penetrated the RED LINE, on his flanks, and he might at any moment have been surrounded'. The Canadian Brigade continued to remain in contact with its infantry until 28 March, when several references to rapidly retiring infantry, both British and French, obviously irritated the artillery brigade commander because the panic uncovered his batteries. It is of interest also that on the same day, 28 March, although low-flying enemy aircraft 'continuously machine gunned and bombed the Batteries, killing a good many horses' they made 'no impression on the batteries themselves'.

In contrast, the experiences of H, Y, and I Batteries of the Royal Horse Artillery supporting 66 and then 50 Division, while still positive, show some problems with incorrect and countermanded orders and lack of ammunition. For example, on 22 March at 9 a.m., the German offensive resumed against 66 Division around Roisel, but 'As no information was forthcoming the [H] Battery fired a map barrage'. Later at 4 p.m., H Battery found itself supporting 50 Division as it defended the rear zone at Brusle, and then at midnight an incorrectly worded message sent H Battery across the Somme River, only to receive orders to return to its starting point at dawn the next day, 23 March. The battery managed to return and opened fire at 8 a.m., only to learn before 9 a.m. that it had to retrace its steps once again, and once more was ordered to recross the Somme River. On this day, not surprisingly, given its rapid changes of position, the battery ran out of 13-pounder ammunition, and was also 'continually engaged with Machine Gun fire from low flying aeroplanes in flights of six or eight at a time'. These aeroplanes were engaged with the battery's Lewis guns, and one aeroplane was downed. This battery did find good German targets on 22 and 23 March, although necessarily in a somewhat ad hoc fashion. The other batteries of the Royal Horse Artillery, Y and I, followed much the same pattern, also obviously following a disjointed retreat, and also finding excellent targets on a somewhat random basis.

Seen from a command perspective, there was general agreement that the artillery support of the infantry in the retreat was a relative failure due to lack of liaison. In other words, the local infantry brigade and battalion commanders had no control over the artillery when they needed it, especially in an emergency, because artillery orders came either from division or corps, and this was too slow in moving warfare. Again, the mobile retreat revealed cracks in the air-artillery liaison, which completely disappeared in March 1918, according to the artillery adviser at Fifth Army. It would seem also that the artillery 'counter-preparation' against the German offensive on 21 March, was not early or strong enough to deter the attack in any way. However, the main lesson from the March retreat for the command structure of the BEF, was that in mobile warfare, decentralization of command was necessary, and neither GHQ nor the army HQs nor the artillery itself had anticipated or trained for this, expecting a slower withdrawal. So, for instance, the CRA of 8 Division 'did not function on the broader aspect of artillery tactics', and after the winter of 1915–16, did no training for mobile warfare. In general, it was said of the artillery that it was either knocked out before it could give support or went too far back to be useful—perhaps an exaggeration, but this does reflect some sort of consensus.

Similarly, air observation for artillery counter-battery work was extremely difficult to achieve in moving warfare, and judging by battery officers' accounts in March, counter-battery work was largely given up, and 'air reports' were few and far between. On the other hand, air support for the infantry was apparently very useful, especially on 26 March, when according to a telephone message from Beddington (GSO 1, Fifth Army) to GHQ, 'without doubt, the concentration of aircraft in the South [in Fifth Army's area, at Chaulnes-Roye, as well as west of Bapaume] had frozen up the attack there temporarily'. What this meant in practice was revealed by Squadron Leader Sholto Douglas, who wrote that all aircraft were concentrated in late March on low-flying attacks in support of the infantry. In 84 Squadron, for the first time in their experience, pilots were presented with perfect ground targets—troops marching in fours along the roads, batteries and ammunition wagons moving across the open. One could thus see plainly what one was attacking.... Troops would scatter into the fields, leaving men lying prostrate in the road; wagons and horses would be thrown into confusion and overturned. One pilot overturned a general's car into a ditch. One felt that one was directly helping to stop the enemy's victorious advance.

Douglas also pointed out that ground fire against his aeroplanes was totally ineffective: 'During the whole of that strenuous fortnight No. 84 Squadron suffered only one casualty: and that was the result of an aerial combat.'62 The importance of the concentrated low-flying RFC attacks in stopping the German advance on 26 March was perhaps overestimated, although the RFC did do considerable damage against German ground forces between about 24 and 26 March. For instance, Major Crofton, with 63 Division, remembered on 24 March seeing the 'Boche coming over the plain [near Le Transloy], about ½ mile away, suffering heavily from M.G. fire from our low flying aeroplanes'.

In fact, the accounts of such successful RFC actions, together with the frequent mention by the BEF artillery of good German targets over open sights, do point up a major German weakness in the March offensive. This was that, contrary to previous interpretations of innovative German tactics in the March offensive, there was a distinct tendency to attack in the old style, and not by infiltration, especially after initial breakthroughs. A series of examples is instructive. William Gordon, defending the Fricourt sector in Fifth Army on 21 March, recalled that while the initial German skirmishers 'were widely spaced', by about 10.30 a.m. 'we saw [German] Infantry advancing in mass on our right front & we managed to do considerable damage with Lewis Guns amongst this horde'. Later that afternoon, after being captured, Gordon noted 'that the Germans had suffered a big number of casualties & transport waggons were collecting the dead. These I saw tied in bundles and thrown into the wagon.' Gordon's story was far from unique. Lieutenant Colonel Clarke, of the Sherwood Foresters, in Third Army, noticed that the German infantry attacked in 'waves', the waves being 30 to 50 yards apart, and troops in rear of the waves moved in column of route. An officer of the 12th Royal Irish Rifles, in Fifth Army, guarding the La Ponche area, found that the enemy offered excellent targets on 21 March once the fog lifted. Then at midday his company noticed a large convoy coming unconcernedly down the St Quentin-La Fère road, and when it came within range, it was completely destroyed with Lewis guns and rifles. Major Ling, the previously mentioned staff officer on XVIII Corps staff, remarked on 'the dense waves of the attack, each man having only to keep touch with his neighbour to ensure a forward movement over the whole front'. Ling theorized that 'these close formations were probably necessitated by the fog in order to maintain a sense of direction. They were hardly close formations so much as thick waves of men almost shoulder to shoulder following one another at short intervals.' In succeeding days, the German offensive tended to use large masses of men to try to overwhelm their opponents—hardly innovative tactics. For example, an officer of 51 Division Artillery reported that on 22 March large bodies of Germans were seen concentrating near Morchies, and for four hours, four batteries over open sights 'had the time of their lives, the losses inflicted by their fire being plainly seen by all. In particular, when the enemy tried to advance in strength between MORCHIES and MARICOURT WOOD, the attack never developed beyond that line, but was broken up time after time.' A little later, some British tanks caused the German infantry to flee, and the enemy in flight presented targets 'that most gunners dream about but that few have ever had the privilege of dealing with. The casualties, from guns and tanks alone, must have been appalling.'

In another area, near Omignon in Fifth Army, Lieutenant Colonel Elkins recorded that on 23 March the A and B Batteries of the Royal Canadian Horse Artillery caught the enemy trying to 'swarm' down the slopes and cross the partially destroyed bridges over the Somme near Morchain, and 'many Boches were killed'. On 25 March these same batteries caught 'large masses' of German infantry advancing along the railway line outside Chaulnes, and fired over open sights until their ammunition was exhausted. Finally, on 28 March, three batteries caught 'massed infantry' coming over the Vrély Beaufort Ridge, and engaged them over open sights. Significantly, the report says that the German infantry eventually gave up attempts at a 'Frontal Advance', and 'commenced to filter in to the valley on either flank'.Several other first-hand accounts indirectly make the same point—that German infiltration tactics were very frequently not applied—and therefore the March offensive was not always as innovative as generally imagined. This applies particularly to the follow-up attacks on the second and succeeding days of the German offensive, but even on the first day, 21 March, perhaps because of the fog and mist, many British reports stress the close formation attacks of the German infantry. For instance, at about 10 a.m. on 21 March, Lieutenant Colonel Crosthwaite, of the Royal West Kent Regiment, defending the line of the Vendeuil road, on the Fifth Army front, reported that 'the Germans seemed to come up against our wire without seeing it in fairly close formation and naturally every one of them was shot down on the wire'. Consequently, when this officer was later wounded and captured, and was sent to the hospital in Maubeuge towards the end of March, it is not surprising to learn from him that 'I had many long conversations with the German doctors who stated that they were receiving three times the number of wounded which they had been ordered to prepare for and that the men coming back from the front at that time were generally of the opinion that the casualties were much too heavy to allow the advance to succeed'.

The fact is that the German infantry tactics were very costly in manpower, and often consisted of old-fashioned mass attacks, attempting to carry their objectives through sheer weight of numbers. Moreover, judging by many British first-hand accounts, by the third or fourth day of the offensive, the German infantry became separated from its guns and therefore suffered heavily when the BEF artillery was close enough to the advance to do considerable damage. On the other hand, the German handling of machine guns and mortars was in advance of BEF tactics; for instance, the German offensive employed trench mortars as artillery, as Major Ling in XVIII Corps pointed out: These trench mortars had been established in the enemy's front system, each with a plentiful supply of ammunition, for some days prior to the attack. They were placed so close together (about 5 yards apart) along the whole front that it was unnecessary to traverse. They were given parallel lines of fire, up and down which they shot until the whole of our front system to a depth of 1500 yards was obliterated, the craters of the shells practically touching.68 This is not the place to analyse the reasons for German failure to exploit the success of their March offensive, whether because of faulty strategy, inability to maintain supplies to their troops, poor artillery support, or just plain exhaustion. But the personal accounts of the front-line BEF defenders can now add a major reason for the slowing down and eventual halt of the German offensive on 5 April 1918, short of Amiens, namely, that German infantry tactics were frequently not innovative, instead they were often just plain old-fashioned and costly. As a Canadian report decided in early 1919, the later disorganization of the German army was brought about by the costly method of the German spring offensive.

Nevertheless, seen from the point of view of early April 1918, the BEF had suffered a serious defeat. There were around 170,000 BEF casualties, some 1,000 guns lost, and a very large amount of territory given up. More serious was the fact that the BEF had very nearly collapsed and been driven from France.70 How did this happen? Various explanations have been advanced, of which Haig's was the earliest, in which he argued that being forced to take over more of the French line, the lack of manpower, and the slowness of the French in providing assistance to the BEF, were the main reasons for the retreat. Not surprisingly, these were all external factors outside of Haig's control, and none of them holds much water. For example, the lack of manpower was belied by Haig's strong wish just before 21 March that the Germans should attack, and by the fact that he sanctioned leave for 88,000 troops on the eve of the March offensive! The official British historian, Edmonds, listed four reasons for the retreat: the fog or mist on 21 March and succeeding days; the lack of training; the reorganization of the BEF battalions in early 1918 before the German offensive: and the German superiority in numbers. Again, these are mostly external factors outside the control of GHQ.

However, the widespread over-confidence of Haig and GHQ before the March offensive dispels most of these explanations, and the first-hand accounts of many officers at the time also contradict these explanations. Instead, officers express puzzlement as to why the BEF did not do better: 'We all felt we ought to have done much better & positions should have been held for longer.' Even the fog is disputed as a negative factor, as one officer claimed bluntly: 'Mist favours the defence. That is beyond dispute. The attacker is moving over unknown ground, he is liable to loss of direction, he has the constant fear of walking into a trap, he realizes that he will be seen and shot at before he can see, and he cannot call for artillery support when he requires it.' This officer concluded: 'There had been a mist every morning for the previous five days. It is not correct to blame the results of all this appalling unpreparedness to the mist.'

But if not the explanations of Haig and Edmonds, what then? Apart from the impact of the German offensive itself, especially the initial bombardment, it has been suggested above that the primary reason for the unexpected and sometimes panic-stricken retreat of the BEF, was the unworkable and misunderstood defence in depth system, and this is indeed the main explanation of what happened on 21 March and succeeding days. This was due to GHQ's inability to comprehend, explain, put into practice and enforce the new defensive system. The BEF was simply unable to adapt to the defence in depth system and make it work, especially the all- important counter-attack component of the system. A secondary explanation, often referred to above, was the poor performance of corps commanders and staff, who often retreated unnecessarily, thus setting off a chain reaction of gaps and disasters down the structured system of divisions, brigades and battalions. Corps commander mistakes were magnified by an inflexible command structure that could not adapt to moving warfare. A tertiary explanation relates to specific errors by the two army commanders, Gough and Byng. Gough failed to understand the defence in depth concept and induced a general retirement that was actually unworkable, thus creating a potentially disastrous gap between Fifth and Third Armies. Byng failed to evacuate the Cambrai salient in time, thus causing his army to retreat in disorder, in fact after four days of the battle Third Army was retreating faster than Fifth Army, and this of course increased the gap between Third and Fifth Armies.Truly, the March retreat in its first six or seven days was a command failure, starting at the top. Nevertheless, the German offensive did come to a halt, especially after a major effort on 28 March toward Amiens. This was due partly to poor German tactics, and partly to better BEF positions with strong machine gun and artillery support. Thus, at the end of March, there was one portent of the future. Lieutenant General de Lisle, GOC XIII Corps, defending Vimy ridge, remarked that the 28 March German 'Mars' attack expected to reach the sea in four days and the German troops carried six days' rations. That they did not succeed on his front was to a large extent due to a reworking of the GHQ three-zone system that had basically failed on 21 March. Now, de Lisle ignored protests from First Army (in which all III Corps served) and organized the defence of the front zone with patrols only, but prepared the rear of the front zone with a resistance line of machine guns, out of range of the much-feared initial German trench mortar barrage.

Then the battle zone contained a trench system with a good field of fire, protected by machine gun pits some 30 to 50 yards ahead of the trench, but connected with it. The rear zone essentially consisted of artillery on Vimy ridge. According to de Lisle The Battle worked exactly to plan. The first attack broke against the Reserves of the outposts [the rear of the front zone], and the 2nd attack was utterly destroyed by the Machine Guns in front of the Battle position.' On the other hand, a bitter action at Moreuil Wood on 30 March showed that German morale still remained very high. Here, the German infantry ran forward with bayonets in order to fight at close quarters with part of the dismounted Canadian Cavalry Brigade, and wounded Germans even refused to be picked up by stretcher-bearers, but seized rifles to shoot their would-be rescuers.74 It was clear that the German spring offensive was far from over, yet decisive success had eluded Ludendorff. At the same time, the BEF was showing greater signs of flexibility in applying the defence in depth concept. What would happen in the next German offensive?

PART II: THE LYS AND THE AISNE, APRIL TO JUNE 1918

In early April, the BEF's First and Second Armies were defending the line of the Lys River, which was initially thought to be a quiet zone. However, the confusion over the defence in depth system which had characterized the BEF in March, was still characteristic of the Lys defence. There was an added concern with 2 Portuguese Division, between the BEF's 55 and 40 Divisions, since the Portuguese were deemed to be unreliable, and this proved to be the case when the German offensive commenced on 9 April. With the rapid retreat of the Portuguese, and the dislocation of some other units, the familiar story of an unravelling BEF command structure was repeated. But one division at least, 55 Division, had learnt the lessons of March and generally held firm, while the German offensive also suffered from the same difficulty of maintaining momentum, and by the end of April the offensive was over. The next German offensive took place on the Aisne River—Chemin des Dames front on 27 May, and was notable for a remarkably intense gas, mortar and artillery barrage. Due also to differences in opinion between the French Sixth Army and the BEF's IX Corps, who shared the defence, there was a disorganized defensive scheme and a disorganized retreat. But both sides were now suffering from morale problems and had become cautious, so that the German offensive ran out of steam even more quickly than on the Lys, in fact by early June.

However, there was one important lesson for the BEF in its defensive battle of March 1918. That was that in a flexible defensive system such as the three-zone defence in depth system, the defence could only work if there was a corresponding flexibility and local initiative in the command structure, particularly as the retreat picked up pace. However, it does not seem that the BEF was able to adjust either at the Lys or at the Aisne, except in the case of particular units. But conversely, neither did the German army discover how to maintain the momentum of an offensive, or minimize casualties.

Even before the failure of the German 'Michael' offensive to reach Amiens, Ludendorff had turned his attention to the Lys sector, where the 'Georgette' offensive was ready to commence on 9 April. Some of the same difficulties as in early March, however, afflicted GHQ both in regard to anticipation of the attack, and uncertainty over the defensive system to be employed. Haig remained curiously fixated on the Arras sector, containing Vimy Ridge, perhaps because of his own penchant for attacking high ground, and despite considerable evidence GHQ did not believe the German attack would be so far north. In late March, GHQ considered there were no German reserves facing the Lys area, and the First Army commander (General Horne, commanding from the La Bassée canal north to the Ypres canal), thought that only a holding attack might be made. Accordingly, when General Plumer (GOC Second Army, commanding from the Ypres canal northwards), visited 78 Brigade around 5 or 6 April he 'personally told the officers...that he was glad to be able to assure us that there was no prospect of a German attack in the Lys sector.' Another commander (General Sir R.Haking, GOC XI Corps), a few days before 9 April, told the troops that they would have some rest, and so they also did not anticipate an attack. On the other hand, the GOC RA of XV Corps was nervous about an attack from around 7 April, and Haking, despite his previous comments, apparently did not like the great silence on his XI Corps front, and told the GOC RA of XI Corps on 7 April that the Germans might attack when the Portuguese, who held the middle of the line with their 2 Division, came out of the line. Clearly, GHQ and the army and corps commanders were vague about German intentions, but there was also the very awkward question of how to set up the defence in depth system, given the problems of 21 March. Strangely enough, there appeared to be a continuation of the same disagreement over what to do on defence, as had characterized 21 March. Partly this was due to the fact that GHQ did not issue a document on defence tactics until May 1918, so the confusion continued.

4

Command and Technology Alignment

From July 1918 onward, the BEF essentially applied two different offensive methods, both of which could potentially save manpower yet at the same time prove effective. The first was the traditional infantry— artillery offensive, but utilizing very much greater amounts of artillery, machine guns and mortars than ever before. The second was the combined tank-infantry-artillery type of offensive. The first method was used at Météren, and the second at Hamel and Amiens. The Amiens assault was particularly successful, and showed what a well-planned tankinfantry- artillery offensive could do when very good infantry and a large body of tanks were used together, having also trained together and become used to each other. Then in late August, under the direction of Foch, a series of sequential attacks were launched by the Allies to loosen the German line. Large numbers of tanks were used, but often in an ad hoc manner, and then at the end of August, the BEF lost confidence in the tanks, which had also been reduced in numbers, and turned back to the first method of traditional infantry-artillery offensives until the end of the war. This traditional option proved successful, although not without heavy casualties, which might have been alleviated if the tank-infantry-artillery method had been continued.

In July 1918, GHQ anticipated a possible German offensive on the Lys front, aiming to enlarge that salient, but determined that local counterattacks could be launched by the BEF in that area to forestall such an offensive. The objective of one such attack by 9 Division on 19 July was the village and hill at Météren. The plan to recapture Météren was to use smoke, gas and heavy artillery fire, followed by the infantry assault. There was an abundance of ammunition available, so much so that one heavy artillery brigade commander remarked that there was even too much ammunition, and so they fired 6-inch howitzer shells into the town of Bailleul just to annoy the enemy. More to the point, the plentiful supplies of ammunition allowed the heavy artillery to dominate the German batteries in the Lys salient. Moreover, seven artillery brigades, and parts of five others, were used to set up a fire plan for this small action, with four belts of fire.

There was a machine gun frontal and enfilade barrage; then further back light trench mortars were used on close proximity targets; then an infantry barrage was provided by divisional field guns with HE, and smoke every fourth round; and finally two brigades of corps heavy artillery worked on rear areas and counter-battery duty. The concept of the attack was to deceive the enemy by using smoke followed by gas in several feint attacks, and then to use smoke followed by men in the real assault, together with the previously mentioned barrage. Prior to this the heavy artillery also worked over the hill at Météren, which overlooked 9 Division, and fired 80,000 6-inch shells and 20,000 8-inch shells, and flattened the hill. An artillery officer with the heavy guns wrote later: 'I told the GOC 9th Division (General Tudor) that I could alter the shape of the Mound [the hill at Météren]...but could never remove it altogether. This never quite satisfied them.'

It is apparent that the attack on Météren was somewhat similar to the earlier Messines attack in 1917—a siege-type offensive—but this time using enormous amounts of artillery fire. There were also one or two twists to the attack that showed a certain amount of ingenuity creeping in. For instance, there was the idea of persuading the German defenders to put on their gas masks every time they saw smoke (since in the previous days smoke had always been followed by gas). Thus when the attack really did commence, but without gas, the defenders would still put on gas masks. Then there was the perennial problem of how to get the assault troops into the front trenches at dawn without being seen by the German air patrols. In this case, General Tudor created a false front trench by painting a black line, about a foot wide, down the centre of 2,000 yards of coconut fibre matting, and this did deceive German air reconnaissance. Also, as at Cambrai, the artillery did not previously register, but still managed to deliver an accurate barrage. Finally, it was a question of waiting for the right wind conditions to carry the smoke toward the German defences, and this required ten days of waiting— although the corps commander, General de Lisle was going on leave on Saturday, 20 July and instructed Tudor to conduct the attack before then! This Tudor managed to do, on Friday at 7.55 a.m., when 9 Division moved forward under the smoke and artillery barrage and captured its objectives in one hour, with very few casualties because the attack was a total surprise.

Not only was the attack a complete success, but the German defenders were indifferent, older than normal, and when taken as prisoners, were disturbed by the fall of their own shells. Moreover, the CRA of XV Corps remarked at the 'ready way in which the Germans surrendered. We saw them in crowds running forward with their hands up. We had never seen anything like it before.... We felt then that the tide had very definitely turned and that the end could not be very far off.' The difference between these defenders and those at the Marne really reflected the difference between divisions with high morale and those with low morale, yet nevertheless, the readiness of the German defenders to surrender showed that the result of the heavy casualties of the German spring offensives was starting to show up. More than this, the success at Méteren revealed one method of defeating the German army in 1918 or 1919, namely, the capture of limited objectives using overwhelming artillery firepower combined with surprise. As one artillery officer at Méteren put it, by this time in the war, the artillery was of 'almost premier importance compared to that of the infantry'.

If the artillery at Méteren had demonstrated one successful offensive method, the attack at Hamel on 4 July demonstrated the other, namely, mechanical warfare, in which the combination and interrelationship of arms and ideas learnt over the previous months were very important. Here finally was the combination of a number of valuable elements: surprise, using 60 of the newly available Mark V tanks, and 4 infantry supply tanks; infantry with high morale (in fact 4, Australian Division plus some American platoons); infantry using Lewis guns and rifle grenades in pairs to overcome machine gun nests; infantry using initiative (with maps issued to all officers and NCOs, and barrage maps given to all company and battery commanders); very limited registration and calibration for the artillery; the new 106 contact fuses available for the artillery; good counter-battery work (41 enemy batteries were neutralized, although counter-battery work on the flanks of the attack could have been improved); an artillery barrage in three belts, involving a combination of shrapnel, HE and smoke, the last being laid down three layers high (interestingly the same smoke and gas routine that was later perfected at Météren was used earlier at Hamel for the first time, although without much success); strong air support, consisting of bombing (135 25-pound bombs were dropped), contact patrols, low-level attacks (10,000 rounds were fired), and ammunition dropping for the infantry (115,600 rounds of SAA), plus air patrols to drown out the sound of the tanks as they came up to the line; and finally, a limited objective (2,500 yards), with minimal infantry involved (10 battalions), and maximum use of tanks.

However, if the elements that were essential to the success of this operation could be listed in order of importance, they would be first surprise, then the previous training of the Australian infantry with tanks and the impact of the new tanks on enemy machine gun resistance, thirdly the élan of the infantry, fourthly the efficient counter-battery work of the artillery, and lastly the smoke and dust screen produced by the barrage. In other words, secrecy, and the bringing together and use of new ideas by all arms, were very significant, all of which showed a new flexibility of thinking that had previously been largely absent.

It was significant that this Hamel attack was organized by Rawlinson, and not by GHQ, since Rawlinson was an advocate both of limited objective offensives and of mechanical warfare. It was he who first suggested the attack to the Australian Corps on 18 June, and he who spent the rest of June persuading the Australians to work with the tanks. Finally, on 30 June, Rawlinson expressed satisfaction with Australian infantry coordination in training with the tanks, and on the same day, Monash, the Australian Corps commander, settled all questions in an open-minded 4-hour and 20-minute corps conference. This was a far cry from the lack of understanding between GHQ and army and corps commanders before the rigid Somme and Passchendaele offensives, even though Hamel was admittedly a far smaller enterprise. Moreover, in line with Rawlinson's thinking on mechanical warfare while serving on the Inter-Allied War Council at Versailles, he stressed the economizing of manpower by the maximum use of tanks, and evidently hoped for big things from the Mark V tanks. According to J.F.C.Fuller, Hamel was a success chiefly due to the tanks. However, he admitted that 'Even in this last operation [Hamel] if they had used us with a little more skill our infantry casualties would have been considerably reduced'. But was Hamel really a tank or an infantry success? Or were there other reasons for the few infantry casualties in the Australian Corps?

A study of the tank battle sheets for Hamel reveals that the tanks did play a significant role in achieving success at Hamel, especially when the Australian infantry were held up. Strangely enough, the tank proved to have several offensive threats—either the enemy ran or surrendered when a tank appeared, or enemy machine gun nests were destroyed by small arms or 6-pounder fire from the tank, or, more frequently, the tank dealt with enemy machine gun nests and infantry by the simple but unpleasant method of running over and crushing them. A typical story comes from Tank 9403, commanded by Second Lieutenant Vickers, who gave the following Hamel Battle History Sheet report:

I proceeded towards the vicinity of [map point] P.9.d. where I encountered a strong post, held by a party of German bombers... where the Australian Infantry were held up. I gave my driver orders to drive over it, & kept up a rapid fire. They succeeded in throwing 4 bombs on the roof of my Tank before I was able to demolish it. I suspected that some were getting at the rear of my Tank with the intention of bombing my petrol tank, so I told my driver to reverse, thus going over some of the enemy. The Australian Infantry then occupied this position & I proceeded to get well ahead of the first wave again. I was then informed by an Infantry man that they were held up by heavy machine gun fire to which I proceeded & found a strong point consisting of 2 machine guns manned by 8 gunners. I drove straight up to their position firing at them. They refused to surrender, so I drove over them. In taking this position I greatly assisted the Aus: Infantry to keep up with those on either flank. I then proceeded & found myself in front of the Infantry, until I reached a small trench containing a few of the enemy. These immediately surrendered. Our barrage was then concentrating a heavy fire in front of me so I had to stop for about 6 minutes. On the barrage lifting I proceeded & encountered numerous German Infantry men who freely surrendered.

Soon after, the Australian infantry consolidated on their objective, and on heading back, the right track of Vickers's tank broke, but the tank was able to proceed to the rallying point, where it was handed over to salvage.7 Other tank battle sheets tell very much the same story of poor German morale, with large groups of enemy infantry readily surrendering, although German machine gunners frequently, though not always, fought on until their posts were crushed or they were killed. In fact, the story of Hamel at ground level is a story of very little or no enemy opposition, due to surprise, a powerful artillery barrage, excellent Australian infantry, the impact of the tanks, and very little resistance. It would appear that the tanks caused a good deal of fear among the German infantry; for example, Lieutenant Wilkinson, commanding Tank 9306, reported that in the village of Hamel 'Very little resistance was encountered; as the enemy gave up whenever we approached him'. The commander of Tank 9372 found that when his tank encountered two heavy machine guns and fired at their crews, 'the teams hurriedly left the guns as I approached'. Then when Tank 9310 patrolled about 150 yards in front of the Australian infantry, the commander, Lieutenant Jefferies, noticed 'a party of between 50 and 80 enemy infantry in a trench, who immediately jumped out and surrendered. Swung my tank continually round them & drove them into the hands of our infantry who took them prisoner.'

In philosophic terms, the tanks had been a necessary but not sufficient factor, in the victory at Hamel. In other words, they had been essential to the success, but they had not achieved it by themselves. But judging by the post-Hamel tank reports, the tanks had been of critical value at certain points in the advance, and against a more aggressive defence the tanks would have been the most valuable arm on the battlefield. However, as Fuller's letter indicates, there had still been tank problems, and it is of interest to note that almost all of these difficulties had been caused by the planning of the Hamel battle, and not by the tanks themselves. First, many tank commanders complained of being unable to cross a sunken road at the start line, and thus several tanks advanced behind rather than in front of the infantry, leading to unnecessary infantry casualties (there were 1,300 total casualties). Secondly, if the infantry followed close to their artillery barrage, as was the custom, the tanks could not be in front of the infantry for fear of being hit by their own barrage. Indeed, Tank 9011 kept 15 to 20 yards behind the barrage, but this was evidently not sufficient because the tank 'was put out of action by a direct hit from one of our own shells'.

Thirdly, because of the start time of 3.10 a.m., the darkness caused the tanks to lose direction, and also targets were not visible. Fourthly, despite tank guides and infantry liaison personnel accompanying the tanks, communication with the infantry was difficult—the bell pull at the back of each tank was not a satisfactory communication system! Finally, the artillery barrage moved too slowly for both tanks and infantry.

Nevertheless, tank casualties were low by First World War standards, only 5 tanks were disabled out of the 60 that started, for an 8.3 per cent loss rate, and at least one of these was hit by its own barrage, as mentioned above. Moreover, as one officer remarked, Hamel was 'to the last phase of the war what Neuve Chapelle had been to the first, a fount of new tactics'.10 It could be expected, therefore, that the mechanical form of warfare as demonstrated so successfully at Hamel would be applied again, perhaps on a larger scale. Yet on 20 July Fuller wrote to Dill at GHQ asking what GHQ intended to do with the tanks: 'As regards the general employment of Tanks either by Armies who have them or the Armies who have not, I think some policy ought to be defined by GHQ because under the present state of affairs we may have all Armies asking for Tanks for small local enterprises and so spoil the market for any considered operation in the future.' In other words, did GHQ know what they were doing, and if so, would tanks be used locally or in a large operation? Dill replied circumspectly, that there were four operations in the wind, but that tanks would not be wasted in 'local enterprises'.

Nevertheless, it was again Rawlinson who actually suggested the Amiens attack to Haig over lunch on 16 July, provided he could have the Canadian Corps, and Rawlinson was delighted to hear Haig saying that he had already decided to do such an attack. It is curious that while Foch had written to Haig on 12 July, proposing an offensive on the British front at Festubert-Rebecq, Haig did not reply until 17 July, the day after Rawlinson had suggested the Amiens offensive, and in this letter Haig now rejected the Festubert option, but argued for a joint British-French offensive to disengage Amiens. This would suggest that the Amiens offensive was basically Rawlinson's idea. However, rather like Haig's imposing of preconditions before approving the night attack on 14 July 1916 at the Somme, Haig insisted that first he had to get the four divisions of Godley's XXII Corps back from the French, and furthermore he would not permit Rawlinson to take over the French line to Moreuil to improve the starting line of the attack. Neither of these objections seems justified, and in particular the take-over to Moreuil would have eliminated an awkward move on the right by 3 Division of the Canadian Corps.

However, at this time Haig seems to have been preoccupied by his subordination to Foch, and the attitude of Foch regarding the use of British troops as reserves behind the French front, nor would he agree to any more French line being taken over by the BEF. Haig may also have delayed agreeing to the offensive because of legitimate concerns regarding the location of the next German offensive, which he thought might be in Flanders. Nevertheless, on 17 July Rawlinson wrote to GHQ outlining his plans for the offensive involving the Australian and Canadian Corps, and stressing the need for secrecy and deceit, the low German morale, and the use of tanks 'so as to save casualties to the Infantry'. In fact there would be a rather thin six tanks per 1,000 yards for each objective. Rawlinson's scheme for an offensive was then conditionally approved by GHQ on 19 July. Rawlinson held his first corps commanders conference on 21 July, in which he said that Haig had not yet approved the offensive because of German attacks against the French and a probable German attack in the Ypres sector, but he obviously anticipated approval. In that case there would be only a very short two to three weeks for preparation. Then on 26 July, at a Fourth Army conference, Rawlinson drew on advice from Foch that General Mangin's counter-attack at the Marne showed that in an attack in depth, all troops should move forward at zero, because leading troops moved faster than reserve troops. In other words, the reserve formations should also move forward at zero hour. Next, on 29 July, at a corps commanders conference, Rawlinson outlined several points. Surprise was the important factor. Heavy artillery was not so necessary because there were no strongly entrenched positions as at the Somme, and because great reliance could be placed on the tanks, which could reach the first objective, the German artillery, at an early-stage. Then open fighting should develop. There was a need for mobile field artillery to follow up the attack at zero, and Rawlinson reiterated the lesson from Mangin that reserves should also move forward quickly. Another conference on 1 August argued that artillery need not fire to cover the advance of the tanks just before zero because the RAF would send over low-flying planes for that purpose. Finally on 5 August, a conference with Haig covered the main points, but Haig, perhaps under pressure from Foch, now stressed the need for Rawlinson to do more with the attack, although Rawlinson obviously wanted a limited objective, attempting to emulate his success at Hamel. This difference of opinion between Rawlinson and Haig was a replay of the mixed signals between Haig and Rawlinson before the Somme, and turned out to be unfortunate, since the attacks on the days succeeding 8 August produced rapidly mounting casualties, while the tanks were essentially reduced to independent actions by the third day. The Tank Corps Report of the battle had this to say:

> It must be noted that the distribution of Tank Units was made for a limited offensive, in which the first object was the reduction of loss to the infantry by the employment of an overwhelming force of tanks. During the first days of August the scope of the operation was greatly extended, too late for any change in the distribution of Tank Units. The lack of reserves was severely felt in the later stages of the advance.

In keeping with the new expanded offensive, Haig also wanted a combined cavalry, Whippet (Medium Mark A tank) and horse artillery force, for the pursuit, and he placed great emphasis on the need for cavalry to keep in touch with the battle. Judging by Rawlinson's diary, Haig and GHQ intervened to turn Amiens from a limited to an unlimited offensive, but did not interfere with the details of the attack, a method of planning that had also occurred before the Somme and Passchendaele offensives. Nevertheless, Rawlinson continued to rely chiefly on three factors: surprise, plenty of tanks and good infantry. Surprise was achieved partly by 'training' the Germans with several 24–48-hour periods of radio and telephone silence as was likely just before an attack; partly by disguising the move of the Canadian Corps through leaving their radio units behind and through the publication of 'lying' orders concerning this corps; partly by deception measures in all units, such as setting up tank wireless detachments in other army areas; and partly by not informing any but the most essential personnel about the offensive until 7 August. In particular Rawlinson avoided saying anything to those units which normally talked the most, namely Q (supplies), medical (including the hardest to disguise—casualty clearing stations and hospitals) and the cavalry. The surprise was so well kept that neither Colonel Hemming, on the field survey staff at GHQ, nor his colleagues at GHQ heard of the offensive. Rawlinson also sought to convert Haig to mechanical warfare at the end of July, by giving him a demonstration of tank-infantry cooperation: 'DH much impressed with the new drill & the development of the use of tanks with Infy.—I think the speed & elan of the Infy. together with the hardiness & speed of the Tanks impressed him.' Rawlinson's simple idea was to use plenty of tanks and good infantry, which he achieved with 342 Mark V and 72 Medium Mark A tanks, more than 50 Mark V* infantry-carrying tanks, and 120 supply tanks. Operating with these tanks were 9 divisions of the best BEF troops in France—the Australian and Canadian Corps—and 3 hopeful cavalry divisions for pursuit. In addition, Rawlinson disposed of considerably more aircraft than at Hamel, some 800 aeroplanes, including bombers, fighters and contact patrols, the latter dropping messages on Tank Brigade HQs and dropping stations, on tank rallying points, and even on groups of Whippets. The aeroplanes were also supposed to attack anti-tank guns, where possible, but this did not work very well. Much has been made of the use of aeroplanes in drowning out the noise of the tanks coming up into the line, but this does not appear to have been successful. A forgotten but important role of aircraft was also to locate and report on derelict tanks after the battle, in order to assist salvage operations. If French aircraft are included in the Allied total (for Debeney was supporting the attack on the right with 42 French Division), there were 1,904 Allied planes as against 369 German planes!

Finally, there were 2,000 guns and howitzers, not counting machine guns, to support the assault with an intense rolling barrage, although there would be no preliminary barrage. As with the other arms, surprise was the key, and the guns were therefore carefully camouflaged. A screen calibration range allowed each gun to be previously checked for accuracy, topography personnel selected battery positions, allowing for gun clearance and range, while field survey provided targets and accurate gun laying. Very important was the BEF's attempt at mobile war, in which detached and forward guns tried to deal with obstacles, and field artillery closely followed up the infantry and tanks. However, this mobile artillery apparently did not manage to get forward to assist, at least on 1 Canadian Division front, while a battalion commander in 1 Canadian Division declared that the liaison of artillery and infantry on 8 August was nil, so much so that 40 per cent of the casualties suffered in his battalion came from short shooting by his own artillery. Moreover, neither machine guns nor light trench mortars could keep pace with the infantry, so the BEF still had a lot to learn regarding mobile warfare. However, the stupendous opening barrage of the Amiens offensive at 4.20 a.m., followed at 4.24 a.m. by the infantry, was a success—'Like Hell let loose' wrote one Canadian officer—and was aided by the surprise and early morning mist, plus thick smoke, and, at GHQ, Birch claimed that the Tank Corps told him that BEF artillery supremacy made the course of the tanks easy that morning.

There is no question that a crucial aspect of the success on 8 August was the surprise element, because the roads leading up to the battle front on 8 August and preceding days had been extremely congested. The Canadian Heavy Artillery GOCRA, Major General McNaughton, wrote home on the early morning of 8 August (around 2.00 a.m.) that if the Germans had known of the offensive, and had put down counter-preparation fire, and long-distance harassing fire on roads and bridges, the Canadian Corps could not have deployed for action. McNaughton also mentioned the constant roar of tanks and transport, which must surely have been heard in the German lines, and so the question arises, was the Amiens offensive really a surprise to the German defences?

In fact, contrary to historians' accounts, the Amiens offensive was not completely unexpected by the enemy, although the time was not anticipated. German prisoner of war statements include the following: 'Prisoner 18 Inf Regt states that they were told on afternoon of 7th that tanks had been seen in Villers-Bretonneux and 201st RIR which had just come out to rest came up...that afternoon.' Another prisoner reported: '152nd IR heard motor traffic and tanks continuously 2 days ago.... Officers are stated [to] have expected our attack but men knew nothing.... Main line resistance however was apparently withdrawn, outpost being 600–700 metres in front.' There were conflicting accounts of whether the 117 German Division knew of the attack, but one German intelligence officer said the attack was expected but not the date, while a German Staff Officer of 109 Division 'states indications of British attack owing to RAF activity but not believed imminent'.

Certainly about half the prisoners denied knowledge of the attack, but what seems to have also damaged the German defence in front of the Canadian Corps was the change-over that took place on the night of 7–8 August, when the 117 German Division replaced the tired 109 German Division, and the new troops obviously had not yet got a grasp of their front. It must also be admitted that those prisoners that did expect the offensive, learnt of the attack only some 24 hours previous to the morning of 8 August. The Canadian Corps Intelligence summary reported in somewhat contradictory fashion that the attack was a complete surprise, with many batteries captured before firing a shot, and the gun teams asleep in their dug-outs, but at the same time that German divisional and brigade staffs had warned of an imminent assault. What seems to have happened was that news of the anticipated offensive did not generally filter through from German staffs to the lower units before the offensive started. Apart from the benefit of relative tactical surprise, the Canadian Corps found on 8 August as it advanced that although there was much in the way of tools and defensive material available to the Germans, very little defensive work had actually been done. The GOC 2 Canadian Division surmised that 'The enemy's positions gave the earliest indication of the lack of morale and discipline in his troops, which resulted from his very severe losses in the Spring offensive'. Thus defences were not strong, in fact were a series of widely spaced strong points rather than established lines, which permitted infiltration, and at the same time German morale was poor, and visibility very poor. Some of these same factors had also occurred on 21 March 1918, and certainly favoured the attacker. A firsthand account by Lieutenant Colonel Cy Peck, CO 16th Battalion, in 3 Brigade of 1 Canadian Division, bears out this viewpoint:

Dense fog hung over the land. Bn. sprang forward with eagerness, at zero hour.... Little opposition for first mile. Very thick pall of smoke. North of Demuin severe fight took place. Piper Paul killed beside me. Bn. moved steadily ahead, capturing ridge after ridge. Temporarily held up at Aubercourt. Tanks relieved situation. Final objective captured about 7.15 am. I returned to HQ Demuin about 8, 1st Brigade passed through & situation after that quiet. The

Canadian Corps plan had been to attack in great depth, with maximum mobility, and not to shake out into artillery formation unless absolutely necessary. Instead infantry were to advance in single file rather than waves, but with large gaps between platoons and companies. Smoke grenades and accompanying Lewis guns, Stokes mortars, machine guns, mobile artillery and tanks, would take care of machine gun nests and strong opposition. Strong points could also be taken by infantry working round them and then rushing them under Lewis gun covering fire. Lessons also learned during May and June were that forward troops should press on, regardless of the flanks, leaving strong points on the flanks to be dealt with later.

Finally, cavalry would pursue. Unfortunately, the mobile firepower side of the offensive did not really work, only the Lewis guns kept up with the fast-moving infantry, and all the other forms of firepower were left behind. In this particular case, it seems clear that there had not been enough training between infantry and tanks for the infantry to understand the limitations of the tanks. Cavalry as a mobile form of warfare was not valuable either and around Beaucourt suffered heavy casualties. An eyewitness, a Canadian horse gunner, saw one squadron nearly eliminated, and he himself was ordered to engage enemy machine guns at 300 yards with fuse zero: 'I now know what it is like to gallop through Machine Gun fire & its not pleasant.'

What occurred on the Canadian Corps front on 8 August was that the tactical surprise, the opening barrage, the heavy mist or smoke, and the rapid infantry advance with rifles and Lewis guns, were all sufficient to overwhelm the German defence on the first day, especially because of poor enemy infantry morale (although once again, as at Hamel, the machine gunners stood firm), lack of strong linked defence works, and initially no German artillery support. Yet it is also clear that the essential mobile firepower support of trench mortars, machine guns, field artillery and tanks, without which an advance cannot be sustained, was missing. There was some success with Whippets and armoured cars, the latter managing to capture a German corps headquarters. However, the advance on 8 August of some 8 miles on the Canadian Corps front, although a dazzling success due to the élan of the Canadian infantry, obscured the fact that neither the Canadian Corps nor the BEF generally had yet mastered the art of combined arms mobile warfare. This was particularly the case with the tanks, which were supposedly the key arm of this offensive, yet a report from 2 Canadian Division noted that by 6.30 a.m. on 8 August, the dense mist had lifted, and tank casualties became heavy from artillery and anti-tank guns over open sights.

This forced tanks to zigzag and use up petrol. By noon on 8 August, very few tanks were left, and the divisional commander put this down to two causes, lack of a smoke screen for the tanks, and lack of petrol and supplies to keep the tanks going. It was also generally acknowledged that the Mark V* tanks carrying Lewis and Vickers machine gunners forward to the final infantry offensive, were a failure. Thus of 34 Mark V* tanks allotted to 4 Canadian Division, only 4 reached their objective, and then only after the infantry was already holding its final objective. This failure was partly caused by tanks being knocked out, for example, 10 were destroyed by a field gun near Le Quesnel, in which case the personnel inside were either burnt alive or shot as they escaped from the flames. Partly also, the infantry in the carrying tanks were overcome by heat and fumes, despite being supplied with a 'special tablet', and had to be dropped off early. Finally, some of the Mark V* tanks were diverted from their task by engaging machine gun nests instead of going straight to their objective. The writer of the report on the Mark V* tanks with 4 Canadian Division shrewdly concluded that the brief period of training was not sufficient, and 'the plans for the operation were hurriedly made'.

On the other hand, German prisoners spoke of the effect on morale of tanks emerging from the mist, and German infantry surrendered freely to the tanks. Moreover, battalion reports of 1 Canadian Division, as opposed to the observations of the divisional commander, frequently remark on tanks helping at crucial moments. For instance, the 3rd Battalion of 1 Canadian Division stated that 'it is very doubtful if we would have been able to have gotten forward [at 10.55 a.m. on 8 August] without considerable manoeuvring and reinforcements if it had not been for the timely intervention of a tank, which exterminated a series of Machine gun nests which held up the whole Battalion'. (However, the statement went on with dry humour: 'A certain amount of difficulty was experienced from the Tanks by their firing their 6-pounder gun upon our men.') The 4th Battalion of 1 Canadian Division also reported that about 10 a.m. on 8 August, 'a very severe fire was encountered from the direction of Ruisseau Wood and slope beyond. A request was sent for tanks, one of which reached the wood…at 10.45 a.m. With the assistance of the tank this wood and the bottom of the slope was cleared of MGs [machine guns] after which the objective was reached with little resistance.'

When such ground-level reports are studied, it can be seen that the tanks were very valuable at critical moments, and therefore it is incorrect to say, as one historian has done recently, that 'the tanks had little impact on the fighting'. It is true, however, that tank performance varied according to geography and tank-infantry cooperation. Thus 54th Canadian Battalion of 11 Canadian Brigade only found the smoke screen from a burning tank to be useful, but their neighbours, the 102nd Battalion of the same brigade, reported that two tanks at Beaucourt Wood enabled the battalion to advance, and later two Whippets enabled the battalion to come to close quarters with the German infantry. The brigade commander summed up the experience of his battalions by remarking that in his brigade all tanks but one were knocked out, and so The tanks proved a disappointment'. In general, there were not enough tanks available for the size of the offensive, and their prior training and preparation with the Canadian Corps were obviously weak.

This was due not only to the speed in which the offensive was prepared (some three weeks), but possibly also because the deception orders of the Canadian Corps prevented full-scale training. In any case, an elementary aspect of the offensive was omitted, namely, protection of tanks against enemy artillery and anti-tank guns through smoke, low-flying aircraft, or mobile field artillery. Not surprisingly, after the 'devastation caused by the anti tank guns in that battle [Amiens]', Brigadier General Elles appealed to the RAF to see if they 'could assist in silencing these guns'. Unfortunately, this was not to be an easy task.

Because of these tank problems on the Canadian Corps front, many tank derelicts were to be seen on the battlefield. One poignant scene was described by a Canadian artilleryman: In the valley lay a crippled tank with a couple of shell holes in her side, within were the crew, terribly mangled a gruesome sight. On a slope less than 200 yards away lay the other actors of the scene, two German gun crews done to death beside their guns...the tank was partly crippled and was returning to the rear. It passed the Hun gunners who stood away from their guns with hands up. But one either unseen or moving too quickly from the group of those who had surrendered, pulled the trigger as the tank passed the line of fire and killed the crew. Another tank saw the incident and destroyed all of the German gunners. Nevertheless, despite this stark scene, it would appear that normally a direct hit by an artillery shell did not mean that the tank was totally destroyed, in fact most were repairable. The analysis also showed that tank crews often survived a direct hit. Nevertheless, if tank-infantry cooperation on the Canadian Corps front had not lived up to expectations, would the story be the same with the Australian Corps, who had already gained much experience with the tanks at Hamel?

An analysis of tank battle sheets from the 8th Tank Battalion, which supported 4 Australian Division, shows that of 35 reports (including those filed by another officer in the case of destroyed tanks), 14 tanks enjoyed considerable success and good cooperation with the infantry, although some were hit by artillery at the end of the operation; 10 tanks worked well with the infantry, and engaged targets, but either suffered engine trouble, or were hit by artillery, mostly while patrolling after the final objective had been reached; and 11 tanks achieved very little, mainly because of engine trouble or because the crews were overcome by heat and fumes. This record was not as good as at Hamel, where smoke and dust had protected the tanks, where the enemy was more disorganized than at Amiens, and where the ground was more suitable than at Amiens. Moreover, a large number of tanks were hit by artillery, 15 out of 35, for a

43 per cent loss rate. However, the percentage of tanks working successfully with the infantry was 68.5 per cent, while those that did not were largely eliminated by engine trouble before the action began.

A report from the CO of 'A' Company, 8th Tank Battalion, stated that all his tanks achieved good cooperation with the infantry by staying ahead as they advanced until they reached the red line objective. There was not much enemy resistance, but 6 tanks out of 12 were hit, for a 50 per cent loss rate. All of this does seem to support the hypothesis that previous training and experience with the Australian Corps provided better cooperation with the tanks on 8 August, and therefore greater success on the battlefield. While the Canadian Corps suffered 3,500 casualties, the Australian Corps suffered less at 3,000 casualties, and while the Canadian Corps captured 114 officers, 4,919 other ranks and 161 guns, the Australian Corps captured 183 officers, 7,742 other ranks and 173 guns. Moreover, the left of the Australian Corps was heavily enfiladed by machine guns and artillery on Chippily Ridge, which had not been taken by III Corps, and it was here that the Australians suffered considerable losses in casualties and tanks. If this problem had been eliminated as anticipated by III Corps, the contrast between the Australian and Canadian Corps would have been even greater in favour of the former.

Some descriptions of tank actions in support of the Australian Corps may help substantiate the above hypothesis. Tank 9308 reported 'perfect cooperation with Infantry Through-out', while the great majority of the 24 successful tanks stated that they had started out either ahead of the infantry as planned, or at least with the infantry. One lengthy battle sheet report, which shows good tank-infantry cooperation, does give the flavour of the fight on 8 August. Second Lieutenant Whittenbury, commanding Tank 9199, stated that his tank had to commence by zigzagging due to two field guns firing at them, and had fired at the flashes, as well as exploding some ammunition dumps, but nevertheless 'I advanced about 1 1/2 miles keeping well in front of the infantry the whole way. Infantry were advancing as far as I could see with no casualties.' After the tank's firing both 6-pounders and Hotchkiss machine guns at dug-outs and gun positions, and causing many casualties, the 'enemy appeared to surrender without any resistance'.

> Then the tank approached a house when it came under heavy fire from loop holes in the walls. The infantry had to stop and lie down. Both 6 pounders put a number of shells in the building and I kept up a fire with the Hotchkiss on the loop holes. As the machine gun fire continued I charged the side of the building three times but could not push the wall in. Fired a few more 6 pounders at 10 yards range and the machine gun fire seemed to cease and the infantry got round the building and in it. An Australian signalled the Tank across to the S side of the road and to the E of the hospital where enemy were using a machine gun. These [sic] were put out of action.

After patrolling in front of the red line objective, the tank fired on some enemy artillery, and then returned to the line where the infantry were consolidating. 'There was no fire on the infantry at this time.' Whatever the differences between the Australian and Canadian Corps, the great achievements of the first day of the Amiens offensive inspired Haig to call for pursuit by 'strong advance Guards', and preparations were hurriedly made that evening to continue the next day. Unfortunately there was great confusion in the early morning of 9 August, with Rawlinson's HQ failing to coordinate the plans for the resumed offensive, and even withdrawing at the last minute a division promised to the Canadian Corps for exploitation, fearing that a German counter-attack might occur. Other examples of confusion included the Canadian divisions, where the times and objective of their attack were changed several times, while 5 Australian Division had to attack with its field artillery in the open, which suffered severe casualties. There were fewer tanks available, and in 2 Canadian Division those that did arrive were late, and did not have a proper smoke screen.

Elsewhere on the Amiens front, 12 Division advanced 800 yards behind their tanks, and cooperation broke down completely. Then in 1 Canadian Brigade, there was very little support from field artillery—indeed the artillery either fired short or actually on Canadian positions. There were some tanks in evidence in this brigade, but these were evidently disorganized, although some did good work at specific moments. As before, the main advance in the Canadian sector was achieved by inspired infantry supported by their own Lewis guns, with some mobile trench mortar activity against enemy machine guns. No doubt the Canadian advance was assisted by the fact that the Germans were still in considerable confusion themselves, and their artillery support was negligible, leaving the machine gunners to fight their usual determined defence. Overall, however, the Canadian Corps had made substantial gains on 9 August, of around 4 miles, and it must be said that this was not due to artillery, tanks, or aircraft, and least of all to the cavalry, but, as the CO of 1 Canadian Brigade wrote, to 'the training in open warfare it received in the Chelers area during the months of May and June last. The diamond formation [in the advance], the Battalion "Scatter" [to avoid artillery fire] and the attack methods [in depth manoeuvrability] there taught were practiced with success.'

Once again, did the Australian Corps perform better with their tanks on 9 August? It cannot be said that they did. For instance, in the case of the 8th Tank Battalion, there were very high tank casualties. 'A' Company lost 3 out of 3 tanks at Vauvillers, and Sergeant Dixon Wynn, commanding Tank 9324, left a memoir of this action. The attack started at 11.40 a.m.: in bright sunlight we knew it [the attack] must be something of a hazard. Our Aireal [sic] Reconnaissance may have revealed the presence of Boche Field guns in the Wood surrounding Vauvillers.... However when we started the attack the second of the seven Tanks and we advanced in single line, not in extended order, and as we ran over the Aussie trenches...the extra resistance stopped the engine, and by the time we had re-started the engine (it took four men to swing the handle) we were the last in line. It was then that the Boche Field guns opened fire from the Wood surrounding the village—only a hundred yards or so away. I saw all the Tanks knocked out at point blank range, the effect was curious, each Tank when hit raised slightly with the impact and then black smoke issued from the Tanks. I remember as the last Tank was hit the Officer Tank Commander getting out with blood running down the tunic of one arm, and one of the crew helping him to run to the safety of the Aussie lines. During this time the Boche was machine gunning them and dust spots were being kicked up on the grass.

Later, Wynn's tank was also hit, but managed to return to the rallying point. There he told the major that his was the only tank to survive, but 'he didn't seemed [sic] surprised'. Wynn remarked that the Australian infantry went on to take Vauvillers, and would have silenced the German artillery that had done so much damage: 'We were usually Brigaded with the Aussies and we knew them to be the finest fighters in Christendom.' One small action cannot explain the entire Australian front, but it was clear that operations were now being hurried, and without regard for proper preparations or precautions for the tanks. This has connotations of the July days of the Somme offensive when casualties were needlessly incurred through GHQ pushing for attacks without knowing the conditions on the ground. By 10 August, tanks were no longer being used in groups on the Amiens battlefield, instead the fighting 'became a series of isolated engagements'. Neither did the fortunes of the 8th Tank Battalion improve, for it was used in a rather strange night attack, starting at 10 p.m. on 10 August. The idea was for the 6 tanks of 'B' Company to precede 10 Australian Brigade of 3 Australian Division along the road to Proyart, which was to be attacked at dawn. However, given the darkness during the approach march, it did not seem likely that the tanks would be able to reply to targets, and it would be hard to keep in touch with the infantry. Understandably, therefore, Second Lieutenant Few, the commander of Tank 9372, recorded that Soon after I had crossed our front line the enemy sent up a considerable number of Very lights and when about 200 yards from his positions heavy Machine Gun fire was encountered. I pushed on replying with my Machine Guns but was unable to locate any of the enemy positions exactly. Owing to the heavy enemy fire the infantry were suffering with a fairly great number of casualties and were gradually losing touch with my Tank. Shortly after, the Australian infantry began to retire, and this tank together with the others simply covered the retirement back to the start line. The story of the tanks after the initial surprise on 8 August was not distinguished. Tanks had suffered very high losses from 8 August onwards, although it is a mistake to argue that by the fourth day of the offensive, the number of tanks had dropped to 6. It is true that there were no tank reserves set aside before the battle, and therefore the only tanks available to continue the offensive would be those that had survived the battlefield. But Tank Corps headquarters reported that 'A total of 688 tanks had been in action by the evening of August 11th; of these 480 had been handed over to Tank Corps Salvage Units as too badly damaged for repair by the crews. Of the remainder all were urgently in need of a thorough overhaul. On the personnel of the Corps moreover the effects of the arduous days and nights of continuous moves and fighting had been severe.' Clearly the Tank Corps was in poor shape, but theoretically there were some 200 tanks still available on 12 August. And certainly by 17 August, there were a very considerable number of 'fit' tanks available, including 122 Mark V*, 242 Mark V, 250 Mark IV and 124 Medium 'A' Whippets. This total of 738 does not include another 314 fighting tanks under repair, and thus the historian John Terraine's comment upon the conclusion of the Amiens offensive that only 6 tanks were available and so 'The German Empire was not going to be overthrown by six tanks' seems inappropriate.

Nevertheless, by 12 August Tank Corps HQ wished to halt further operations with tanks, unless they mopped up after the infantry. Significantly, Tank Corps HQ also decided that tanks must be kept intact in groups and not detached in dribs and drabs, that in future attacks one third of the tank force must be kept as reserves, and that smoke grenades should be used to protect tanks. The last instruction recognized the fact that tanks were being knocked out far more readily than had been anticipated. But the obvious reason for this was the failure of the planning staff, whether at corps, army, or GHQ level, to protect the tanks from antitank guns through the use of smoke, artillery, aircraft, or better infantry-tank tactics. What the battle of Amiens actually showed, therefore, was that the combination or coordination of arms was not yet working in the BEF. In fact, in the days succeeding 8 August, the Amiens offensive was being run as an infantry offensive, supported by other arms. This was explicitly expressed by Brigadier General Griesbach, GOC 1 Canadian Brigade, who remarked that 'as to the tactical handling of Tanks, I am persuaded that we cannot sit down and allow the Tank people to dictate the tactical use of the Tank, except insofar as its mechanical possibilities are concerned'. Griesbach pointed out 'that [on 11 August] some 15 Tanks were "done in" outside of PARVILLERS [actually 12 out of 15], probably by the same anti-tank gun or battery. This meant that Tank after Tank went up against an impossible situation and was lost to the use of the attacking infantry. This was magnificent, but it is not war.'

Griesbach suggested instead a three-phase advance for the future, in which phase 1 saw the normal set-piece attack with tanks leading infantry under a barrage, then phase 2 saw the tanks 200 or 300 yards behind the infantry, who dealt with the anti-tank guns, and finally came phase 3, where tanks would be used as a reserve, working under the orders of the battalion commander. Griesbach therefore still envisioned an infantry-centred assault, although now with better infantry cooperation, but still with little appreciation of the difficulties of the Tank Corps in regard to crew exhaustion and the overhaul of the machines. It remained to be seen, however, whether the fighting of the next three months of 1918 would mark 'the first successful use of high performance teams using high performance machines in the attack', as the historian Dominick Graham has written of 1918 generally. This was all the more critical because the other element of mechanical warfare, the aircraft, had also suffered very considerable losses in the Amiens offensive. On 8 August, 96 of 700 day-flying aeroplanes had been written off, mainly the low-flying bombers and fighters. On 9 August, the RAF lost another 45 planes, and similar casualties continued on the following days. Mistakes had been made, partly the lack of fighter escorts and partly the costly decision to attempt to bomb the Somme bridges with low-level attacks when railway junctions would have been more appropriate, given the arrival of five fresh German divisions by train. The history of 8 Squadron gives some idea of why the technology of the air was suffering from the same malaise as the tanks on the ground. Technology was not yet the answer unless thoroughly integrated with the traditional arms. In fact, according to Squadron Leader Leigh Mallory, it is clear that 8 Squadron, as a tank contact squadron, was losing control of its role already by 9 August: With an advance of 12,000 yards [on 8 August] the difficulties of communication became acute. It became practically impossible to communicate with the Tank Battalions, and very difficult to get in touch with the Brigades. Distances were great, the roads were bad, and blocked with traffic, and it was naturally impossible to communicate by phone.... It became increasingly difficult to find the positions of the Battalion Dropping Stations, and when we did get their positions, the [identification] strips were frequently not out; however, the Brigade Dropping Stations hardly ever failed us.

Leigh Mallory also noted that after 9 August, when tank actions 'became a series of isolated engagements...it became very difficult to find out when the tanks were going into action'. It is not surprising also, in view of tank casualties, that 8 Squadron's role concentrated 'more and more on Anti-Tank gun work, which grew more and more successful, as fresh experience was gained'.31 The inference is that mechanical warfare was still in the process of being worked out.

Meanwhile, in 8 Squadron, patrols had to be in the air, watching for the tanks to start, in order to commence their role of dropping messages concerning advances on the relevant dropping stations. This role, however, did not apparently prevent the pilots from undertaking low-level attacks as opportunities offered, as the story of Captain West and his observer, Lieutenant Haslam, on 10 August, illustrates. Captain West noticed some enemy activity near Roye, and although this was some 8,000 yards from the front line, he immediately flew over there, and wrought great havoc among limbers and transport with his bombs and machine guns. Just as he turned to fly back to our lines he was attacked by 7 Fokker biplanes. With almost his first burst, one of the hostile machines...shot his left leg off between the knee and the thigh with three explosive bullets. In spite of the fact that Capt. West's leg fell helpless amongst the controls, and he was wounded in the right foot, he managed to fly his machine back and land it within our lines. Meanwhile Lieut. Haslam, who was wounded through the right ankle, had been keeping the hostile machines at bay with his Lewis guns, and managed to bring one of them down.... Capt. West...was subsequently awarded the Victoria Cross, and Lieut. Haslam was awarded the D.F.C.

With actions such as this, 8 Squadron found itself in the same boat as the tanks, namely, with heavy casualties: 'The Squadron establishment of machines was 18. On August 8th and 9th, 9 of them were completely written off.' In addition, besides this 50 per cent loss rate, 'no less than 10 machines had to be repaired in the squadron'.

What was happening with both tanks and aircraft was that, within certain limits, the technology was capable of successfully engaging in mechanical warfare, but the tactics, cooperation and protection for these machines of ground and air had not yet been worked out, partly because more experience was needed, but partly because the emphasis remained with the traditional arms. However, what had been achieved by mechanical warfare, especially the tanks, was that it had made mobile warfare possible in 1918. The MGRA of Fifth Army acknowledged this in September 1918, when he wrote that operations were now mobile, because tanks 'made it possible to capture strongly defended lines of trenches and localities'. Meanwhile, back on the Amiens battlefield, the traditional arms of infantry and artillery were now fighting the offensive, and on 10 and 11 August there were mixups as they strove to continue. For example, on 10 August, 4 Canadian Division did not start on time to support 1 Australian Division in their joint attack, and on 11 August, 4 Canadian Division postponed its attack, waiting for 12 Mark V tanks, which never did show up. Currie then ordered 4 Canadian Division to cancel its assault, but meanwhile 32 British Division, operating in the Canadian Corps area, postponed its attack for 2 1/2 hours without telling anyone, so that the French next door suffered heavy flank losses. When it did attack, 32 Division itself took nearly 1,500 casualties because the artillery barrage got ahead of the infantry. Evidently the Amiens offensive was winding down, and because the front was now reaching the old Somme trenches, the corps commanders were getting anxious about stiffening resistance within the context of a mass of uncut wire and trenches.

However, on 10 August, Foch stressed that the frontal advance should be continued, although he also drew Haig's attention to the possibility of flank attacks by the BEF's Third Army. Rawlinson emphasized Foch's ideas regarding flank attacks by Third Army to Haig on 10 August, 'as I suggested a week ago', and confronted Haig over Foch's main concept of pushing straight ahead, with the amazingly frank question: 'Are you commanding the British Army or is Maréchal Foch?' Nevertheless, Haig consented to Foch's demands for a further advance.

Then on 11 August, Currie decided that the offensive must be broken off, to which Rawlinson again provisionally agreed. But under pressure from Foch and Haig, Rawlinson felt compelled to organize a limited objective, set-piece assault for 15 August (later postponed until 16 August), which would employ a barrage and as many tanks as possible. Even so, Rawlinson feared a heavy casualty list, but was prepared to carry out the offensive. But on 13 August Currie objected to the 15–16 August offensive plan, and Rawlinson once again agreed, saying that finesse was needed and not a sledge hammer. So on the morning of 14 August, Rawlinson took photographs of the very difficult mass of wire and trenches to be attacked to Haig, and asked for the offensive to be cancelled. He also, as before, proposed instead a future surprise Third Army attack on Bapaume, with Fourth Army pressing on simultaneously. To Rawlinson's surprise, 'This he [Haig] agreed to without a murmur'. According to Dill (GS at GHQ), this was the only time that Haig listened to advice, in this case to break off the offensive, and so on the afternoon of 15 August Haig went to see Foch and persuaded him to agree to the change of plans. Thus the sequence of events in breaking off the Amiens offensive was from Currie to Rawlinson to Haig to Foch, showing that, as in 1916 and 1917, the further the commander was from the battlefield the less grasp he had of reality. Thus Henry Wilson said of Haig on 10 August that he was more prosy and full of platitudes and principles than ever, while Maxse felt GHQ to be ignorant and out of touch.

Despite this convoluted decision-making process in cancelling the resumption of the Amiens offensive, a change in Allied thinking had also taken place. It seems to have been initiated by Foch, who on 12 August set forth new tactics in a letter to the commanders-in-chief of the French and British armies:

In the presence of the resistance offered by the enemy, we must not try to reach him by pushing forward simultaneously along the whole front.... Instead of this, we must make concentrated and powerful attacks against the important points of the region...against those whose capture by us will increase the disorganization in the enemy's ranks, and more especially jeopardize his lines of communication. Foch also recommended two attacks on the extreme flanks of the Amiens offensive, one by the BEF's Third Army toward Bapaume-Péronne, and the other by the French Tenth Army toward Chauny. Foch's concepts seem to have been incorporated by Haig on 13 August, when Haig's diary entry spoke of reinforcing where the enemy was weakest and not where he was strongest, and by corps commanders such as Haldane, who on 13 August reported in his diary that Foch wanted to bite off bits of the German front in several places, because the Germans were now demoralized. (It is of interest that others besides Foch were also now realizing that new methods were required, thus a thoughtful letter from Birch to Lawrence in April 1918 declared that deliberate linear offensives under massed artillery were no longer possible, what was needed now were small operations to seize tactical points.)36 However, Foch mixed in with his plans the requirement that the Amiens attack be pushed ahead, and it was this decision that Haig refused to accommodate on 15 August.

But it is significant that the next operation was to be Third Army's attack toward Bapaume, supported by Fourth Army, as originally suggested by Rawlinson, and sanctioned by Foch, while the French Tenth Army did attack toward Chauny as envisioned in Foch's plans of 12 August, with the BEF's First Army attacking north of Arras on 26 August. These are the successive blows that Foch sought, and regarding which he had already set out the principles in a wide-ranging document read to the Allied commanders-in-chief on 24 July, and basically agreed to by them. The document called for movements 'executed with such rapidity as to inflict on the enemy a succession of blows'. In this sense, Foch was the principal strategist of the moving warfare that developed after Amiens and until the end of the war, although most historians do not agree with this verdict.

However, a number of BEF senior officers at the time supported the concept of Foch as the primary architect of strategy in the second half of 1918. For example, in mid-September 1918, Rawlinson wrote that Foch deserved credit for attacks all along the front: 'It is good war', and later in September he noted: 'Under Foch's tuition and the lessons of four years of war, we are really learning and the synchronisation of the various attacks has been admirable.' Similarly, in September Haldane reported that it was Foch's idea to attack all along the front until a breakthrough came, and in October 1918, Haldane noted that he was pleased to hear the word strategy, because until Foch took over 'one never heard the word "strategy" mentioned'. At GHQ, the counter- battery coordinator, Hemming, also listed Foch's arrival as Supreme Allied Commander as one of the key reasons for the successful offensive operations of 1918.

The GOC of the Canadian Machine Gun Corps, Brigadier General Brutinel, stated that 'One is impressed by the efforts made by Marshal Foch on his assumption to command, to break down the tendencies to particularism of the Allied Armies'. Brutinel believed that 'the results to be obtained by creating under the stress of battles the feeling of the unity of front and command...[were] so great that it was good policy to subordinate everything to that ideal'. Detractors of Haig such as J.F.C.Fuller were also predictably in favour of Foch, and Fuller considered that having Foch as combined Commander-in-Chief fully compensated for the German successes in the spring offensives.38 On the other hand, Edmonds, who was no great admirer of the French, saw no strategy to Foch's advance. Edmonds believed there was no attempt to cut east-west communications, and no use of troops in the Lorraine area.

According to Edmonds, all that happened was that the line gradually crumbled, and then pursuit took place by mobile columns, without much support from the tanks. But Edmonds is not quite accurate, Foch did try to cut east-west communications, for example, as early as May he issued orders to cut the lateral railway lines near Amiens and Hazebrouck, and his 24 July plans for local offensives were specifically designed to free lateral railway communications, starting with the Amiens-Paris line. Then in regard to Lorraine, the American St Mihiel operation took place in the Lorraine area, although it is true that the French Eighth Army was not scheduled to attack into Lorraine until November 1918. However, to be fair, Foch's 24 July document shows that his main strategy was the delivery of rapid successive blows so that the German army would be set on the move and, most important, would not have time to switch reserves around to meet these sequential thrusts. Basically this is what did occur, and so Foch's strategy must be judged a success. Nevertheless, Liddell Hart's judgement of Foch also seems sound, namely, that Foch's constant calls to attack really succeeded in 1918 because these continuous demands for offensive action sooner or later coincided with the right conditions.

It might also be noted here that the French, too, had been attacking in August, despite the attitude of the BEF and some historians, that the BEF was the only effective army in the field, and Haig the only effective commander. For instance, those actually observing the French army often had a positive image of French operations. Thus a Canadian liaison officer with the French First Army reported strongly on the action of French artillery (the 75s) in clearing Wood 'Z' on 14 August 1918, as 'something else', and then on 18 August when the French attacked the Bois de Bracquemont, the French opening barrage was withering and the poilus were brave and 'gai'. Later that night the French had to retake the wood after a German counter-attack had recaptured it, and this the poilus did. As the liaison officer noted: 'They know no fear and they are a useful army.'

Returning to the operations of the BEF, the next offensive of 21 August was evidently planned to be a repeat of Amiens as a two-corps tank-infantry mechanical style attack, with as much surprise as possible. It is interesting to note that GHQ attempted to conceal the point of attack (between Albert and Arras) by asking for normal wireless activity by Third Army on its front (it was doing the attack), while the move of the Cavalry Corps from Fourth to Third Army was concealed by keeping the Cavalry Corps wireless sets in Fourth Army. (Presumably the presence of the exploiting Cavalry Corps would give away the location of the offensive.) It turned out, however, from prisoners' statements, that the tanks rather than the cavalry were located by the enemy, since they were heard assembling. Fog had prevented the usual trick of aeroplanes flying up and down to drown the noise of tank engines. Nevertheless, IV and VI Corps were to lead the advance, but now because of tank casualties there were only 183 tanks available as opposed to the nearly 600 at Amiens, although the frontage was much narrower than at Amiens, and so the percentage of tanks per yardage was not much different. This was to be the second major offensive blow of 1918 after 8 August, and like Amiens, was initially thought of by Byng (Third Army GOC) as a limited objective assault, although it was to be a straightforward frontal attack on a narrow front, which tended to expose the flanks.

Dense fog on the morning of 21 August both helped and hindered the offensive as it rolled forward at 4.55 a.m. in the semi-darkness. Interestingly enough, Haldane as commander of VI Corps saw the attack as a success due to the tanks, and indeed the old story repeated itself— where the infantry was properly trained in tank-infantry cooperation, as in VI Corps, and when tanks had proper protection, all went well, but where the corps commander, Harper, of IV Corps, was ignorant of the tanks, and where tanks had little protection, the attack had problems. Thus Lieutenant Colonel Butler's 12th Tank Battalion, cooperating with 99 Brigade (GOC Brigadier General Ironside, the future CIGS) of 2 Division, VI Corps, had remarkable success, despite being equipped with obsolete Mark IV tanks.

For several days previous to the offensive, schemes and discussions between tank and infantry personnel produced excellent understanding between the two sides, and as a result 12 tanks started on 21 August, 12 tanks took all three objectives, and 12 tanks rallied at the end of the day: 'Cooperation with the infantry was perfect and all tank commanders left their tanks and discussed the situation at the different objectives. Several MG nests were reduced when indicated by the infantry, several bunches of prisoners were handed over to them.' This success was caused partly by the previously mentioned training and liaison with the infantry, but also by good communications via car for the CO and runners, by the dense mist, by the careful reconnaissance beforehand, and by the weak resistance of the enemy, 'the Germans who had not run away generally surrendering freely on the close approach of Tanks'. On the other hand, due to the thick mist the Mark V tanks accompanying IV Corps troops failed to keep in touch with the infantry, who thereupon had to borrow Mark IV tanks from another tank battalion to get them to their objectives. Undoubtedly, despite the official explanation, this loss of touch between tanks and infantry was due to poor training beforehand and poor cooperation during the battle itself in IV Corps.

It is of interest that the report of 3 Division (VI Corps) by the GOC, Major General Deverell (an infantryman not particularly interested in tanks), regarding 21 August, made no mention of training with the tanks beforehand, and obviously saw the whole battle as a purely infantry action. According to Deverell, the tanks were there to assist the infantry rather than to cooperate as equal partners, and so it is not surprising that his comments were generally negative: 'The old Mark IV tank is most unreliable. It should be kept for village fighting, or for very short advances to clear up a situation and in drawing up plans for an attack, if allotted Mark IV tanks, they should be regarded as a very subsidiary arm, and not allowed to influence the plans in any way.' Then Deverell went on to admit that before 21 August, 3 Division had 'never really operated with tanks at all, and, though very able lectures had been given, the want of training and actual experience with Tanks was very much felt both by the Infantry and the Tanks'. Hence, the poor results of the tanks with 3 Division on 21 August were certainly to be expected.

However, there were also some basic problems with the mechanical- style offensive of 21 August, which was explained in a report by Lieutenant Colonel Karslake, GSO 1 of the Tank Corps:

The [German] system of a deep outpost zone up to 3,000 yards in depth requires careful consideration before Tanks are employed. In conjunction with this system the enemy keeps the majority of his guns about 5,000 yards back from their front line. This is just too far for effective counter battery work against all the batteries and too far for the initial surprise to let the Tanks reach the guns before they recover from the first shock. In this battle the hostile guns were placed in this way and caused considerable trouble.

In other words, the German defences had become much deeper in order to accommodate the BEF tank-infantry-artillery method of assault. Karslake suggested a possible answer: 'The solution appears to be for the infantry to work forward with the artillery but without Tanks until it becomes possible for the Tank assault to take place within 3,000 yards of the hostile artillery, at any rate until some better method of protecting Tanks from hostile guns is developed.'44 That better method was thought after Amiens to be air support, yet 8 Squadron, detailed to destroy anti-tank guns, found the going tough:

August 21st was quite the most disappointing day's work the Squadron had with the Tanks.... The morning was very foggy indeed, and it was quite impossible for the machines to leave the ground till 11.00 am.... The wind being in the East, the fog had cleared on the German side of the line first, thus allowing their aeroplanes to fly on the line unmolested for an hour or so. Also, just as the fog lifted, our Tanks, especially Whippets, were just approaching the ACHIET LE GRAND railway, thus presenting a magnificent target to the isolated German anti-tank guns situated on the railway embankment, which immediately opened fire scoring many direct hits on our tanks. In other words, the delay in getting machines into the air, which meant a delay in catching up with the battle and finding out where the tanks and infantry actually were, plus the sudden lifting of the fog, meant that the anti-tank work of the aeroplanes was poor.

There were other difficulties on 21 August. For example, 17 Division complained that its corps did not coordinate the attack at all, but that each division operated separately. But the greatest problem was between Haig and Byng, since at 10.30 p.m. on 21 August, the latter wanted to pause before continuing, while Haig, with his usual impetuosity, ordered resumption of the attack as soon as possible. The war was no longer like 1916 and 1917, wrote Haig, requiring step by step advances in regular lines, but now armies must push ahead where ground was being gained. Therefore Byng gave instructions for a resumed offensive on 23 August. Haig also told Haldane that the Germans could not counter-attack because they had no reserves, therefore, it was possible to push to distant objectives. In effect, Haig was sounding like Foch, sooner or later the constant admonition to attack and seek distant objectives was going to coincide with the right conditions. However, conditions were not quite right on 23 August because BEF troops had suffered very severe gas casualties on 22 August, and the German policy of extra-deep defensive zones, permitting advances of 3,000 to 4,000 yards, was sufficient to hold the line, albeit with 8,000 prisoners lost. Divisional commanders also complained to Haig on 23 August that German machine gunners were giving trouble, and tanks were going back at the end of the day's patrol, leaving infantry vulnerable. Not very usefully, Haig suggested using artillery to counter machine gun nests.

Despite these complaints, 23 August was another effort at mechanical warfare, this time on a much larger front of 33 miles, with both Fourth and Third Armies attacking straight ahead, using some 110 tanks. The anti-tank gun work by aircraft was very successful on 23 August, and 8 Squadron dropped 111 bombs on anti-tank guns and fired 18,000 rounds of MG ammunition at these guns. Much the same results were achieved by 73 Camel Squadron. However, resistance increased, and according to Tank Corps HQ, Tanks encountered a much greater resistance in this action than at any time since the offensive began; a large number of machine gunners fired their guns until run over by the Tanks. These guns were equipped almost exclusively with armour piercing bullets and all the tanks returned from action pitted like thimbles.' On the other hand, the cooperation of the infantry was good on this day, and most tank casualties were incurred after the infantry had reached their objectives, when the tanks were used as a protective screen. Lieutenant Colonel Karslake declared: 'This is wrong; they are much too vulnerable to artillery fire to be used in this way.' Once again, a close look at operations on the ground may illuminate actual conditions.

Twelve tanks of the 8th Tank Battalion were allotted to 32 Division, operating with the Australians south of the Somme on the Herleville-Chuignolles front. There was no preliminary barrage, and in any case no wire to cut or serious defences to reduce. The barrage was stated to be a mixture of HE and shrapnel, with 10 per cent smoke, but something must have changed because almost all tank commanders complained of dense smoke. Thus Tank 9372 reported: 'Picked up Infantry at tape line but owing to extreme density of smoke barrage was very difficult to maintain direction and keep in touch with Infantry. At [map point]...heavy MG fire was encountered but again owing to the smoke barrage it was impossible to locate MG.' Later this tank ditched, and then caught up with the infantry who had reached their objective. The tank was then directed to a wood from which sniper fire was coming, but all the tank could do was circle the wood firing at invisible targets, although this was sufficient to silence the snipers. However, apart from excessive smoke, most tank commanders also reported that German defenders were using a new technique to defeat the tanks, which was for the infantry to fire red lights at the tank, thus providing markers for the German anti-tank guns to open fire, even in the smoke.

In this 8th Tank Battalion action, the tanks were quite successful. Only 1 out of the 12 was put out of action, and a further 2 had mechanical problems, for a good survival ratio. Most of the 12 tanks also enabled the 32 Division attack to continue at certain key moments. But ironically, smoke protection was now too good and created loss of direction, the tanks were unsuitable for eliminating machine gunners and snipers in woods, and German anti-tank defences were starting to become more sophisticated with infantry signal lights directing artillery fire onto tanks and with the use of anti-tank rifles and armour-piercing machine gun bullets. However, the tanks continued to be allotted in groups along the line, for example, 12 Mark IV tanks made a decisive contribution to the capture of

Gomiecourt by 3 Division on 23 August, according to the division commander as reported by Tank Corps HQ: 'The Div.

Commander [Deverell GOC 3 Division] stated that the success of the show was almost entirely due to Tanks.' And 12 tanks assisted materially in the capture of Loupart Wood on 24 August. However, it is clear that tanks were now being used in 'penny packets', that tank losses (both heavy tanks and Whippets) were averaging 40 to 50 per cent, due to artillery fire, mechanical problems and ditching, that crews were very tired, and that even 'fit' tanks needed mechanical overhauling after every battle. In other words, tanks and their crews were not usefully adapted to the kind of offensive that attacked every day over a period of many days.. In this favoured method of assault by GHQ, who wished to pursue the enemy relentlessly, tanks and crews were quickly worn out, although comparatively few tanks were actually permanently destroyed. This use of tanks therefore was not the best application of the weapon, although at certain key moments tanks did make the continuation of the advance possible. Comments by Tank Corps HQ, and by Haldane, the VI Corps commander, showed the way things were going. In regard to the state of 3 Tank Brigade at 8 p.m. on 25 August, Major Hotblack, GSO 1, Tank Corps HQ, remarked of the 9th Tank Battalion: '10 Tanks are moving tonight to West of Telegraph Hill and are due to operate with 2nd Canadian Division about dawn. Owing to fatigue of crews and lack of time for Reconnaissance or Liaison with the Infantry these Tanks cannot be relied upon to obtain good results if used tomorrow 26th.' Similarly, tank crews of the 11th Tank Battalion, due to attack at dawn near Arras the next day, 26 August, 'are also tired and have had no time for Reconnaissance'. The VI Corps commander, Haldane, evidently understood what was going on, for on 25 August he decided not to use tanks the next day, and in fact 'The Corps Commander does not intend to use Heavy Tanks until the HINDENBURG LINE is reached, or until really heavy opposition is encountered'. Not surprisingly, Lieutenant Colonel Karslake of Tanks Corps HQ told Haldane on 29 August that VI Corps was the only corps where tanks were used properly, i.e. with economy of force.

Elsewhere, in other parts of the line on 23 August and following days, tanks were hardly mentioned, as in 3 Division, where 76 Brigade had the use of 8 Mark IV tanks on 23 August in advancing to take Gomiecourt, the very same attack where tanks were reported by the divisional commander to Tank Corps HQ to have been decisive in the success of the assault. But in the 3 Division report, these same tanks apparently could not advance due to their being under enemy artillery observation, and also had trouble with the terrain: The Tanks had difficulty crossing the Railway and arrived too late to be of any assistance.' It is hard to reconcile the two statements, unless the 3 Division commander was simply being nice to the Tank Corps. Instead 3 Division gave the reason for its success as the action of troops closely following the barrage, the bombardment of Gomiecourt by heavy artillery, and the covering fire of the machine gunners. Indeed, 3 Division's report included a lengthy anecdote by an escaped prisoner of their Machine Gun Battalion to highlight the part played by the machine gunners:

About 7 am a party of the enemy emerged from a dugout on the Sunken Road about 20 yards away and rushed our position. I shot one officer through the head with my revolver, then we were taken prisoners with about 12 GORDON HIGHLANDERS, two of whom were wounded. We were taken along the Railway and put in a small sandpit with three of the enemy to guard us. We tried to take our wounded with us, but a German officer refused to let us get them all. This officer started beating one of the GORDONS with a stick and told him to hurry up. He said he was going to shoot the two Machine gunners because they had inflicted heavy casualties on German troops. At that moment a German Colonel appeared who was very nice to us.... Just then our barrage opened at 11 am. We were hurried to ACHIET LE GRAND and the Germans took refuge in a dug-out and left us at the top of the stairs. We saw our fellows advancing and waved for them to come on and they took prisoners all the Germans in the dug-out about 3 Officers and 50 men...we told the KRRs [King's Royal Rifle Regiment] about the Officer who had beaten the GORDON with the stick: the KRRs then bayonetted the officer.

The reports of the offensives of 21 and 23 August and following days show that two separate and often uncoordinated battles were really going on—the traditional artillery and infantry attack, and the mechanical-style attack. A German officer captured on 21 August said that a BEF attack with infantry, artillery and tanks would always get through; one with infantry and artillery alone would get through three times out of four; but one with infantry and tanks unsupported would get through only one time out of four.

This was a reasonable evaluation of the divergence that now occurred in the BEF—between a manpower, traditionally oriented army, and a mechanical-warfare oriented army. Edmonds noticed this divergence when he commented that after 8 August, 'it is to be greatly regretted that no massed tank attack was made, not even planned', instead tanks were used in penny packets as available, and not saved up to be used in mass attacks as at Cambrai and at Amiens. Critics invariably say that few tanks were available to be used in mass attacks, but Edmonds points out that between 8 August and 27 September, 582 tanks were salvaged and only 14 were beyond repair. Tank Corps HQ reported that 630 tanks were available on 8 August, but that between 8 August and 31 August, 1,184 tanks were in action, meaning that tanks were being used several times over. Weekly tank state reports also show the specific availability of tanks in France.

Thus on 19 August, soon after the Amiens offensive, there were in France 242 fit Mark V tanks, with 153 under salvage and repair; plus 250 Mark IV fit tanks, with 85 under salvage and repair; and 124 fit Medium A Whippets, with 36 under salvage and repair. There were therefore on that date 616 fit fighting tanks, not counting Mark V* or gun-carrying tanks, with another 274 under salvage and repair. Then on 30 August, after the offensives of late August, there were 261 'fit' fighting tanks, 156 in the process of being salvaged and 102 under repair, for a total of 519. A week later on 7 September, there were 177 'fit' fighting tanks, 382 in the process of being salvaged and 121 under repair, for a total of 680. By 19 October, 317 'fit' fighting tanks were available, with 402 under repair or temporarily 'unfit', and 349 being salvaged, leading to a total of 1,068. Finally, on 9 November, at the end of the war, 235 'fit' fighting tanks were counted, plus 550 temporarily 'unfit' and under repair, and 306 being salvaged, for a total of 1,091. In other words, tanks were sufficient in number to have been saved for other mass tank attacks. The Tank Corps also suffered considerable personnel casualties of 561 officers and 2,627 other ranks between 8 August and 20 October—but here again these might have been saved for mass attacks, and personnel could have been replaced at a higher rate. The divergence in the BEF between the two styles of warfare was actually precipitated, not by tank casualties, and not entirely by the changed circumstances of a German breakdown in morale and the consequent moving warfare, but by a second manpower crisis (following the first at the end of 1917), which produced a difference in opinion between Lloyd George, Churchill and the Army Council on the one hand, and Haig, GHQ and several senior officers on the other hand.

The opening shot was fired by the Army Council which sent a letter to GHQ on 23 August saying that only 42 active divisions would be maintained in France, and with a battalion strength of 900 rather than 999 men each. Furthermore, despite GHQ opposition, 1 Cavalry Corps HQ and 1 Cavalry Division would be disbanded, and the men used for the Tank Corps and other purposes. Three thousand tanks would be delivered, and the Tank Corps increased to 55,000 men. Therefore, when on 25 August Rawlinson asked Haig for more divisions for his Fourth Army, because his divisions were tired, Haig denied him any divisions. And so, on 29 August, Rawlinson, previously a strong supporter of the tanks, and of mechanical warfare, wrote to Henry Wilson in reaction to the Army Council letter: All you have got to do is to keep our infantry up to strength and not waste man-power in tanks and aviation. They won't win the war for you as the infantry will. We cannot beat the Boche without infantry. Tanks, aeroplanes, etc., are great helps, but they cannot and will not win for us by themselves, so do not let Lloyd George think they will, and persist in developing them at the expense of the infantry.

This line of thinking was repeated by Haig, who on 27 August had been discussing manpower problems with the Adjutant General, and who in early September wrote his wife that 'Too many men are being sent to air Service, Tanks, & such fancy jobs, & not enough to Infantry who can win the war!' For the opposition, Wilson clearly continued to be keen on tanks, telling Haig on 21 August that he wished the BEF now had 4,000 to 5,000 more tanks, and that the army should have looked more to the future, and then on 27 August telling the War Cabinet that 'Complete [tank] losses were small and the German machine gunners had been unable to do anything against the tanks'. Churchill also fought hard for an increased Tank Corps in August, through his Ministry of Munitions. Then in early September Churchill sent a long letter to Lloyd George, arguing for men to be sent to the tanks rather than to the infantry, claiming that tanks and training would ensure BEF success, although he conceded that there was strong resistance to putting more men into the air force and it would be necessary to cut back considerably on the proposed expansion of air manpower. Finally a letter from Wilson to Haig at the end of August expressed the War Office concern with Haig's traditional manpower style of warfare: 'Just a word of caution in regard to incurring heavy losses in attacks on the Hindenburg line as opposed to losses when driving the enemy back to that line.' In other words, Wilson and the War Office did not want more offensives like the Somme and Passchendaele. In fact there was considerable justification for this manpower caution because Wilson reported on 7 September that the BEF had lost 650,000 men since 21 March, and 110,000 since 8 August. Thus by 23 September, Milner was warning Haig that if he knocked this army about there was none to replace it.

At the end of August 1918 therefore, the BEF had arrived at a turning point in its prosecution of the war. In fact this was the precise point at which GHQ moved away from mechanical warfare and back toward the traditional manpower-oriented, infantry-artillery style of war. This was curious because at just the same time—late August 1918—the Ministry of Munitions believed that 'an augmented tank programme was considered to be at the moment the most vital requirement of the allied armies in France as a means of reaching decisive results.... The first class priority in favour of tanks was renewed.' But commanders such as Rawlinson, who had converted to the methods of mechanical warfare at Hamel and Amiens, now, when it came to the question of whether his army was going to be allowed to attack or not, because of manpower concerns, thought only of manpower, and returned to his roots as an infantry commander. Hence when Davidson at GHQ told Rawlinson on 6 September to ease up in his push forward, Rawlinson's response was to tell Clive and Wilson that the BEF needed more men. Similarly, on 7 September 1918, Haig was very insistent to his army commanders to be careful about preserving manpower, but as with Rawlinson, the reasoning behind this was so that the infantry-centred warfare could still continue, in spite of manpower problems. Already at the end of August Haig had signalled his belief in the infantry-centred attack by telling his army commanders that Tanks must join the Army', and must manoeuvre on similar lines to the infantry, in accordance with the pre-war FSR [Field Service Regulations] volume 1. Tanks must also come under the control of the (infantry) commanders of local attacks. Haig also stressed the value of his prewar ideas concerning the 'Advanced Guards of all Arms'. Whatever else was going to happen, Haig and the top echelon of GHQ ensured that the fighting of the rest of the war was not going to resemble the mechanical warfare offensives of Cambrai, Hamel and Amiens. Ultimately, in the context of a crumbling German defence, and the almost desperate wish to finish the war in 1918 and not wait for Fuller's Plan 1919 in the next year, Haig and some of the senior officers of the BEF reverted to the emotionally comfortable principles of the prewar days rather than the potential of a new style of warfare. As Dawnay at GHQ wrote in September, having talked to Rawlinson, Maxse and others, the BEF was 'back to our old pre-war principles, which prove their soundness every time'.

GHQ's rejection of the mechanical alternative was enshrined in its significantly entitled policy document, 'Tanks and their employment in cooperation with other arms', of August 1918. The traditional nature of these regulations was revealed when the MGRA at GHQ, Birch, read a proof copy in July 1918 and wrote on the document that there was too much emphasis on the artillery turning the enemy's defences into a crater field, in which case the tanks could not be used. Birch commented that 'Last year there was a general tendency to devote more time and ammunition to the enemy's defences than was really necessary'. Despite Birch's objections, the relevant paragraph was not changed, and the emphasis remained on the traditional heavy artillery preparation, regardless of whether this was useful or negated the effectiveness of the tanks. The document itself stressed the pre-eminent role of the infantry as the central factor of the battlefield, and the subordinate role of all other arms, including tanks: 'It is their [the tanks'] duty, just as it is the duty of the artillery, machine guns and trench mortars, to assist the Infantry to gain superiority of fire.' Even though the tanks 'can materially assist the Infantry.... It is unwise, however, to place too much reliance upon mechanical contrivances.' Nevertheless, the document did grudgingly admit that 'As the speed of tanks is developed, and their machinery perfected, it is possible that their tactical employment may develop and that their role may become more independent'. Although the document was ostensibly concerned with the tanks, it is curious that the role of the infantry and artillery wound up as the central feature of the new regulations, and presumably of the battlefield.

GHQ cannot be faulted in the very important sense that the war was won. Yet it is probable that the full adoption of mechanical warfare would have saved lives, for although the German army fought a rearguard battle for the rest of the war, BEF casualties were far from light, indeed from 7 August to 12 November these casualties totalled 314,206, and this sum includes only the infantry, cavalry, Tank Corps and Machine Gun Corps, but excludes the artillery and all other subsidiary arms and services. Thus a full BEF casualty list for the period from Amiens to the Armistice in November would amount to some 400,000, to say nothing of French and American casualties. There was no easy way to win a war in 1918, but it is of interest that Tank Corps casualties from 8 August to 10 October 1918 were only 3,188, and from 21 August to the end of the war, were just 2,416. Thus Tank Corps casualties for Amiens by itself would have been some 700. Yet it was this tank-infantry battle that proved to be the 'black day' for German arms and which gave momentum to the 1918 German collapse. In this same battle, BEF infantry and cavalry casualties for the period 7 August to 20 August were 33,382. In contrast, BEF infantry and cavalry casualties for the period 21 August to 17 September were 105,943, and from 18 September to 11 November were 158,440. But from 8 August to 31 August, the total number of tanks engaged was 1,184, while from 1 September to 20 October, the total number of tanks engaged was only 706. These figures, although the dates do not precisely coincide, do suggest that when infantry fought with the advantage of properly mounted tank offensives, infantry casualties were much lighter. There are several other variables, but the figures tend to support the statement by Edmonds that the saving of tanks for surprise, mass tank attacks should have been done, and they strengthen the hypothesis that GHQ's concern with traditional and pre-war principles actually resulted in a costly final two months of the war.

5

War and the Movements

The two and a half months of the war produced, initially, the development of what can be called semi-traditional warfare. This meant set-piece offensives, with very heavy reliance on artillery, and to a lesser extent on machine guns and mortars, and occasionally the use of tanks, to get the BEF infantry forward. Innovative ideas emerged at corps, divisional and lower levels, while GHQ became less relevant. Nevertheless, BEF casualties were very high due to German firepower defences, while on the other hand German casualties of around 1 1/2 million (mostly deserters and prisoners of war) in the second half of 1918, showed that the German army could stay in existence only by relying on machine gunners and the artillery. Then in the last 30 days or so, mobility returned to the battlefield, mostly because German units retreated to a new line of defence almost every day. Set-piece attacks were still used by the BEF, as well as open warfare tactics, while GHQ gave carte blanche to the army commanders. The war ended not with any decisive offensive or breakthrough, but gradually, through the wearing-down strategy that Haig and GHQQ had applied since 1916, and through the use of ever larger amounts of traditional or semi-traditional technology.

The essence of the last 70 days of the war was the effort of the BEF to adapt to a mixture of set-piece and mobile styles of warfare. These had nothing to do with the prewar principles preached by the top brass at GHQ, but resulted from developments at army, corps and divisional level. This learning process coincided at the end of August with pressure from Haig, whose strategy was a simple continuation of his classic 'wearingdown' concept, which had not changed from prewar days, and which he expounded to Churchill on 21 August. Haig wanted men to press forward relentlessly where ground was being gained, which would lead to the 'breaking up' of the enemy, and then the BEF must take very great risks to keep the battle going. In effect what this meant was a straightforward advance on several fronts, but especially along the Arras—Cambrai road. Under this pressure, army and corps commanders such as Byng, Horne, Rawlinson and Currie pressed their frontal attacks in late August longer and further than was prudent. Thus Haig complained of Byng's caution on 22 August, and then, on 25 August, when Horne professed anxiety about the Hindenburg Line, because two of his First Army divisions had come sharply up against it, Haig gave Horne the not very useful advice at 2 p.m., for an attack early the next morning, that the way to take it was from the rear. That same day, 25 August, Haig complained that Currie, the Canadian Corps commander, was 'sticky' in planning the Canadian Corps assault on Monchy-le-Preux and the Drocourt-Quéant Line, and so Haig took the very unusual tack of seeing Major General Burstall, the GOC of 2 Canadian Division, who, wrote Haig, would do the job whatever Currie might feel about it! The Canadian Corps was in First Army, and Haig noted that 'Horne was quite satisfied'. When the Canadian Corps attack on 26 August turned out well, Haig wrote rather patronizingly to his wife that the Canadians were fitter now because of their experiences south of the Somme, that is, the Amiens offensive. However, Haig was less pleased on 30 August, when Currie wanted extra time to prepare for the forthcoming Canadian Corps set-piece attack on the formidable Drocourt-Quéant Line, and so he again berated the Canadians for their stickiness.

Haig's anxiety to keep the German army on the run was understandable, since he was convinced, correctly, that the German army was demoralized. But this haste resulted in poorly prepared attacks, as was the case with the Canadian Corps on 28 August. Burstall, for example, complained that his 2 Canadian Division attack that day failed because the barrage was thin, the wire was not cut, there was a strong machine gun defence, and his men were very tired, having had only a few hours' sleep in the last eight days. Army commanders felt the same pressure from GHQ, but basically launched offensives according to their own ideas of how to attack. Rawlinson, for example, favoured short advances under well-prepared powerful artillery barrages, and it is interesting to note that when 5 Australian Brigade carried out the daring capture of Mont St Quentin on 31 August, the day before a major set-piece offensive was to be launched by Rawlinson's Fourth Army which included St Quentin as a distant objective, Rawlinson's private reaction was allegedly to say 'You've spoilt a bloody good battle.' Publicly, Rawlinson of course praised the Australian performance, but he was obviously irked by the alteration to his carefully planned offensive, and his diary entry has an artificial ring to it: 'I was overjoyed.'2 But while Haig was pressing his army and corps commanders for results, it is interesting that a contradictory note appears, namely, a concern with casualties. On 27 August, Maxse from GHQ told Haldane that the reason behind the BEF pushing where the enemy was weak, but stopping where the enemy was strong, was to save men. Then on 3 September, Haig himself lectured Haldane that he must not force the enemy back, but must push the Germans back gradually in order to save men. Finally, on 7 September, Rawlinson remarked that Haig was so insistent on saving manpower that he ordered there would be no attacks in Fourth Army exceeding brigade strength without reference to Rawlinson.

The situation at the beginning of September 1918, therefore, was pressure from the top for results, but at the same time, explicit orders to save manpower. Meanwhile, army, corps and divisional commanders were trying to work out how to conduct mobile warfare, bearing in mind the two potentially contradictory messages coming from GHQ. How to do all this? There had certainly been a mental change in the BEF from the time when Rawlinson told his commanders at the Somme on 1 July 1916 that 'the attack must be made in waves with men at fairly close intervals in order to give them confidence'. Now, on 23 August 1918, Lawrence wrote to the army commanders counselling the use of advanced guards to get through the enemy outpost zone, then tanks to break the main line of resistance, with the 'usual enveloping tactics' of the infantry, followed by a rapid advance on points of tactical and strategic importance. But specific lines on a map as objectives, hostile groups holding out, and flanks, could all be ignored, and instead infantry were to press ahead to capture points of tactical and strategic importance such as road and railway centres. If these were captured, then the ground in between would fall automatically. These ideas were of course a radical departure from the set-piece attacks of 1916 and 1917, and marked an emotional change from the rigid thinking of those years.

GHQ had now finally abandoned its preoccupation with ground gained, and with its overpowering hierarchical desire to exercise rigid control over offensives. Nevertheless, Haig, Lawrence and Davidson at GHQ still unquestionably had a mind-set which focused on the traditional warfare of infantry, artillery and cavalry, despite Lawrence's mention of tanks, and the result was a series of mixed signals. Mobile operations were required, but full-scale mechanical warfare was discarded as a model, and so the BEF found itself at a transitional stage of warfare. The result was that each army, corps and division tried to develop its own answer to the new conditions and, understandably, usually fell back on semi-traditional methods. As might be imagined, confusion ensued. For example, on 8 September, Haldane remarked that Haig had ordered him not to rush and lose men, but his army commander, Byng, was ordering Haldane to attack strongly on a narrow front, and Haldane concluded: 'Truly not one of them seems to know his own mind and it has been so ever since the war started.'

Haldane concluded that the uncertainty came from higher up than Byng. The tactical confusion at the beginning of September was anticipated in a letter from the Deputy CIGS to the CIGS in the middle of July 1918, which complained of lack of doctrine, lack of uniformity in training, lack of driving power from above, and lack of a means of collecting information and thinking about it. The ambiguity in ideas was reflected in an unauthorized song composed at GHQ in the summer of 1918 which related how everyone did what they wanted tactically, until Major General Dawnay at GHQ decided on common training and doctrine. However, the song concluded that some armies liked this and some did not. Dawnay himself wrote pessimistically to Maxse in early September, remarking on indications of a revival of tactics in the armies, but doubting that his efforts were doing any good. There also exist various other letters to Maxse, the Inspector General of Training at GHQ, around the end of August and beginning of September, which indicate the great variety of responses to the new conditions.

For example, Aylmer Haldane stressed the need for the offensive in depth; Lieutenant General Alec Godley reported that the advanced guard formations were the hardest to carry out, and that the use of heavy artillery by divisional commanders was poor; Lieutenant General Shute (GOC V Corps) said that other commanders had different ideas from Maxse; Major General H.L.Reed (GOC 15 Division) had great difficulty in dealing with the German machine gun screen as did Major General C.J.Deverell (GOC 3 Division); Lieutenant Colonel Wetherly (GSO 61 Division) argued that infiltration tactics in his division were not used, and that machine guns, artillery, trench mortars and smoke grenades were all individually deficient because he believed that the fire-power of all arms was the key to success; while his divisional commander pointed out the importance now of the advanced guard, but wanted infantry tactics to operate at the company and not platoon level; Currie, the Canadian Corps commander, wrote on 5 September that he wished to see Maxse to tell him about the many useful lessons his corps had learnt in the recent fighting; while Maxse himself apparently wanted a series of GHQ training schools to replace all corps schools. All this discussion of ideas was a healthy sign, yet what it indicates is that GHQ, unlike the German OHL, did not impose tactics and ideas on the BEF, rather army, corps and divisions organized their own methods of fighting, which they were to use for the rest of the war.

This sense of useful anarchy is reinforced by a brief review of BEF tactical ideas from August and September 1918, which show different levels of command producing their own tactics according to experience and the type of weapons involved. For example, at divisional level, 17 Division complained at the end of August that

V Corps was not coordinating divisions at all, and in September that the key was for the division to work out the best way of organizing artillery cooperation with the advanced guard. Then from 27 August, two 6-inch mobile trench mortars became available and greatly assisted mobile warfare in this division, which then developed its own vanguard method of advancing. All this was useful learning by experience, and the same thing occurred in 3 Division, where the chief lesson of the period 29 August to 2 September was 'the necessity for adapting ourselves at once to the requirements of more open warfare'. The 3 Division commander also called for a training period as of great importance for learning the new open warfare. Meanwhile at the corps level, the Canadian Corps laid down 'a definite Corps tactical doctrine' of its own, albeit with input from German documents translated by GHQ and from Dawnay's 'Notes on recent fighting'. The corps also issued its own instructions on the employment of artillery, machine guns, and so on, in combination with the infantry. Again, the Canadian Corps devised its own plans for the 26 August assault, including the concept that as a result of experience at Amiens, tanks should follow rather than precede infantry.

This doctrine was in advance of GHQ's policy on tanks which did not emerge until 1 September, when Lawrence usefully argued that the proper use of tanks was not to deal with the outpost zone, but to break down the main line of resistance.

At the army level, Major General Vaughan (MGGS Third Army) issued Third Army's own doctrine in September for the use of heavy artillery during the war of movement, which essentially decentralized the heavy artillery and allotted it as much as possible to each division under a temporary Divisional Heavy Artillery Commander. Third Army also noted a new twist: 'The latest theory is that all batteries should carry out equally counter battery or bombardment work.' On the top of the document is an interesting handwritten note from Vaughan to Major General Uniacke, Deputy to Maxse at GHQ, which emphasizes the separation of GHQ from its armies in the development of doctrine: These notes are mostly from personal observation—I wd have liked to talk of [sic] them with you or your officers—but you do not give me the chance. Can you not come to lunch one day?'

Third Army's ideas were later endorsed by Colonel Rawlins, historian of the artillery, who believed that from mid-August following there was a big advance in the BEF in the handling of heavy artillery through affiliation of these guns to division, who pushed them well forward, even into the front line. Yet, in contrast, Uniacke at GHQ argued that during the advance of 29 August, Corps HQ still controlled the heavy artillery brigades, who had a direct line with infantry brigade HQs through liaison officers. Uniacke stated that therefore divisions did not need their own heavy artillery. A different tack was taken by the Canadian Corps which automatically allocated a mobile heavy artillery brigade to each division after each set-piece barrage was completed. Even in October, there were still debates in the BEF about the affiliation of heavy artillery to divisions and even brigades, but it appeared that the GOCs RA at corps were beginning to relent, and when the fighting was really mobile, then the heavy artillery was reluctantly handed over to infantry brigade commanders.

The point of this discussion is to show that apart from the general concept of the advanced guard, the tactics of mobile warfare were being developed independently of GHQ, through experience of what was actually happening. In fact, GHQ had become irrelevant from the tactical point of view, as all units developed an array of their own ideas in struggling to adapt to moving warfare. A useful standpoint from which to view tactics is the brigade level, where the brigade commander was in daily contact with the fighting. Thus Brigadier General Griesbach, GOC 1 Canadian Brigade, reported to his division commander some interesting criticisms after the Canadian Corps had successfully broken through the Drocourt-Quéant line on 2 September: 'I would say that in the attack on the DROCOURT QUEANT Line there was too much quick success, coupled with very heavy fighting which brought about a certain amount of disorganization.'

This was because the reserves got caught up in the fighting because they were only 1,000 yards behind the attack. 'In trench to trench fighting, this distance may be satisfactory but in open warfare the Reserve Brigade ought to be nearer two miles behind than 1,000 yards so as to keep intact and uncommitted until the last.' Turning to machine guns, Griesbach stated that The offensive use of our Machine Guns still leaves much to be desired. They followed along and took up successive defensive positions…I am now of opinion that having regard for the difficulties of transport and the apparent lack of a definite offensive doctrine, Machine Guns must be attached to Infantry and specific orders given by the Infantry Commander.' Next, Griesbach considered the artillery, and declared. Our Artillery also requires to be ginned up in the matter of offensive fighting. Trench warfare ideas still apparently prevail and our Artillery have not yet to any extent got into action over open sights at targets of opportunity. Up to the present, I have only intimated my intention to the Artillery Commanders. In future I will assume the responsibility of ordering guns forward…. What I refer to is the matter of doctrine and training which to some extent might be secured by combined training and in the absence of that, greater social intercourse with an interchange of ideas.

Griesbach also noted that communications between brigade and battalions was poor, although it was good between brigade and division, but 'it is obvious that we cannot continue to lay wires at the present reckless rate.' In regard to the tanks, Griesbach only mentioned that when the brigade was held up at the Buissy Switch beyond the Drocourt-Quéant line, 'A couple of tanks would have breached the line with ease'. Finally, Griesbach reported that 'The training of officers in open warfare still leaves much to be desired. We have not the time to train them here. They should be training before coming to France.'

Griesbach's surprisingly frank discussion of problems in adapting to moving warfare shows that even the progressive Canadian Corps, which had found the training period of May and June 1918 extremely valuable in teaching open warfare methods (including the diamond formation, the battalion 'scatter', and infantry envelopment attack methods), and which had the experience of Amiens and the late August righting to reflect on, found there was still a very great deal to be learnt. For example, a battlefront message from 1 Canadian Brigade to 1 Canadian Division, timed at 4.35 p.m. on 3 September, suggests the difficulty of counter- battery work on the move: 'Troops on forward slope being pounded by enemy Artillery. I propose tonight to withdraw 2nd Bn to BUISSY Switch and Rear. Counter battery work urgently needed. Get aeroplanes to locate hostile batteries & we will cooperate. We appear to be meeting with no serious opposition except Artillery which is severe.' As a means of comparison, a brigade commander in another division of the Canadian Corps, Brigadier General Odlum, GOC 11 Canadian Brigade, reported his experiences of the fighting on 2 and 3 September. Once having easily broken the Drocourt-Quéant line, wrote Odlum, enemy resistance stiffened, and enemy machine guns could not be dealt with because they were too far away for the Stokes and 6-inch mortars, and too numerous and scattered for the infantry alone to deal with them. Basically, no further advance could be made without either an artillery barrage or 'adequate tank assistance'. Odlum commented on the failure of his infantry firepower to take on machine guns and other targets at over seven hundred yards range; the poor communications system between brigade and division, and between battalions and forward companies; the need for decentralized command so that forward commanders could make quick decisions; the 'comparative failure of the air force. Enemy fighting machines practically had their own way'; and the repeated failure of his and other brigades to help flanking formations gain ground. Odlum also noted the lack of cooperation between machine guns and infantry: 'It is more and more apparent that in open warfare Vickers gunners and battalions must work very close [sic] together.... The need for Brigade MG Coys, is more apparent than ever.'

The common thread in the conclusions of the two sets of Canadian brigades' reports, was the failure to coordinate arms and weapon systems after the support of the artillery and tanks had been outrun, despite earlier training. Hence, if the innovative Canadian Corps was experiencing the pains of organizing the cooperation of all arms in the new warfare, so must the rest of the BEF have been experiencing similar or worse difficulties. Even in the BEF's dependable 3 Division, it is interesting to note that the divisional commander, Deverell, laid a major part of the blame for the checks his division received on 2 September to 'the complete failure of the tanks operating in this Sector'. Yet a report by the CO of a tank company operating with 3 Division on 2 September was scathing: 'Nine Mark IV tanks started at 5.30 [a.m.]. Our barrage was satisfactory, but our infantry were not [2nd Royal Scots]. No touch whatsoever was possible with them. They seemed lost, in bunches, without officers generally, and entirely without knowledge of what was happening or what to do next.

They had no information of the situation at any time, and the whole show lacked cohesion.' The commander of the 12th Tank Battalion commented later: 'Bosche observation balloons were up, guns firing in the open at tanks without air force co-operation, no infantry support, led to the natural result of eight out of nine tanks being left on the field, and highly trained crews were sacrificed.' It is true that in another sector of 3 Division, Mark IV tanks and Whippets failed to appear, due to mechanical problems and ditching, but Deverell's summary conclusion that 'the Tanks proved of no value on the 2nd September' shows how poor tank-infantry cooperation was in this good division when it came to mobile warfare, to say nothing of air-ground cooperation. All of this is indicative of the serious tactical problems in organizing the combination of arms for moving warfare in the BEF in early September, problems which GHQ was not really in a position to solve.

Yet ground was being gained on the BEF front, and the Drocourt- Quéant line had been broken quite easily. Thus Lieutenant Colonel Cy Peck, CO 16 Canadian Battalion, wrote of the Canadian Corps breaking of this line under a barrage:

First part of advance fine—1 battery firing short, Easily snapped Drocourt Quéant line, Great number of Hun prisoners. Held up by MG fire on right flank about 300 yards beyond above line. Ordered tanks ahead but they did not go. Returned to above line under intense fire. After being held up an hour resistance on right slackened & whole Bn advanced to first objective.

What is clear is that the German army was now giving way when artillery or tanks were applied, and in fact was defending with machine guns and artillery, rather than with men, especially where geographical features such as high ground and forward slopes made the BEF advance vulnerable to firepower. Unquestionably, a key reason for the success of the BEF in August and September was the declining numbers and morale of the German army. For example, in the afternoon of 3 September, Brigadier General Griesbach's troops easily took the Buissy Switch position, and then at 4.45 p.m. Griesbach put his field glasses to his eyes and looked east toward the Canal du Nord: I could see with my glasses every evidence of confusion on the part of the enemy...Guns, Lorries, Convoys moved Eastwards on the roads and parties of the enemy infantry were everywhere in flight toward BOURLON WOOD. Enemy mounted officers could be seen galloping hither and thither, endeavouring to rally their men but apparently without avail. I noticed, however, a very singular thing. In many places there came moving Westwards through the retiring infantry, parties of enemy Machine Gunners, trudging stolidly forward to the Canal Bank, apparently oblivious to the retirement going on about them.

This was to be a scene repeated many times in the next two months, particularly as the German army ran out of reserves. It is not always recognized how depleted the German army on the Western Front had become by late 1918. The German Official History estimated that from 18 July to the Armistice, the German Army had lost 420,000 dead and wounded, and a further 340,000 as prisoners of war, for a total of 760,000 casualties, plus an unknown number of desertions or refusals to serve, which may have been as high as 750,000 to 1 million. This was on top of the 1 million or so lost between March and July 1918, during the German offensives, so that the German army suffered a possible total loss of some 2,760,000 casualties and deserters during 1918. Moreover, the highest losses occurred in the Mobilization or Attack divisions, containing the elite of the German army, leading to the fact that by June 1918, 27 of 36 Mobilization divisions in the Flanders area had been decimated. As an example of divisional losses, the German 214 Division came into the line south of the Scarpe on 19 May, and then was overrun by the Canadian Corps at Monchy-le-Preux on 26 August.

When it was withdrawn on 28 August, it had lost 24 officers and 1,147 other ranks in unwounded prisoners alone. The division came into the line again on 24 September, but by the end of October the battalion strength ranged from 10 officers and 25 other ranks to 20 officers and 150 other ranks. Another example is that of the German 201 Division, which on 6–7 September had 5,400 men, but by 19–20 September had only 1,000 men. The division gave orders to search farms, villages and dug-outs for stragglers, but without much success, so that the 402nd Regiment had battalion strengths of 40 men in the 1st battalion, 42 in the 2nd, 35 in the 3rd, plus 36 signallers, 17 staff and 65 in the machine gun company. A final example is that of 113 German Division, which on 21 September had 5,508 men on paper, but only 2,556 actually in the trenches. On 1 October, this division was withdrawn, having lost a further 1,600 men in prisoners alone.

These incredible losses could not be made good except by breaking up divisions, to the extent of 5 German divisions disbanded in May 1918, 2 in July, 9 in August and 10 in September. It is also worth noting that the estimated fully 'fit' German divisions on the Western Front had fallen from 98 on 1 August 1918 to 75 on 16 August, and 47 on 1 September. This number had again fallen to 14 by 14 October, and finally to only 4 on 11 November.

Moreover, the whole of the German 1919 class had been drafted to the front by early August 1918, and although the 1920 class of recruits (those born in 1900) was available in divisional field recruit depots in October, these youths of 18 were drafted to the front line only on 22 October, too late to appear. Thus in September 1918, German drafts contained very few new recruits, only 0.4 per cent; while 94 per cent were returned wounded from disbanded formations, or men transferred from other fronts (Russia); and 5.6 per cent were 'combed' from the air service, transport, signal, technical and lines of communication units. Therefore, when it is said that the German army began to fight with machine guns and artillery rather than with men, it was because the German army had literally run out of men in the second half of 1918.

Of course not only were German numbers declining, but so also were morale and discipline. The failure of the German spring offensives had obviously depressed German morale, and even in April 1918 one story revealed a certain desire to fraternize. Opposite Aveluy Wood on 23 April, the German and BEF trenches were very close to each other, and a British officer going down a trench happened to meet a German, who popped up and said 'good morning'. He was shot. Then a 15 year-old German soldier did the same, but he was spared. Later, in May and June 1918 there were reports of indiscipline, looting and refusal to go into the front line. In fact, the failure of the German spring offensives—the so-called Peace offensive—was really the turning point of 1918. Then came the psychological blow of the French counter-attack on the Marne in mid- July, which effectively put an end to German offensive hopes in the war, and by the time of the Amiens offensive in August, Brigadier General Burstall noted that 'The enemy's positions gave the earliest indication of the lack of morale and discipline in his troops, which resulted from his very severe losses in the spring offensive'. A German officer noted that after the Marne and Amiens actions, 'morale from that date began to go down rapidly'. Then in September, an officer in the German 187 Division argued that morale and discipline had been greatly reduced by their elastic defence tactics, which led men to believe that ground was of little value, while both officers and men displayed lack of character. In the same month, German prisoners also told strange stories; for example, of a company attack ordered by 1 Reserve Guards Division, but the NCOs and men refused and threatened the company commander with violence.

Only when the battalion commander came around, promised that the attack was a light one and gave cigarettes to all concerned, did the company promise to attack. Then there was the prisoner's report that the 103rd Regiment of 58 German Division had mutinied, and killed both the regimental commander and his adjutant in a dug-out, because they were too severe with their men. Another prisoner told the story of the riot in Cambrai in September, when Prussian and Bavarian troops came to blows over loot, and one Prussian officer was thrown to his death from a third- floor window. By October, it was common for drafts to try to escape from the train bringing them to the front, so that one prisoner from the German 187 Division said that on about 20 October, some 150 out of 300 men deserted on their way to the front, and threw their rifles and equipment out of the train. Another captured German from the 167th Regiment of 22 Division, but formerly of the 61st Landwehr Regiment in the Ukraine, stated that complete disorder prevailed in the Ukraine, and that German officers had no control over the men. While in Brest Litovsk, he witnessed several German officers attacked, and when travelling to the Western Front, 60 to 70 men from his regiment deserted, and indeed wherever the train stopped garrisons were brought to the station to prevent trouble. The war itself was by 1918 frequently referred to by German soldiers as the 'Great Swindle', and in November there took place the well-known mutiny of the German navy.

With such problems it is truly remarkable that the German army held together from August to November 1918. This was all the more surprising in that the critical turning point for the irreversible collapse in German morale occurred as early as mid-July 1918. In fact, it is entirely possible that the war could have ended in the late summer of 1918. Yet the German army did actually do better than simply hold together, as is evident from the BEF casualty figures of more than 300,000 in that same period. Moreover, from time to time, the German defenders launched violent counter-attacks, for instance, as reported by Currie, the Canadian Corps commander, on 1 October: 'The Germans have fought us here very, very hard.' Currie mentioned further heavy German counter-attacks on 11 October, and again on 12 October, and even on 10 November, there was heavy machine gun fire from the canal near Mons. The next day, Currie wrote that the German machine gunners in Mons were all volunteers and stayed firing at their posts on 11 November until they were all either captured or killed. Currie also mentioned the hard fighting on 6 November when XXII Corps was forced back across the Honelle River by severe German counter-attacks. Other corps told the same story, as in Haldane's VI Corps, where he noted on 21 October that since the operations of 21 August, his corps had buried 3,987 British troops, but only 1,808 Germans.

The same day, Major General Vaughan said that after the next fight, the corps' bolt was shot, that the French were doing nothing, and that in the BEF only the Third and Fourth Armies were fighting hard (although these last two points were obviously incorrect). At lower levels also, there were many accounts of Germans fighting hard, for example, a soldier in the 43rd Canadian Battalion reported that at roll call on 3 October, only 27 men out of 125 in B Company answered 'Here'. The rest had been casualties of an accurate German artillery box barrage. Then the CRA of 31 Division wrote that on 3 September the Vaulx area was full of German dead, and on 12 and 13 September that the Bosche had fought strongly for Havrincourt. Similarly the adjutant of 29 Brigade Field Artillery, remarked that at Verchain on 25 October the Germans had put up a stiff fight, and there were many dead Germans lying around.

The contradiction between declining German morale and at the same time occasional stiff German defence is explained by the fact that the German army fought hard at certain critical points, for example, in defence of the Hindenburg Line, the Canal de l'Escaut and Cambrai, but otherwise simply retreated. Then, while many German divisions were unreliable, some maintained a kind of stubborn morale and fought on, regardless of events, while other hand-picked units were capable of fierce counterattacks, such as the 55th Regiment of the German 220 Division on 30 September. Finally, while the German infantry was generally poor in later 1918, the artillery and machine gun units remained the determined core of a dogged firepower defence, even in November 1918.

It is also the case that heavy BEF casualties were often caused by hastily arranged attacks, such as the 4 Canadian Division assault on 30 September. The problem then, for the BEF in September, was how to adapt to moving warfare, how to penetrate the very deep machine gun and artillery defences of the German army, and especially how to crack the Hindenburg Line in late September. If this could be broken, then the war could probably be ended in 1918.

The BEF drive against the Hindenburg Line in late September was part of the wider four-front sequential effort by the Allied forces suggested by Foch, which was to break open the German front once and for all. Hence, 26 September was to be a Franco-American offensive between the Suippe and the Meuse; on 27 September the BEF First and Third Armies (including the Canadian Corps) were to attack toward Cambrai; on 28 September a northern attack was to be launched by the Flanders group of armies (including the BEF's Second Army); and on 29 September, there was to be an offensive by the BEF Fourth Army, with American divisions, plus the French First Army, attacking toward Busigny. What was significant about the BEF portion of these offensives, apart from their sequential 'loosening' aim, was that they were set-piece traditional infantry assaults, under very heavy and well-organized artillery preparation and barrages, including the new mustard gas BB shell, and with very effective counter-battery components. They were therefore not to be tank-infantry mechanical type offensives, because although some 230 tanks were rounded up, these were dispersed along the line and not massed, with the majority going to Fourth Army in the south. Thus, for example, only 24 tanks were allotted to the Canadian Corps for 27 September, with 8 tanks going to each of the three divisions leading the offensive, and clearly the tanks could not be decisive with these isolated numbers. Part of the reason for this general dispersal of tanks in the BEF was that the ground was not always suitable for their use, for example, along the St Quentin canal, but also partly because GHQ's policy had reverted to large-scale semi-traditional offensives, relying on artillery to get the infantry forward, reminiscent of the battles of the Somme and Passchendaele.

Hence the September offensives were not aimed at completely surprising the German defences as at Hamel and Amiens, and so the tanks were used primarily as auxiliary weapons. This reversion to the artillery and infantry-centred style of warfare was noted by Lieutenant Colonel Karslake (GS Tank Corps), when he was told in September by Major General Birch (MGRA at GHQ) that 'You tank people must close down your demands. Heavy artillery, not tanks, will win the war.' This 'traditional' viewpoint was confirmed by Haig on 3 October, when he wrote to Churchill with a repetition of his prewar concept of the classic 'wearing-down' process: 'I hope everything will be done to maintain the army at full strength [Haig meant the infantry] in order to beat the enemy as soon as possible...if we allow him any breathing time at all...much of the work of "wearing him out" will have to be started afresh.' A similar message was conveyed when Foch remarked that in September and October, 'The government in London, being inclined to give aviation and tanks a perhaps exaggerated importance in relation to the combatant forces as a whole, favoured the suppressing of some infantry divisions'. Foch claimed that at a conference in France on 7 October, with Lloyd George presiding, he succeeded in persuading London to maintain the same number of divisions, even if manpower in each was somewhat reduced.

As an example of the semi-traditional BEF offensives in late September, it is of interest to note the artillery preparation for the Fourth Army attack on 29 September. Due to the capture of high ground overlooking the Hindenburg Line on 18 September by the Fourth Army, observation was good, and Fourth Army artillery responded with a mustard gas BB shell and high explosive bombardment from 10 p.m. on 26 September to 6 a.m. on the next day, then a 48-hour bombardment on strong points, telephone exchanges, and particularly the entrances of tunnels (where gas shells were freely used), before the actual offensive on 29 September.

There was also continuous harassing fire, and wire cutting of lanes by 4.5- and 6-inch howitzers using the now widely available 106 instant fuse. Counter- battery work was efficient, and long-range work was undertaken from 26 to 28 September, with gas shell, 26,000 rounds of 18-pounder artillery, and 6,000 6-inch howitzer shells, which produced a wide, though not devastating distribution of enemy casualties. This preparation caused the German defenders to go into their dug-outs and not man the defences on 29 September, while the barrage also prevented the blowing up of bridges at Bellenglise. The success of this artillery-based offensive also has to take into account the fact that the German divisions defending against Fourth Army had all previously been heavily engaged, that German air and artillery were now inferior, that the German scheme of defence of the Hindenburg Line had been precisely learnt from captured documents and that observation was good for the Fourth Army artillery.

Because of the widespread nature of the offensives of late September, it will be convenient to follow the fortunes of just the Canadian Corps in their offensive on 27 September, as a means of focusing the narrative. The task of the Canadian Corps was to assault and cross the Canal du Nord on 27 September on a narrow front, because this was the only point where the canal was passable, and then fan out to capture Bourlon Wood on the right, and certain villages and high ground on the left. The success of this operation was undoubtedly due to the careful set-piece preparations which preceded the attack, especially by the artillery. Reconnaissance of the assembly areas, of the canal crossings and of the attack area was carefully done, 'and as the days passed an astonishing quantity of valuable information was secured and I [Brigadier General Griesbach] think that the smooth working of all plans and arrangements during the attack is attributable to the work done during the preparation period'. This information came from Canadian night patrols, from air observation and photographs, from captured prisoners, and from a BEF pilot and his observer who were shot down over German lines beyond the Canal du Nord on 20 September. These two airmen managed to escape at night back across the lines, and reported that the Germans had very few trenches, but were using dugouts and connected shell holes. The airmen crossed the canal by a lock which remained usable, and also reported a significant fact, namely, that although large belts of wire of the much- vaunted Hindenburg Line were discovered, this wire was not much of an obstacle. The wire was 'in belts of about 50 feet across and 3 feet high, on wooden stakes with a few corkscrew iron stakes in front. The wire is put very loosely together and in several places was seen to have been lately repaired. No difficulty was encountered in crossing it without much noise as it is so loose, also numbers of gaps were found in it.' The airmen also noted that German alertness was lax; for instance, when they were resting close to a dug-out, 'a German appeared out of it in his shirt: he took a long look at them and went back again'.

The Canadian Corps artillery also dominated the area; for example, harassing fire was stated by German prisoners to have 'caused many casualties...seriously hampered the movement of artillery and guns and...rendered some roads impassable'. The creeping barrage itself on 27 September was very heavy, with one field gun for every 20 yards, and five zones of fire moving forward. As the commander of 1 Canadian Brigade said to his troops before the battle: 'As you advance, more metal will be thrown over your heads on the enemy than in any previous action in which you have been engaged.' The corps counter-battery fire was very effective, and as the attack went in 'a withdrawal of [enemy] artillery seems to have begun almost immediately. In any case, the fire, although heavy, was not well placed and our [1 Canadian Brigade] casualties were not severe from it.' The corps staff report maintained that 'hostile shelling has been generally light', and that the enemy artillery on 27 September 'was put out of action by capture or shell fire'. It also appeared that the enemy artillery was short of ammunition due to destruction of enemy dumps and very heavy harassing fire on German routes of approach. Finally, enemy barrages had been poor and disorganized, limited almost entirely to targets of opportunity and harassing fire. Certainly, 11 Canadian Brigade reported that at first, 'the enemy's artillery fire was considerable but this soon fell away'.

With this artillery superiority it was not surprising that the corps commander, Currie, felt some confidence in the likely success of his offensive, although the army commanders Byng and Horne were doubtful (probably because of the initial narrow front and then fan-out plan), and there was still the matter of enemy machine guns. But there were other factors also which assisted the offensive, for example, the age of the enemy wire entanglements, so that 'the men walked through these entanglements as they can always do unless under heavy fire'. Another useful factor was the unsuitable German defence, which consisted of interlocking but isolated dug-outs, from which infantry and machine gunners emerged to fight, but German policy was 'to leave these isolated detachments to fight it out or to hold out until a counter-attack restored the situation.

These dug-outs and positions were selected and built when the morale of the German Army was very different from what it is now and I [Brigadier General Griesbach] think that this system of defence…[was] a German miscalculation.' Finally, a German officer later asserted that the 27 September Canadian Corps attack was a complete surprise to the Seventeenth Army as the attack had been expected N. of the SCARPE. The passage of our tanks over the CANAL-DU-NORD also completely surprised them…. He [the German officer] attributes our success on that day to surprise, to the use of tanks, and to the fact that the 187th Division—which he classes as an indifferent division—put up no fight and enabled us to turn the flanks of the divisions to the N. and S. Apart from the usual reference to the tanks, the officer may well have been correct regarding an element of surprise and the poor morale of the defenders. Certainly all these factors, and the others mentioned, plus the careful set-piece preparations, and the artillery dominance, must go a long way to explaining the success of what at first sight seemed to have been a risky operation. There was also the factor of determination by the Canadian Corps infantry, but there was not, apparently, overwhelming support by the tanks. The tanks did supply effective assistance at times, for example, on the 1 Canadian Brigade front, but also got stuck in the canal and, at least on the 11 Canadian Brigade front, did nothing. Indeed, Brigadier General Odium wrote critically that three tanks were allotted to his 11 Brigade, but the tank commander…stated that his tanks were old [presumably Mark IVs] and could get no further than the edge of BOURLON WOOD, from whence they would have to return to the canal to be refilled. He further objected on the score of the condition of his personnel, which he said was not good. I informed him that, as it was apparent he would not be of any assistance to the Brigade, I had no further time to waste with him.

There was probably more to the story than Odium allowed, but in any case the attack opened at 5.20 a.m. as an infantry assault under the artillery barrage, and the idea was to mount a whirlwind advance that would mop up the canal crossing in only six minutes, and then a further rapid advance over several hundred yards to a hedgerow position to consolidate. This would allow the main forces to follow behind and fan out as previously arranged. Essentially, the attack followed the rolling barrage, and met little opposition, while the enemy counter-barrage fell behind the advancing troops. Progress was rapid until a railway embankment provided protection for the enemy machine guns, and the barrage was lost. At the lowest level, Private Foster, 38th Canadian Battalion, recalled that on the morning of 27 September, he helped capture a machine gun and 30 or 40 men from a dug-out, but by this time, the barrage had moved ahead:

> The artillery observer seeing this ordered the barage [sic] to fall shorter at our particular point, meaning to help us out of our difficulty, but by this time we had won the position ourselves but nevertheless the barage fell short. It landed on us instead of the Germans. We being terrified at this jumped into the hole that the Germans were in. For a moment we were at a loss to know what to do. The officer said 'I have no orders what to do in a case of this kind.'

Eventually a 1914 vintage soldier rescued the situation by grabbing some green 'O.K.' flares from the officer, 'in spite of the officer trying to prevent him. He shot the two green flares high into the air. The second one had no sooner burst into a green light when we could hear the artillery lift, and we were once more free.' The platoon once more followed the barrage until they were again held up by more machine guns. Ultimately, Private Foster wound up lost beside the railway embankment, where he met the colonel of his battalion, who was also lost. They managed to find the battalion, and spent the night beside the railway embankment. This episode reveals the importance of the artillery barrage, the ease with which machine guns could hold up an attack, the flexibility of the forward artillery observation officers, and the problems of moving warfare, not least for inexperienced junior officers!

The first day of the offensive had been very successful, but in an almost exact copy of the earlier evolution of the Amiens offensive, and the advances in late August, the succeeding days contained both useful advances, and unhappy experiences, due to haste and disorganization. One example of the latter was the attempt by 4 Canadian Division to continue the attack on 30 September at 6 a.m., after issuing orders late on 29 September. In 11 Brigade this resulted in an 11 p.m. conference of battalion commanders. The night was also very dark and guides were unobtainable for the battalions. Brigadier General Odium vented his frustration in his later report:

From the start the operation did not go well. It was based on false assumptions, namely that the enemy was beaten and would withdraw, and that a smoke screen would be an ample protection for the left of the attack against the fire that would naturally be expected from BLECOURT Valley and the high ground south of ABANCOURT. The result showed that the enemy had no intention of withdrawing. As for the smoke screen, the less said the better. It was a total failure. According to Odium, 'The failure of the attack was due to the haste with which it was thrown in and the failure to protect the exposed left flank. The promised smoke screen simply did not materialize.' The report of the 4th Battalion Machine Gun Corps explained what happened: 'This was an exploiting scheme [that is, not a set-piece attack with artillery], and it was proposed to put a smoke barrage on the villages on the right flank.... Owing to the high wind this proved useless, and our troops encountered heavy machine gun fire.' Under the circumstances 'Some infantrymen started to the rear and this made a bad influence on the remainder, especially as they were weak in numbers and very well worn out. It did not appear that the situation was an exploiting situation, which apparently was the idea of the scheme.'

The next day, 1 October, 11 Brigade attacked again, but this time the battalion commander received orders at 12.15 a.m. on 1 October, for an attack at 5 a.m.! However, Canadian Division artillery provided some sort of an artillery barrage, and a little progress was made, although by around midday the fighting strength of the 87th Battalion was down to 3 officers and 74 other ranks. The GOC 87th Battalion reported that there was 'very heavy shell fire and heavy machine gun fire from the direction of Blécourt. The situation was very obscure and units were badly mixed up.' In one of the mixed-up units was Claude Craig of 54th Battalion, 11 Brigade, who wrote of the heavy shelling and of a 4.1-inch shell that landed among his company:

> I was only blown up and shaken a bit. We still kept going ahead and before we knew where we were we were right in the thick of it. By it I mean the [enemy] barrage. It sure was a peach and the worst that I ever went through. We lost an awful lot of men going through and after we were through we had the Machine Gun fire to put up with.

Afterwards a friend told him that his battalion had 50 men left out of the original 435. What was evidently occurring was that in the pressure to keep mounting attacks every day at an early hour, battalion conferences were having to be held only four or five hours before each attack took place, meaning that battalions had to move up in the dark, over ground they were not familiar with, suffering from fatigue and heavy casualties, and so not surprisingly the organization at corps, division and battalion level was faltering. For example, Lieutenant Colonel Cy Peck, CO 16th Battalion, in 1 Canadian Division, wrote in his diary that on 30 September 'Very ambiguous orders' were received, and then there were sudden orders to attack early the next morning. Peck implied there was a command problem. As far as the 1 October assault was concerned, it seems that after initial success, the Canadian artillery barrage had been lost, and the infantry battalions were essentially on their own against enemy artillery and machine guns.

This analysis is supported by the report of 1 Canadian Brigade, which noted that the barrages did not take account of the curve of the railway line and embankment running through the sector, and fired in straight lanes, so the brigade came under heavy machine gun fire. Moreover, the CO of the 1st Battalion complained that 'the barrage was very ragged' and contained 200-yard gaps, with some guns firing late, so that the troops could not keep up to the shrapnel barrage. In 1 Brigade, there was also the problem that the neighbouring Imperial 32 Brigade, which had the key task of capturing the all-important high ground on the left, proposed to attack with a strength of only three companies. The 1 Brigade commander, Brigadier General Griesbach 'strongly disapproved of his [the Assistant Brigade Major of 32 Brigade's] plan and told him so and asked him to convey my observations to his Brigade Commander which he promised to do'. Whether he did or not, the thin attack by 32 Brigade failed, and caused most of the problems later that day. Griesbach also paid tribute to the enemy artillery, machine guns and aircraft, which all acted boldly.

The Canadian Corps had attacked with verve and determination from 27 September to 2 October, had rapidly crossed the Canal du Nord, but had then become bogged down in very costly fighting around Cambrai and to the north of the town. The Canadian Corps had shown great courage and dash, but had underestimated the opposition of the German Seventeenth Army, who poured in divisions, but it must also be said that the severe Canadian casualties—30,806 from 22 August to 11 October, two thirds of which were incurred in the Canal du Nord and Cambrai battles—caused some soul-searching in the Corps. Currie himself seems to have admitted that things had gone wrong, but not to have known what the problems were. For example, when Brigadier General Griesbach complained to 1 Canadian Division about hastily arranged artillery barrages in the period after 27 September, Currie replied to Griesbach saying that such rushed barrages were useless and affected the morale of the infantry, and that he hoped very much he was not to blame. In fact, a close look at battalion battle reports shows that the hurry in organizing daily attacks at a late hour every evening for an early morning attack the next day was one major reason for things going wrong. At the same time, the inability to provide fully effective artillery barrages after the first day of the offensive, appears to have been the other major cause of the Canadian Corps' problems and casualties.

The corps also suffered from some Imperial divisions on its flanks who did not keep up or did not keep in touch. It is also the case that the Canadian divisions were still working out mobile warfare techniques in the heat of battle, for instance, just to take the Canadian

Machine Gun Corps, the lessons learned from 27 September to 2 October were quite numerous. These included the mistake in tying down batteries with too definite instructions; the need for attaching batteries definitely to battalions; the necessity for a reserve of guns under brigade control; the complaint that the infantry expected too much firepower from the machine guns, when in fact they had 32 Lewis guns per battalion, while the real task of the machine guns should have been consolidation in holding the line; the provision of extra firepower at the end of the attack, when infantry casualties were greatest; and finally, that the forward guns should be well forward, because when fatigue and casualties lowered infantry morale, the infantry frequently rallied around well-organized machine gun batteries. Then, in reference to the attempt to make field artillery mobile, and place some guns well up with the infantry, 1 Canadian Brigade decided to attach one field artillery battery to each battalion in 1 Brigade during open warfare. But this did not work, and little firing was done. The brigade commander noted: 'we still have much to learn in the use of Artillery in an operation of this sort.'

On the other hand, some aspects of mobile warfare had been successfully worked out, for example, the Canadian Corps advanced guard system of October 1918: 'Each of the front Platoons were designated "combat patrols" and each of these patrols threw forward "contact patrols". Each of these patrols threw forward two or three scouts. This plan was worked out in December and January last when the Brigade was training in the CHATEAU TENBY Area.' Some machine gun units also worked well, as noted in a letter from Lieutenant A.L.Barry describing the crossing of the Canal du Nord on 27 September: 'You can tell your GHQ opponents', he wrote to Colonel Lindsay, that we advanced about 8 to 9 miles from the position of assembly.... No difficulty was found in keeping up with the infantry—in fact the leading section of the right company arrived between Orsy le Verger and Epinoy [in the centre of the corps' attack] 20 minutes ahead of the leading infantry & were responsible for the majority of the guns captured in the area by shooting the horses & driving off the personnel trying to get the guns away.... Close liaison was kept with the infantry by having MG officers with Battn. Head Quarters—ie Two companies went with me & Brigade group commander at Bde HQ. One Cpy. Commander with leading Batts., One with support Bttn. This makes communications easier. However, in summary, the Canadian Corps seems to have been more successful when engaged in set-piece attacks, such as 27 September, or earlier on 8 August at Amiens, and on 2 September at the Drocourt-Quéant Line, rather than in continuous attempts to follow up such set-piece victories.

Elsewhere, 29 September was the date of the Fourth Army's major assault on the Hindenburg Line, and here there were hopes that the presence of some 180 tanks would materially assist the previously described extensive artillery preparations for the infantry offensive. Results were mixed on the left, however, due to great problems with preliminary attacks two days before by two American divisions, which prevented a proper barrage taking place on behalf of the Australian Corps. But on the right, 46 Division of IX Corps stormed across the St Quentin Canal, and provided a critical breach in the Hindenburg Line.

The tanks did not have a good day, with about 50 per cent being knocked out, principally by anti-tank artillery. By now the German defences included 'tank forts', encompassing artillery, machine guns and infantry protection, and there were field artillery batteries attached to the infantry for close fighting. However, it would appear that, as before, artillery and infantry support for the tanks was poor, and this, together with German preparations, to a large extent accounts for the tank casualties. There were other problems too, including too much smoke, the bunching together of tanks, unsuitable tank tactics, and the use of more tanks than necessary in particular areas. As far as the 8th Tank Battalion was concerned, the cooperation between the tanks and 5 Australian Division, normally excellent, was uncharacteristically weak on 29 September, due no doubt to the previous mix-up with the two American divisions. Coming up in reserve on the afternoon of 29 September, and with no possibility of surprise, 5 Australian Division found itself under murderous machine gun fire, and therefore the Australian infantry did not keep contact with the tanks. This was a primary cause of the problems that the tanks of the 8th Tank Battalion encountered when starting at 3 p.m. on 29 September.

Reports from the 8th Tank Battalion on 29 September show that very often the tanks initially had excellent targets, and advanced successfully before being hit. In almost every case, it would seem that the tanks generally did not have artillery, air, or infantry support, and therefore could not be expected to survive the anti-tank artillery. For example, the Camel aircraft of 73 Squadron were flying contact and anti-tank missions, but often appeared to report the situation after the tanks were in trouble. Thus one aircraft was attracted to Magny 'by a tank throwing out its red flares. They found that several tanks had been knocked out by a gun firing from the orchard on the southern edge of Magny. This they attacked with their bombs and MGs silencing it.' Altogether the Camels on the whole front fired 14,000 rounds of machine gun fire and dropped 88 bombs on anti-tank guns throughout the day.27 The impression is of a Camel squadron doing its best, but on the whole failing due to lack of numbers. Certainly the tank reports of the 8th Tank Battalion make no reference to air, or any other support.

Hence, Tank 9199, under Lieutenant Arding, started at 3 p.m. in support of the 15 Brigade of 5 Australian Division, and reported that Hostile shelling was very severe & the enemies defence consisted of many MG nests. I was able to pick out three of the latter and used my 6pdr. gun with effect. The infantry were unable to move forward in face of the fierce MG fire. I accordingly returned to the infantry in order that I might best form an idea what part of the enemies defences was giving most trouble: the MG fire seemed to be coming from all directions. I moved forward again in the direction of CABARET WOOD FM [farm] & fired on a light field gun position there. Before I could come within near range of the FARM my tank was hit. Similarly, Tank 9385 under Second Lieutenant Dunlop started at 3 p.m. with the same Australian brigade and division, and went around the bank to the left of Cabaret Wood Farm.

When the enemy Infantry saw the tank they left their trenches & retreated under the fire of all possible guns of the tank, my driver, firing with his revolver whenever a slight cessation of enemy MG fire permitted. During the whole of the time from leaving the bank we were under direct fire from enemy field guns in the farm & on our left…. We crossed the trench & on reaching a point level with the farm I asked for news of the movement of our own infantry & was told that they were not following up behind, so I asked the driver to return…. Fortunately we managed to get fairly near to our own front line before we were finally put out of action altogether by a shell smashing up the right track.

This last account is of interest since it seems to indicate that the tank commander actually expected the tank to be hit.

Even when starting with the first attack at dawn on 29 September, tanks were still vulnerable for the same reasons. Tank B53, commanded by Lieutenant Jefford, moved at 6.30 a.m. from the west of Bellicourt toward the dangerous Cabaret Wood Farm:

During my progress the front of the tank was swept by a hail of MG bullets from numerous positions both in the trench positions in front of Farm & from the Farm itself. I turned round when I was within 50 yards of the enemy as I found our own infantry had not advanced, also in order to outflank, if possible, the enemy who were holding the line in large numbers…. My left gun using case shot knocked out a MG & gunners in rear of trench, my right gun using steel shot kept down fire of MGs and Field Guns & I observed many hits from my own front Machine Gun among the enemy in trench. During my progress to get back to ascertain the position of our own infantry, my tank was hit twice in the R.Sponson, taking the door away.

The story was much the same for Tank 9372, which left Bellicourt and headed toward the village of Nauroy, where the German defence had created a strong point. Being unable to go through the village, the tank received two direct hits, but not before 'we blotted out two Anti-Tank guns & six machine guns which were visible'. Tank 9332 started at 5.30 a.m., but at 9.30 a.m. was spotted by enemy aircraft, which brought down shell fire with the use of flares. However, the tank survived until 10.30 a.m. when the mist lifted and a field gun on a ridge put three shells through the tank. There was a different story, however, for Tank 9034, commanded by Sergeant Vicary, which started at 5.30 a.m. as many of the others did. But this tank and the accompanying infantry cooperated well, so that the tank knocked out machine guns holding up the Australian infantry, while the latter requested the tank to wait while they dealt with an anti-tank gun. Later on, the tank stopped because of engine trouble, and the crew suffered from petrol fumes and were 'badly shaken', yet this was one of the few tanks that was not actually hit.

One cannot escape the conclusion that tanks were being wasted through lack of support, especially when called upon to advance after the first assault had taken place. The conclusion of the historian John Terraine, that 'the tanks of 1918 were not war winners', does not take into account the possibility that with proper protection, and with serious infantry and artillery training in how to cooperate with tanks, very much more might have been accomplished with this weapon. Instead the tanks were used as a lesser partner with the infantry, and consequently suffered a very high casualty rate. In fairness, it must be noted that in September, before the major offensives at the end of that month, there were attempts to find out how to shield tanks from anti-tank guns. Lieutenant General Braithwaite, IX Corps commander, suggested that howitzers or long-range trench mortars mounted on tanks would be the answer, while Rawlinson believed that 6-pounder guns mounted on tanks could knock out antitank guns. Birch, MGRA at GHQ, suggested that the 6-pounder gun was hard to lay accurately from a moving tank, but that the 18-pounder gun was good against anti-tank guns. However, Birch said that such guns should not be carried on tanks, because horses were still better! Lieutenant Colonel Karslake, from Tank Corps HQ, appeared to sum up the discussion by arguing that smoke and speed were the best antidotes to the anti-tank gun defence. Nothing much could be done about the speed of the tanks, but smoke was used on 29 September, although it turned out either to be too heavy or not available at key moments.

Nevertheless, despite tank losses, the Hindenburg Line was broken on the Fourth Army front, partly as a result of the greatest artillery effort of the war (945,052 rounds fired between noon 28 September and noon 29 September), based upon the plans of the Hindenburg Line captured on 8 August at 51 (German) Corps HQ; partly because of German disorganization, low numbers, declining morale and lack of reserves; and partly because of some innovative ideas in IX Corps, especially the action of 46 Division in crossing the St Quentin Canal with the aid of life jackets. However, it was the artillery preparation and the creeping barrage, plus early morning fog, that really got the BEF troops through the German defences, and so if there was one element which really made the difference on 29 September, it was the artillery.

Thus the IX Corps heavy artillery programme firing all night for two nights before 29 September, literally swept away all obstacles, including German batteries, Brigadier General Mackenzie, GOC IX Corps heavy artillery, remarked in his diary that the wire at the canal had been thoroughly destroyed, and that forward artillery intelligence officers had been within 100 yards of the front line, making sure that the artillery task was properly done. Mackenzie commented that the success of the artillery at the Hindenburg Line showed what heavy artillery really could do. Another significant element of the barrage was the use of 30,000 mustard gas shells, which arrived in Fourth Army only on 20 September. Hence, the surprise use of these mustard gas (BB) shells on individual targets and on hostile batteries from the night of 26–7 September to the morning of 29 September was very effective, especially against hostile batteries, because it was the first use of mustard gas by the BEF. In regard to the effect of the artillery in late September and early October, Major van Straubenzee of the BEF artillery observed: 'Hun infantry no longer seem to stand a barrage and the sight of it coming now frightens them.' Major Burne, brigade major for 32 Division Artillery, confirmed this fact in regard to breaking through the Hindenburg Line:

I don't believe now that Ludendorff's new defence system will worry us much. We just push along till we get stuck, bring up ammunition, put down a barrage next morning, get on to the next line, whether 1000 yards or 2 or 3 miles, come up against more opposition, and repeat the operation. His guns are not now numerous enough to interfere and prevent our operation. I studied the captured [German] Hindenburg Line Defence Scheme closely before the battle. The artillery programme was laid down in minute detail, but it simply did not come off.

With the breaking of the Hindenburg Line and its reserve lines on 5 October, and the capture of Cambrai on 9 October, the fighting became open warfare. Already on 1 October, Haig essentially gave carte blanche to his army commanders Byng and Rawlinson: 'They agreed that no further orders from me were necessary, and both would be able to carry on without difficulty.' Even before this date, in mid-September, Haig felt that it was now merely a process of 'breaking-up' the enemy lines. As far as Haig and GHQ were concerned, the last stages of the war in October and November did not require very much involvement. In fact, the major problem for Haig in the last 40 days or so, apart from discussions about armistice terms, was the attempt to get the BEF's Second Army back from French control. Second Army had been used with the Belgian army, commanded by the King of Belgium, and under Foch's orders, to advance in the general direction of Brussels. For what seems to have been a matter of chauvinism rather than military necessity, Haig wanted it back. Foch's disinclination to return Second Army obviously rankled Haig, who wrote rather stiffly to his wife on 24 October: 'But the British must operate in the field under my orders.' Fortunately, this matter, which had really become a personal quarrel between Haig and Foch, was settled on 28 October with the return of Second Army to the BEF. Meanwhile, on the battlefield, operations settled down into a steady pursuit of the German army in a semi-traditional style of warfare. As far as the tanks were concerned, with the exception of 8 October, they 'were only used in very small numbers, just when the Germans put up stout resistance'. On the other hand, a liaison officer with the French Army reported in late October that 'French troops will not advance without tanks'. Ironically, air cooperation improved at this late stage, because smaller-scale actions were easier to coordinate. Hence on 8 and 9 October, two squadrons (8 and 73) worked with 82 tanks against the villages of Sérain,

Prémont, Brancourt and Villers-Outreux, dropping 200 bombs and firing 25,000 rounds at anti-tank guns over the two days. An account of one action over Sérain shows a hint of the future:

Lieut Trites (pilot) and Lieut Hicklin (observer) saw the Tanks taking SERAIN. As the Tanks were approaching the village Lieut Trites dropped his bombs on various parties of Germans who were in the village. He then saw the Tanks surround the village, one going right into the centre of it. Another attacked the orchard just to the south, mopping up parties of Germans. Another Tank came round the north of the village and was approaching a small valley in which were two to three hundred Germans, who were in dead ground. On seeing the Tank approaching, the Germans fled east; Lieut Trites and Lieut Hicklin then fired their machine guns into them doing great execution. They also saw another Tank capture several MG posts to the north of SERAIN. Lieut Trites then dropped a message on the 3rd Battalion to whom the Tank belonged.

However, for the period until the Armistice, the decentralized mobile warfare of the next month almost exclusively involved artillery preparation and then infantry occupation. As the CRA of 57 Division wrote: 'The Infantry have no difficulty in reaching their objectives up to the limits of the creeping barrage. The Germans are then captured, killed, or have retreated to their next offensive line, possibly 6,000 yards in the rear. The infantry then advance this far without difficulty and are then brought to a standstill against the next line.' This simple form of warfare was confirmed by another artillery officer who said that the assault was carried out by the artillery, and then the infantry occupied, but the infantry could not exploit beyond the limit of the creeping barrage. The BEF artillery was also aided by overwhelming superiority because from midsummer 1918 following, for every shell the enemy sent over he received ten or twenty back. In the bombardments which preceded the great engagements of the summer and autumn of 1918, the British artillery dominated to such an extent that the enemy retaliation was largely blind. Shooting by the map was the rule throughout. Even that was smothered to a very great extent by the accuracy of the fire of our own guns and the necessity he was under of keeping his heavy guns far back to avoid capture. The dominance of the artillery was essential by this stage in the war because BEF troops were tired, units were low in manpower, and morale was not as high as before due to the continuous fighting. Rawlinson noted in his diary on 27 October that the US Corps in his army was now out and no good for a month. The Australians were not going to be any good until late November, and his XIII and IX Corps were used up. Consequently Rawlinson's Fourth Army could not keep up the pressure since there was simply no manpower left, although by early November the situation seemed to have improved because of lower casualties. Even in the normally ebullient Canadian Corps, the GOC of 2 Canadian Division remarked in early October, that the new infantry drafts had little idea of how to attack enemy machine guns, and that 3,000 men had not been replaced. By November 1918, the same GOC stated that his division had received replacements of 30 officers and 5,000 other ranks since August, but this was 90 officers and 4,200 other ranks fewer than casualties.

Therefore, the division was not as efficient as before. At the lower levels there was also a sense of war weariness, and a concern with the heavy casualties, although there was optimism that the war was close to the end. Nevertheless, the Canadian Corps continued its active advance, capturing the major town of Cambrai due to an innovative night attack at 1.30 a.m. on 9 October, following short artillery crashes every fifteen minutes on key targets. The enemy was caught by surprise, and in process of withdrawal, and apparently 2 Canadian Division also captured a small German party with orders to set fire to Cambrai. There were fires burning in the town, but whether from shelling or wilful intent, was not clear. Regardless, there were few casualties in actually capturing Cambrai, and at 9.50 a.m. Currie ordered relentless pursuit of the German defenders.

For the remaining month of the war, the Canadian Corps did pursue the German army in front of it, although hindered by Allied railway congestion, which prevented the bringing up of artillery ammunition on all of the BEF fronts. Rawlinson even reported that the Cavalry Corps had been pulled out, since they did no good, and merely blocked roads. Indeed there seem to have been general problems of logistics at this stage, as might be expected. Hence one Canadian anti-aircraft officer noted: 'our H.Q....are at present at least 30 miles behind the line, & we have to get our rations from them.... Such insanity as drawing rations for 5 sections 30 miles over bad roads when H.Q. could easily be with the second line section...Too much whisky and fast life is responsible for it all. It is nothing short of criminal.'

However, by this stage, the Canadian Corps had adopted two styles of warfare in the closing days: either extremely heavy artillery bombardments and creeping barrages, as at Mont Huoy and Valenciennes on 1 November, or fairly rapid mobile warfare. The latter showed adaptability, with various types of units spearheading the advance. Thus, cavalry patrols, forward machine guns, motor machine guns, forward artillery, 6-inch Newton trench mortars, light trench mortars and armoured cars all played their part. However, although orders were to push on with determination, brigades and battalions were not to become engaged in regular actions unless under orders to do so, or unless absolutely necessary, and heavy casualties were not to be incurred. The Canadian Corps found that the enemy would withdraw every night, and touch with the retreating Germans would not be regained until around noon the next day. Then resistance would stiffen during the afternoon, so that further advance towards evening would require a serious engagement. The Canadian Corps would avoid this, knowing that once more at night the retreat would recommence.

In the last month 11 Canadian Brigade adopted an unusual method of progress: The Brigade, which advanced on a one battalion front (thereby undoubtedly reducing to a minimum the casualties incurred) was disposed with battalions forming a chain in depth, each battalion leap-frogging in its turn and assuming the front line duty. Each tour of duty in the front line averaged from 24 to 36 hours, varying according to the opposition met and the time taken in overcoming it. Headquarters in all cases were occupied in accordance with orders from Brigade and were located with a view to forming a chain on one central line of communications...each unit being usually responsible for the link immediately forward of it. All short lines were cut out, and Brigade and battalion commanders operated from signal office phones. This proved a great success, and enabled the chain to be strung out to great depth without interruption of telephonic communication...Headquarters for all units were in all cases located and laid down from the map.

Mobile warfare had thus become a structured science rather than an art, and where opposition was met with, usually machine gun nests, it is remarkable how often these were disposed of either by 6-inch Newton mortars, or by infantry Lewis gunners, or in the case of the 87th Canadian Battalion, very frequently by armoured cars. Thus on 21 October, the battalion approached the villages of Buevrages and Bray, and adopted the apparently normal method of sending in an armoured car to report on opposition:

They [the armoured car] engaged enemy MGs throughout their task killing a Boche officer and clearing the road, this allowing the infantry to occupy the main road along the whole Brigade front before dusk without further assistance. During this dash Corporal Anthony greatly distinguished himself by walking in front of his car and steering it by hand to a place of safety under machine gun fire, when the steering rod was broken.

As far as the Canadian Corps was concerned, the final action of the war was the capture of Mons on the night of 10–11 November. This turned out to be controversial, since Currie was accused after the war of incurring unnecessary casualties in this late action, although he did not wish for a set-piece attack and told divisions to avoid casualties. On the other hand, Currie reported that there was heavy machine gun fire from the canal on the outskirts of Mons on 10 November, and he must have known that his instructions to take Mons, even by encirclement, and without casualties, would put pressure on his divisional commanders to attack. This is supported, to some extent, by Burstall, GOC 2 Canadian Division, who found out from prisoners that the German strong rearguard defence was scheduled to leave Mons at 11 p.m. on 10 November. Perhaps because of this Burstall ignored orders from the Canadian Corps at 10 p.m., and stayed with his earlier orders to his 6 Brigade. In any case, by 11 a.m. on 11 November, 2 Canadian Division was well east of Mons, and had used mobile trench mortars and field artillery to silence the still active German machine gunners. In this action 2 Canadian Division suffered casualties of 22 officers and 343 other ranks. In the afternoon of 11 November, Currie hastened to Mons for a formal entry, but by then the war was over. A final footnote to the armistice of 11 November, however, occurs in the story of a Canadian soldier, Private Oborne, whose war came to an end in a way that was symbolic of the great confusion of the German army. Private Oborne was captured on 31 October, and then found himself hitched to a wagon with 20 other prisoners, dragging supplies to Germany. Private Oborne continued to pursue this task until 14 November, when he was released. The German guards had not known that the war was over until then.

6

THE SURRENDER OF SINGAPORE

On 15 February 1942, the British garrison at Singapore surrendered to the Japanese, in what Winston Churchill described as 'the worst disaster and largest capitulation in British history'. The defeat dispelled the traditional view that Japan was a second-rate Oriental power, not possessing the military potential to challenge the West. For the following three and a half years, Britain struggled to regain its empire in the Far East, against an enemy whose fighting capabilities and will to resist surrender proved more resilient than ever believed possible. Intelligence enabled the British to understand their Japanese opponent, and played a crucial role in helping them develop the methods needed to conduct a successful war effort.

Since professional intelligence organizations started operating at the turn of the twentieth century, their activities have taken on a rapidly growing role in shaping the conduct of international conflicts. Yet, the subject has remained largely unexplored. It is not an exaggeration to argue that historians have either taken intelligence for granted or overlooked it. To complicate matters, the majority of academics correctly believe that intelligence is a business carried out with exceptional secrecy, and those involved are reluctant to expose its activities, whether successful or otherwise. Nevertheless, a popular notion, and one not entirely accurate, is that the relevant documents remain forever closed or have been systematically incinerated, all in the interest of national security. A more realistic explanation has been put forward by Christopher Andrew and David Dilks, who illustrated how intelligence remains the 'missing dimension' of history, mainly because official secrets laws have only recently allowed public consultation of the archival material. Thus, the assumption, that one cannot conduct a serious academic study on intelligence due to lack of evidence, is untrue.

Intelligence activities undoubtedly had a significant impact on the Second World War, as revealed by F.H. Hinsley's official history, which illustrated how effective intelligence speeded up the war effort against Germany by almost two years. On the Asia–Pacific front, there remains room for exploration.

Much of the literature has focused on signals intelligence and the clandestine services. Richard Aldrich explained how inter-service rivalries hindered the performance of the British and US secret services. Edward Drea and Ronald Lewin described how signals intelligence aided the US forces in their island-hopping campaigns in the Pacific theatres. An equally pressing issue, namely *qualitative intelligence*, or assessments concerning the performance of Japan's armed forces, has remained largely uncovered. Historians such as Arthur Marder, Wesley Wark, John Ferris, Antony Best and Thomas Mahnken have discussed Western perceptions of Japanese military capabilities before the outbreak of the Pacific War. The question of how Allied images of Japan evolved during the course of the war itself has yet to be answered.

The existing historiography on the Pacific War does not contain many works on British intelligence for further reasons. When viewed alongside the existing literature on the war against Germany, Britain's conduct of the Far Eastern conflict has not attracted much scholarly attention. This is mainly because the Asia–Pacific theatres were of secondary importance for Britain. The official histories on British grand strategy focused mainly on Europe and North Africa, devoting only a fraction of each volume to Asia. The literature on the campaigns in Southeast Asia has either emphasized how the theatre was a backwater in Britain's global war effort, or tended to focus on filling the gap with detailed narratives describing the accomplishments of its forces. In addition, because the United States devoted significantly more resources, Britain's contribution paled in comparison. The works on the Asia–Pacific conflict have treated the British participation as such. The official histories on British intelligence went as far as to argue that, because Britain's engagement in the Far East was minor, its intelligence activities there do not demand scholarly research. The neglect is not entirely justified, and Britain's operations against Japan were significant for other reasons. Recent studies by Williamson Murray have highlighted how British forces in the Far East, while having suffered some of the most severe military defeats to befall their nation, managed in the end to achieve a markedly higher standard of efficiency than their counterparts in Europe and North Africa. Consequently, by autumn 1944, while Montgomery's armies on the Continent were stalled at Arnhem, General William Slim's XIV Army in Burma was steadily advancing against determined Japanese resistance. Such an achievement begs a further investigation of the underlying reasons.

The study aims to further fill the gap surrounding the impact of intelligence on the Second World War, and will analyse the evolution of the British defence establishment's assessment of Japan's strategy and war capabilities between the outbreak of the Sino-Japanese War in 1937 and Japan's final defeat in August 1945. At all levels of Britain's war effort, the battlefields of Burma, the headquarters of General Slim and Admiral Lord Louis Mountbatten (Supreme Allied Commander, Southeast Asia Command), the corridors of Whitehall and Cabinet War Rooms, intelligence had a pivotal influence on strategy, operational planning and tactical doctrine. It showed the British how Japan's armed forces were a resilient foe, but at the same time, one that could be overcome with adequate resources and proper methods of use.

Two key questions will be tackled; the first is the way in which the British used intelligence to gain a realistic picture of their Japanese adversary. The term 'intelligence' will be used to describe the full range of information drawn upon to evaluate the enemy. To use a term coined by practitioners, the work focuses on 'all source analysis'. The majority of studies on intelligence tend to concentrate on information obtained via human agents (humint), or the interception of enemy communications, commonly known as signals intelligence (sigint). Nevertheless, a number of sources provide vital intelligence, and yet do not receive due attention. For example, during the Pacific War, captured documents provided a unique insight into how the Japanese military operated. In addition, because sigint and humint were not always reliable, for a host of reasons, the Allies looked towards photographic reconnaissance, or imagery intelligence (imint).

The particular conditions of wartime also enabled the British to draw upon types of intelligence not available in times of peace, the most important of which was observations of the Japanese armed forces in action. Incidentally, information obtained through firsthand encounters was the single most valuable source.

The book will tend to focus less on how intelligence was used for daily planning purposes, and concentrate more on how the material was employed to formulate what has been called 'net assessments', or in simple terms, an overall calculation of the enemy's strategy and capabilities.

Second, the work will illustrate how the British used intelligence to plan an effective war effort in the Far East. It will illustrate further examples to support Michael Handel's observation that intelligence is a 'force multiplier', or an instrument which allows the economical use of limited resources. At the same time, one needs to bear in mind that intelligence was only one factor which shaped Britain's war effort. For starters, Handel has argued that intelligence is of little value unless accompanied by military strength. The British experience in Southeast Asia was no exception.

In addition, Britain's conduct of the Pacific War was influenced by a number of circumstances where intelligence rarely made a difference. No amount of good intelligence could compensate for the fact that commitments in the European theatres substantially limited Britain's capabilities in the Far East. Because Allied policy during the Pacific War was largely dictated by the United States, British strategy often had to be formulated in accordance. Under the circumstances, intelligence was relegated to secondary importance in the decision-making process. These limitations not withstanding, intelligence made a distinguishable contribution to Britain's war effort.

The prospects of accurately gauging the Japanese depended largely on the experience which Britain's armed forces had in confronting the challenges they faced. One of the central arguments of the book is that Britain needed to fight Japan in order to understand what it was capable of doing. Prior to December 1941, the British miscalculated Japan's war potential, mainly because in the absence of a direct confrontation, a realistic assessment was not possible.

The evolution of British intelligence after the commencement of the war also illustrates the crucial role combat experience played. When the Pacific War broke out, the British were unfamiliar with their opponent. At the strategic level, the absence of previous engagements where British forces had to operate across the vast land and sea masses prevailing in the Far East, and against an enemy with substantial strengths, complicated calculations of the effort required. At the battlefield level, military com manders faced formidable difficulties developing the appropriate tactics. In certain areas, notably amphibious operations and jungle warfare, the British had to build up their capabilities virtually from scratch.

The British were able to develop an adequate war plan only after gaining sufficient combat experience. The defeats at Malaya and Burma in early 1942 proved that British forces were inadequate. The turn of the tide after the US victory at Midway in June 1942, followed by the Allied counteroffensive in the Pacific theatres after the recapture of Guadalcanal in January 1943, revealed that the Japanese could be defeated. However, in Southeast Asia, the British continued to face a steep learning curve. The key lesson drawn from encounters with the Japanese was that they could be defeated only if British forces substantially enhanced their own strengths and efficiency. The failure of the first Arakan offensive in winter 1943, followed by the stalemate which prevailed until the early part of 1944, meant that British assessments concerning the Japanese demonstrated caution. It was only in the aftermath of the Japanese reverses at Imphal and Kohima in spring 1944, culminating with the total expulsion of Japan's armies by the following summer, that apprehensions were substantially alleviated.

THEMES AND ISSUES

The subject of British intelligence during the Pacific War touches upon several themes which are crucial to any study of the conflict. Throughout the work, five issues will appear regularly: (1) Britain's role in the Pacific War, and the place which the conflict took in British grand strategy; (2) the challenges which the Allies encountered in fighting the Japanese; (3) the organizational ethos of the British defence establishment, or what specialists in strategic studies have described as 'military culture', and the manner in which it influenced intelligence activities; (4) the nature of the Anglo- American alliance; and last but not least, (5) the race issue.

The first issue to be addressed, and one that is essential for properly contextualizing British intelligence during the Pacific War, is the contribution which Britain's forces made to the Allied war effort. The war against Japan was mainly undertaken by the United States, Britain being a junior partner. The existing literature correctly argues that Japan was defeated in August 1945 first and foremost because the US brought to bear its economic and military preponderance. Britain's operations in Southeast Asia did not deal a decisive blow, and its victory was due to the fact that it had aligned with the winning side.

Nevertheless, Britain's conduct of the Pacific War does form a significant area of military history and intelligence studies. After the fall of Singapore, Britain was by no means prepared to write off its presence in East Asia. On the contrary, Prime Minister Churchill and his Chiefs of Staff (COS) stood side by side with their American counterparts in demanding that the Pacific War end with Japan's unconditional surrender and the total destruction of its war-making capabilities. Britain also continued to have imperial interests in the Far East, and one of its key wartime objectives was to regain its colonies in Burma, Singapore and Malaya. The achievement of this aim was essential if Britain was to remain a Great Power. Britain also had to secure its interests without over-relying on US assistance and allowing the latter to dictate the postwar settlement. Intelligence provided Britain with a valuable instrument for devising a strategy that was suitable for accomplishing its war aims. The second core feature is the challenges which the Pacific War posed. The intelligence obtained through combat experience accurately portrayed the obstacles the Allies had to face. The first of these was the unpredictable nature of Japanese strategic and operational planning. While intelligence provided Slim and Mountbatten with reliable information on current Japanese dispositions and strengths, the issue of future developments was a matter for guesswork. The British therefore had to formulate their plans on the understanding that the results could not be foretold, while ensuring that their own forces were prepared for a variety of scenarios.

The uncertainty was compounded by the air of apprehension arising from a greater challenge, namely the resilience which Japan's armed forces demonstrated. Indeed, the campaigns in Asia and the Pacific presented some unique problems for the Allies. Encounters with Japan's forces revealed their capabilities to fight prolonged wars of attrition, in spite of their inferior numerical strengths and technological capabilities. The geographical expanse of Japan's conquests and its ample forces precluded the prospects of an easy victory. The Japanese army, navy and air services employed tactics that inflicted substantial delay and damage. Added to this was the Japanese soldier's insistence on fighting to the finish. The intelligence pointing to the various obstacles was used to enable the British to deal effectively with the situation facing them, and attain their war aims at an economical cost.

The third theme alluded to will be the organizational ethos, or service culture within the British defence establishment. After all, if intelligence is to be employed properly, its consumers need to recognize its value. The subject of military culture and its effect on strategic practice during the interwar period and the Second World War has been explored by a number of historians, including Allan Millett, Williamson Murray and David French. One can detect a number of ways how service culture led the British defence establishment to use intelligence effectively. Among the most important was the fact that Britain was initially operating from a position of weakness, and this feature has been cited in a number of works comparing the Allied and Axis intelligence systems. Allied decision-makers needed to concoct a plan where their forces could overcome their opponent with limited resources. To achieve this objective, it was essential to know which enemy strengths to avoid and the shortcomings to be exploited. Hence, the Allies made a greater effort to improve their intelligence capabilities.

Britain's performance during the Pacific War clearly supports the above contention. The trauma arising from Japan's victories in Southeast Asia during 1941–1942 led British commanders in the Far East, as well as the planning staffs in Whitehall, to admit the need to improve their own forces. British war plans were based on a calibrated evaluation of the Japanese, so that further reverses could be avoided, and victory achieved at an acceptable cost. Intelligence was therefore treated as an integral instrument. The British willingness to draw the appropriate lessons from its setbacks stood in stark contrast to the Japanese experience. Japan's defence establishment scorned intelligence for a variety of cultural reasons, the most important of which was a widespread taboo against questioning the prospects of winning. The victories achieved by the Imperial Japanese Navy (IJN) and Imperial Japanese Army (IJA) during the opening stages of the conflict reinforced the sense of superiority, and removed any incentive for conducting a methodical evaluation of the Allies. The neglect had some unfortunate effects on Japan's war effort. The concluding chapter will compare how Britain and Japan used intelligence during their campaigns in Southeast Asia, and explain how military culture gave rise to some of the differences. The fourth theme which will appear frequently is the nature of the Anglo-American alliance. One of the key indications of the state of inter-Allied relations was the collaboration achieved by their intelligence services, or lack thereof. Furthermore, Britain's ability to obtain adequate information on the Japanese often depended upon the help of its American ally.

Intelligence cooperation between the alliance partners reflected how their relationship was simultaneously one of harmony and competition. On one hand, the United States and Britain agreed that their ultimate objective was to secure Japan's unconditional surrender.

British intelligence reports demonstrated how Whitehall supported the Americans' wartime goals. At the Cabinet level, the Joint Intelligence Committee (JIC), which held ultimate responsibility for intelligence assessment, was tasked to produce detailed analyses concerning Japan's position in all theatres, including the Pacific, an area where the British were not heavily involved, but one which formed an integral part of the Allied war effort.

At the same time, inter-Allied intelligence relations reflected some of the differences within the coalition, and indicated how the British and Americans were fighting separate campaigns against the same opponent. While the United States viewed the Pacific theatre as the focal point of operations, since it provided the most direct avenue for launching assaults against the heart of Japan's empire, influential sections of the British government, notably Churchill and a large portion of his war cabinet, argued that the reconquest of Southeast Asia was a top priority.

The discrepancy prevailed until the late stages of the conflict, and the disagreements manifested themselves in intelligence cooperation, especially at the theatre level. The Americans were in a position to share a large amount of intelligence with their British ally, since they had made significant progress in decoding Japan's military communications and gained considerable experience dealing with the methods used by its armed forces. Yet, the sharing of material did not run smoothly. Cooperation appeared limited to the level of intelligence collection, with minimal efforts to coordinate efforts at the stages of the analysis, dissemination and implementation. The incomplete state of Allied cooperation had a number of significant effects on Britain's intelligence activities.

The fifth, and final theme is the contentious issue of race. Racial factors played a key role in shaping the conduct of the Pacific War. While the ethnic divide between the Allies and the Japanese visibly affected the opposing sides' views of each other, few historians aside from John Dower have covered the subject. During the years preceding the outbreak of the conflict, one can detect a number of ways in which ethnocentric prejudices led the British to snub the Japanese.

The outbreak of the conflict saw the British shift to a more rational view, and as the war progressed, racial stereotyping gave way to professional evaluation. Assessments of Japanese strategy focused on what the available intelligence had to tell, and one cannot detect any notable instances where racial biases tainted the process. At the battlefield level, the British did identify some cultural factors which influenced the performance of Japanese forces, and assessments often focused on the enemy's 'national characteristics'. At the same time, intelligence staffs and military officials painstakingly sought to base their hypotheses on a judicious analysis of the information they obtained, and were careful not to reach conclusions unless they could be proven by empirical evidence. For this reason, generalizations were made with reserve. Towards the end of the Pacific War, British views of the enemy were complex. The difficulties involved in defeating the Japanese created a certain level of animosity. At the same time, their dedication generated respect. The book will argue that while cultural views of the Japanese had a distinct impact, British intelligence was based more on logical analysis than racial prejudices.

STRUCTURE OF THE INTELLIGENCE MACHINERY

No work on intelligence studies is complete without explaining the structure of the apparatus, and how the information passed through the four main cycles, namely collection, analysis, dissemination and decision. For much of the period covered by the study, intelligence operated at two separate but interconnected levels, in Whitehall and in Southeast Asia.

Within Whitehall, after 1939, a central body in the form of the Joint Intelligence Committee was tasked to provide finished assessments to policymakers. The information was drawn from the service departments, namely the War Office, the Admiralty and Air Ministry, as well as civilian ministries such as the Foreign Office, Treasury and Board of Trade. The service departments and government ministries relied on an array of raw intelligence, including sigint, reports prepared by attachés in British diplomatic and consular offices across Japan and East Asia, as well as military personnel and private citizens who provided information. The main problem facing the intelligence machinery was not the lack of centralization, but resource shortages. Because Britain was preoccupied with its war effort against Germany, European affairs received priority, and intelligence operations in the Far East were a secondary concern.

The organizations operating in Southeast Asia also faced similar difficulties. The Far Eastern Combined Bureau (FECB) had neither the man power nor facilities to collate the volumes of material it received. Clandestine organizations such as the Special Operations Executive (SOE) and Special Intelligence Service (SIS) found themselves without the finances necessary to employ skilled agents and to foster useful contacts within Japan. The setbacks during the opening phases of the Pacific War led to the development of a more efficient apparatus. Within Whitehall, the organization remained more or less the same, with greater resources devoted to Japanese intelligence matters. At the theatre level, a marked difference existed in the efficiency of the different services' intelligence directorates (Figures I.2 and I.3). Army intelligence's machinery was the most elaborate, with air intelligence a close second, and naval intelligence remaining derisory until the closing stages. The contrast was due to the fact that the British army bore the brunt of the fighting in Southeast Asia. Hence, it was in greater need for intelligence, and its apparatus was likely to be more sophisticated. The Royal Navy, on the other hand, remained inactive for much of the conflict, thus negating the impetus for creating a resourceful organization at the theatre level.

NOTE ON SOURCES

A brief word on archival sources is in order. The secretive nature of intelligence activities means that the relevant documents often face destruction, and the available evidence consists only of the material which the producers have deemed fit for public inspection. Also, from a logistical point of view, it is physically impossible to find the space to house all of the paperwork. The result is often a fragmented collection, where gaps and mysteries emerge frequently. In the case of British intelligence during the Pacific War, there are a number of 'black holes' which the historian must confront. For example, the FECB's records were destroyed at the start of the war so as to prevent them from falling into enemy hands, and hard evidence of its activities prior to December 1941 is difficult to obtain. A large part of the evidence on British intelligence is made up of finished reports, such as, JIC appreciations, service bulletins and memoranda written by senior military officers. While the material provides a reasonably clear idea of the tone of net assessments, information on more basic questions, such as the material on which the reports were based, is often left wanting. Equally mysterious are the bureaucratic processes which gave rise to the final report, and how differences over interpretation between the responsible individuals and parties were resolved.

Likewise, at the bottom end of the cycle, there is plenty of raw intelligence indicating the type of information being received. However, many of the papers have been kept in their original form, and there is little hard evidence to show how they were processed. The consumers' views remain open to conjecture. Despite these difficulties, the available records allow an informed study of how British intelligence operated during the Pacific War, and they suggest that its activities made a valuable contribution.

AMBIGUITY AND COMPLACENCY

During Japan's attack on Southeast Asia between December 1941 and early 1942, Britain found itself virtually powerless. The British and Commonwealth forces were ousted from the Malay peninsula in a little over two months, and in February, the IJA conquered the bastion at Singapore. The inadequate state of Britain's defences played its part in facilitating Japan's victories. Nevertheless, to state that poor intelligence was the primary cause for Britain's setbacks is farfetched. Numerous historical works, as well as firsthand accounts by the commanders responsible for planning Singapore's security, have debated whether the capitulation was inevitable. The final explanation must follow the postmortem of General Sir Henry Pownall, commander of the British forces in the Far East. According to Pownall, commitments in Europe and the Middle East took priority, and preoccupations with matters closer to home significantly diminished the prospects of using military force to protect Britain's empire in Asia. Security thus had to be achieved by other ways. An understanding had to be sought where Japan agreed to respect the integrity of British interests. Of equal importance was to secure US support in placing diplomatic and economic pressure. By late 1941, Tokyo was determined to expel the Allied powers from Southeast Asia, and the prospects of avoiding war were slim. One is tempted to conclude that even the most accurate intelligence could not save Singapore. A more realistic argument is that poor intelligence led Britain to miscalculate the Japanese. The available evidence did not convincingly suggest that Japan had the intention and capacity to achieve Far Eastern hegemony. On the contrary, it gave good reasons to conclude otherwise. The result was a general air of complacency within the British defence establishment, which dictated that a conflict against Japan was unlikely, and even in such scenarios, Britain would not face acute problems in safeguarding its empire. While faulty intelligence did not cause Britain's strategic shortcomings, it led the British to mistakenly believe that their strategy against Japan was adequate.

FLAWED ANALYSIS, STRUCTURAL DEFICIENCIES, OR INADEQUATE INTELLIGENCE?

Britain's misperceptions of Japan prior to the Pacific War can be attributed to a lack of reliable intelligence. Some of the recent works have correctly argued that the British used a flawed method of assessment, which was based on the assumption that Allied forces would prevail in all circumstances, and Japan would not risk a conflict that it knew it could not win. While analytical defects were present, their significance cannot be understood without examining the nature of the intelligence that shaped British calculations. The main factor which prevented a forecast of Japan's intention, to conduct a total conquest of Southeast Asia, was Tokyo's ambiguous behaviour. Despite Japan's aggression in China during the 1930s, along with exhortations for eliminating Western influence in the Far East, the government and military did not have a definite plan for southward expansion until the final months preceding the outbreak of war.

The assumption that Japan wished to move cautiously was supported by credible intelligence. Following the outbreak of the Sino-Japanese conflict in July 1937, Japan's involvement in China restricted any enlargement of its operations. The occupation of French Indochina during 1940–1941 showed that the navy and army had sufficient resources to expand southward. Yet, Japan's inability to prevail in a prolonged war of attrition, along with the government's apprehension over confronting an Anglo-American coalition, gave grounds to conclude that Tokyo would not encroach upon British territories.

Assessments of Japanese military capabilities were likewise affected by inadequate intelligence. The British did not understand how the IJA, IJN and Japanese air forces (JAF) had developed the capacity to challenge their Western counterparts. Japan had also successfully concealed its rearmament programme through military secrets laws and travel restrictions, thereby substantially limiting the information British intelligence could obtain. The material reaching intelligence staffs in the Far East and Whitehall mostly emphasized the difficulties Japan's armed forces faced in subduing the Chinese. If suggestions of incompetence arose from faulty assessment, the available material did not help.

The structural weaknesses of the intelligence machinery also have to be analysed in view of the lack of serious threat indications. Whereas past experience revealed that Germany could challenge Britain, Japan had to prove its potential. As a result, the service departments devoted their scarce intelligence resources towards European matters, and invariably placed secondary importance on Asia. Japanese security laws also discouraged efforts to collect intelligence from secret sources. The only area where British intelligence made significant progress was Japanese diplomacy. Starting in 1919, the Government Codes and Cyphers School (GCCS) regularly produced decrypts, known as Blue Jackets (BJ), of messages transmitted by the diplomatic services of Britain's rivals. This source provided an insight of the Japanese Foreign Ministry's (*Gaimusho*) objectives. However, efforts to collect intelligence on crucial aspects such as military strategy and capabilities met limited success.

Clandestine services were also unproductive. Throughout the interwar period, Whitehall faced a shortage of finances, which precluded adequate support for the SIS, and the latter could not operate effective agents in any part of the world. Personnel for Japan and its overseas possessions were not available in sufficient numbers until the mid 1930s. By then, Japanese travel restrictions severely curtailed espionage activities. The situation was further complicated because Colonel Piggott, the military attaché in Tokyo between 1937–1940, insisted that his aim was to foster closer ties with the Japanese, and the presence of British special operatives could alienate his hosts. As a result, SIS activities remained meagre. Operations in other areas, notably Malaya and Singapore, suffered a perennial lack of funds. Britain's apparatus for intelligence analysis suffered equally from apathy. A central organization, the Far Eastern Combined Bureau, operated in Hong Kong since 1935 (Figure I.1). In 1938, following the Japanese advance into southern China, it relocated to Singapore.

Aside from breaking Japanese army and navy ciphers, the FECB analysed the performance of Japanese forces, and was able to obtain a reasonable amount of information on their operations in China. Again, the main problem was that London could not provide proper financial support, hindering the acquisition of the manpower to thoroughly collate the intelligence. In addition, there were few personnel with the skills needed to evaluate an adversary using a complex language as Japanese. The organizations within Whitehall suffered similar problems. The War Office, Air Ministry and Admiralty maintained their own intelligence directorates. In addition, the Industrial Intelligence Centre (IIC) handled economic matters. In September 1939, with the outbreak of war in Europe, the IIC was incorporated into the Ministry of Economic Warfare (MEW). The service departments collaborated with the IIC and MEW over matters concerning Japanese raw materials supplies and armaments production. In all of the above organizations, the sections responsible for Japan were poorly funded and under-staffed.

At the highest level of the machinery were the Cabinet and its committees, with the Joint Intelligence Committee being the most important. Founded in 1936 to provide a centralized body for assessing intelligence used by the Cabinet, the committee's functions grew throughout the late 1930s. Following its reorganization in summer 1939, the JIC became the chief producer of appreciations for the COS. In May 1940, with Churchill's accession to power, it took the additional task of producing operational intelligence reports for Britain's defence planners. Preoccupations with Europe limited the attention it could devote to the Far East.

The final structural feature which deserves attention is the cooperation between Britain and its allies. Intelligence was exchanged periodically with the other European colonial powers in Asia, namely the French and Dutch, as well as the Chinese. However, the most valuable partners were the Pacific Dominions, namely Australia and New Zealand, and more importantly, the United States. In particular, the Americans achieved considerable progress in penetrating Japan's communications, and were in a favourable position to aid the British. The latter's collection capabilities were limited to traffic passing through listening posts in Hong Kong, Singapore and its island possessions in the South Pacific. The US services covered the gap with a chain of intercept centres stretching from Alaska to Hawaii, while their stations in the Philippines were closer to Japan's home islands. Thus, Anglo- American collaboration offered potential benefits.

Yet, cooperation remained unsatisfactory for two key reasons, the first of which was the divergence of policy between Britain and its allies, and the level of exchange reflected some of the conflicting interests. Second, regardless of the amount of collaboration, Japanese security arrangements meant that the Allies faced persistent problems in obtaining intelligence.

At the level of collection, the British made progress in securing expertise of Japanese ciphers from the United States. The Americans had made considerable inroads since the early 1920s, and possessed a clear lead. In summer 1940, following a request by Lord Lothian, British ambassador in Washington, President Roosevelt dispatched a high-level mission to London to discuss the standardization of arms. In August, General George Strong, representing the US Army, informed the COS that the Americans were about to break the Japanese diplomatic code, commonly known as *Purple*, and were prepared to share the secrets. The offer was made in the hope that the British would divulge information on the German *Enigma* ciphers which the Americans had been attempting to obtain. Shortly thereafter, in February 1941, the GCCS secured a replica of the *Purple* machine from representatives of the US Army's cryptographic mission. The FECB also joined its counterpart in the US Navy, OP-20-G, in an effort to break the Japanese Navy's JN-25b code. A few months later, in June, an agreement was signed whereby US military authorities passed on to Singapore all intelligence on Japanese communications. British cryptanalysts were thus able to overcome the obstacles they had faced since the Japanese introduced more complex systems in 1939. Nevertheless, the British and Americans were unable to coordinate their activities, mainly because they were conducting separate efforts to contain the Japanese, and as such, the interests of their services rarely coincided. Whereas in the Atlantic, there was agreement that the sea lanes were vital for Britain's survival, 'no such meeting of minds was visible in the Pacific'. British strategy centred around protecting the Empire. Its war plans called for defending Singapore and the sea communications to Australia and New Zealand. US strategy, on the other hand, aimed to stay on the defensive in the Pacific, and thereafter regroup for attacks on Japan's main forces in Asia. The Americans regarded Southeast Asia as a British responsibility, and devoted minimal efforts towards intelligence activities there. During the weeks leading up to the attack on Malaya, US naval authorities could only point to indications of a possible attack on the Philippines and Thailand. Cooperation at the level of analysis also appeared minimal. The JIC and service departments rarely referred to conclusions reached by their US counterparts. As late as November 1941, British officials in Washington stated that they had yet to determine the reasons for lack of US assistance. The rigid demarcation of Anglo-American zones of interest continued to affect collaboration even after the outbreak of war highlighted the need for integration. The sharing of intelligence between Britain and its Dominions was also hindered by political wrangling. Whitehall was reluctant to let Australia and New Zealand pursue an independent strategy, and thus held back support for their intelligence communities. By the mid 1930s, the Dominions established their own naval intelligence services. Although their activities were constrained by lack of financial resources, they operated intercept stations which picked up Japanese radio traffic, and used direction finders to track the IJN's movements. The Dominions also contributed codebreakers to the FECB; however, their intelligence capabilities were left wanting. At the outbreak of war, the Royal Australian Navy and the Royal New Zealand Navy were unable to decode any of the IJN's signals, at a time when the material could have provided clues concerning the impending invasion of Malaya.

Simultaneously, the Japanese restrictions on foreign intelligence activities meant none of the Western Powers could make a proper assessment. The problem was particularly apparent in the area of Japanese military capabilities. The US services faced the same difficulties as their British counterparts, namely an inability to collect reliable information on Japan's rearmament programme. Under the circumstances, it was difficult to envisage allied cooperation enabling British intelligence to create a more precise image. British misperceptions were, for the most part, due to the lack of signs that Japan posed a danger. The analytical faults, along with the deficiencies of the intelligence machinery, were often byproducts rather than the cause of flawed images. To understand why Britain failed to predict the developments that transpired at the opening stages of the Pacific War, one must investigate the problems arising from the absence of credible threat indications.

ROOTS OF BRITISH PERCEPTIONS OF THE JAPANESE MENACE, 1931–1937

Britain's preoccupation with Germany did not render it oblivious to the Japanese menace. Following the abrogation of the Anglo–Japanese alliance in 1922, British leaders were aware that war was a distinct possibility. However, for much of the 1920s, the USSR and Comintern, with its alleged sponsorship of subversive movements in India and China, was viewed as the principal challenge in Asia.

Japan's occupation of Manchuria in 1931, followed by its withdrawal from the League of Nations, convinced Whitehall to alter its position. In 1933, the SIS placed Japan above the USSR as a power whose activities needed to be monitored, and stated that its attempts to enhance its political and economic control over China created some of the most pressing concerns for Britain's security. Japan's renunciation of the Washington naval arms limitations in 1934 and the signing of the Anti-Comintern Pact with Germany in 1936 provided further indications that Tokyo was aligning itself with the 'revisionist powers', and that its policies aimed to alter the *status quo* in East Asia. Despite Britain's awareness of the growing dangers, the situation was complicated by the lack of resources to defend its worldwide empire. When the end of the Anglo–Japanese alliance became imminent, the Cabinet approved the Admiralty's plans to construct a facility at Singapore, which was to serve as Britain's main base in the Far East. The working assumption was that the Royal Navy would dispatch its main fleet to Singapore. Japanese incursions against Malaya were to be contained, and the final phase envisaged an advance towards Japan's home islands in an attempt to sever its oceanic trade routes. Restrictions on defence spending delayed the construction of the base during the 1920s. After 1933, following Hitler's accession to power and the commencement of Germany's rearmament programme, Britain focused on Europe. The economic effects of the Great Depression also curtailed military spending, and jeopardized Britain's ability to provide surplus forces for the Far East.

As a result, during the 1930s, the British steadily downsized their war plans. The 1931 Naval War Memorandum reiterated the lynchpin of the Royal Navy's strategy, namely that after arriving at Singapore, the fleet would proceed to Hong Kong, and then establish bases for the blockading campaign against Japan's home islands. However, in 1934, at a COS meeting, the War Office and Air Ministry representatives informed the Admiralty that air and ground forces for operations north of Singapore were not available. As the decade progressed, the feasibility of dispatching a fleet to Singapore became questionable. At the June 1937 Imperial Conference, the COS informed the Australian and New Zealand representatives that the fleet's size would depend on whether Britain was engaging Germany and Italy at the time. It was in these fragile circumstances that Britain found itself when the Sino-Japanese conflict erupted only a month later.

THE OUTBREAK OF THE SINO-JAPANESE WAR AND ITS EFFECT ON BRITISH PERCEPTIONS OF THE JAPANESE MENACE, 1937–1939

On 7 July 1937, following skirmishes at the Marco Polo Bridge near Peking, the IJA launched a full-scale invasion of China in an attempt to secure dominance over the Asiatic mainland. The outbreak of the Sino-Japanese War confirmed suspicions that the subjugation of China was a key Japanese objective, and compelled Britain to pay closer attention to possible encroachments upon its interests.

The conflict also provided the first test of Japan's ability to wage a protracted war. By summer 1939, the available intelligence cemented the popular belief that the economic and military costs of the China campaign had significantly limited Japan's capacity for further expansion. Thus, despite Britain's difficulties in defending its empire, the threat of a Japanese invasion was considered minimal, so long as the China incident remained unresolved.

The drain on Japan's economy was the most notable consequence. Because the bulk of Japan's resources was committed in China, ventures which entailed further costs were deemed unlikely. Observations following the outbreak of hostilities revealed that Japan's finances could support its war expenditures only with the greatest difficulty. Economic intelligence also showed how Japan's narrow production base disabled its industries from providing sufficient amounts of armaments and munitions.

Although the effect on Japan's war-making capabilities was open to conjecture, evidence of deficiencies hinted that additional ventures would impose strains that its economy could not absorb, and its policies would be shaped accordingly. In September 1939, the COS actually stated that a prolonging of Sino-Japanese hostilities was potentially advantageous, for the costs were most likely to prevent Japan from trespassing upon the British Empire. Japan's dependence on imported raw materials also provided a means to aggravate its economic difficulties, and laid the grounds for predicting that its ambitions would be limited by fears of Western retaliation. Economic sanctions were a double-edged sword which presented challenges and opportunities. In their contribution to the COS's *Far Eastern Appreciation* of 1937, the IIC confidently concluded that in the event of war against the British Empire and the United States, Japan's economy could be disrupted through a distant blockade of its trans-Pacific trade route and shipping lanes to Europe. At the same time, to be effective, economic sanctions had to be imposed over an extended period, given Japan's possession of stockpiles. In addition, because the United States was Japan's most important trading partner, American participation was necessary to ensure that its economy was strangulated. Finally, until sanctions took their toll, Britain faced the possibility of Japanese attacks against its interests in the Far East. These points were brought forward in an enquiry conducted during autumn 1937, by the Cabinet's subcommittee on trade matters. The government of PM Neville Chamberlain thereafter refrained from sanctions.

Nevertheless, the mere prospect of economic isolation held prospects of moderating Japan's policies. In winter 1939, signals intelligence revealed that Japan was reluctant to transform its Anti-Comintern Pact with Germany into a formal military alliance, owing to worries that Britain and the United States might cease the export of vital raw materials. Japan's military commitment in China also hindered its ability to take on additional enemies, since the majority of its troops were tied down and the conflict showed no signs of ending. In early 1938, Dobbie, the General Officer Commanding (GOC) Malaya, and Percival, his chief of staff, warned that a Japanese overland attack against Singapore was likely, and in order to counter such scenarios, the defence of the entire Malay peninsula was vital. However, the War Office replied that Japan was too preoccupied to embark on such a complicated expedition. Although the conclusion was not based on accurate figures, it was based on observations suggesting that Japan's operations in China were likely to continue absorbing its strength.

BRITISH INTELLIGENCE ON JAPANESE STRATEGY, SEPTEMBER 1939 TO DECEMBER 1941

British assessments of the Far Eastern situation following the outbreak of the Second World War in Europe continued to predict that Japan would behave cautiously. The available intelligence provided vague hints of further expansion. To complicate matters, the threat of British and American retribution appeared to be restraining Japan. A southward advance entailed a possible confrontation against Britain, in which case US intervention could not be discounted. Japan could not bear the costs of such a conflict, and the evidence pointing to its limited resources suggested that Tokyo would avoid confrontation with a combination of Allied powers.

The optimism arising from indications of Japan's weaknesses had two effects on Britain's handling of the situation. First, policymakers maintained that the threat of economic isolation and military reprisals was sufficient to deter a Japanese advance into Southeast Asia, and that Britain did not need to substantially reinforce its territories. Second, by early December 1941, when intelligence provided reliable indications of an imminent invasion of Malaya, the British were accustomed to seeing such scenarios as unlikely, to the point of downplaying the danger signals.

The outbreak of war in Europe in 1939 complicated Britain's position in the Far East, while at the same time giving Japan favourable opportunities to undermine Western interests. Germany's conquest of France and Holland during spring 1940 exposed Indochina and the Dutch East Indies, and Japan lost little time in exploiting the power vacuum. Among Tokyo's objectives were to improve its economic situation by obtaining privileged access to sources of raw materials, and bolster its strategic position by establishing bases in Southeast Asia. Japan also took advantage of Britain's preoccupation with the defence of its home islands against Germany, by pressuring Churchill's government to cease supplying arms to China.

Even more alarming, the Japanese possessed sufficient forces for a southward advance, in spite of continued difficulties in liquidating their commitments in China. In an attempt to subdue Chiang Kai Shek's nationalists, Japan's military leaders attempted to strangulate China's lifelines. In autumn 1939, Japanese troops occupied Hainan island, thereby severing China's access to the sea. During summer 1940, through an agreement with the Vichy French government, the Japanese acquired bases in northern Indochina for conducting air raids against the Chinese hinterland, where Chiang had relocated his headquarters. Both moves indicated that Japan could extend its operations without significantly diverting manpower and equipment from China.

At the same time, Britain's involvement in the war against Hitler restricted its ability to contain the Japanese. In August 1940, the COS warned that the cumulative effect of Germany's onslaught against the home islands and trans-Atlantic lifelines meant that even in an emergency, the Royal Navy could not protect Singapore. Despite the mounting evidence of Japan's ability to invade Britain's colonies, as late as autumn 1941, the available intelligence did not firmly point to such moves. While the JIC did forecast Japanese strategy precisely, this was due to intelligent guesswork rather than good intelligence. The fact of the matter is that until autumn 1941, the government and high command remained undecided over Japan's long-term policy. The main objective was to subdue China, with southward expansion a secondary goal. Tokyo had acknowledged that further territorial annexations could result in hostilities with the United States and Britain, but was circumspect about such scenarios. For example, in June, after the trade delegation to the Dutch East Indies failed to secure oil concessions, General Sugiyama, the Army Chief of Staff, rejected invasion on the grounds that it could provoke Allied intervention. The army and navy also disagreed over Japan's objectives. The IJA insisted on preparing for a confrontation with the Soviets on the Asian mainland, while the IJN envisioned an oceanic war against the United States and Britain. The Japanese did not view the occupation of southern Indochina in July 1941 as a prelude to a southward expansion. The aim was to place Japan's forces in a favourable position to conquer the oil resources of Southeast Asia if the need arose, and in the meantime, continue with the China operations and remain on guard against the USSR.

Only in September, after the United States and its allies imposed oil embargoes and froze Japan's overseas assets, in retaliation for the conquest of southern Indochina, did policymakers in Tokyo decide that an occupation of the British and Dutch colonies in Southeast Asia was imperative. Nor was it until November that the high command approved Admiral Yamamoto's plan for a pre-emptive strike against the US Fleet at Pearl Harbor. In any case, the secrecy surrounding Japan's war plans negated any prospect of predicting its strategy.

Britain's miscalculation therefore did not result from a flawed reading of the Japanese leadership's mentality. It was based on a mistaken notion concerning the rationale likely to guide the future course of Tokyo's policy. The British assumed that Japan would seek all means to avoid war against an Allied coalition, and did not foresee how the presence of Allied forces in Asia, combined with the effects of the economic sanctions, would encourage rather than dissuade the government and military elite to take a gamble. Churchill held a deep-seated belief that the Japanese were inherently cautious, as illustrated in his remark to the War Cabinet Defence Committee in May 1941, '[the Japanese] would enter the war when they thought that [the British] are on the point of defeat, so that [Japan] could gather the spoils without danger . . . '. In predicting that Japan would behave cautiously, the British relied on a method of analysis which intelligence theorists and practitioners have defined as 'projection', a tendency to project one's values onto the adversary, or 'mirror imaging', that is, assuming that the other side would follow the same principles as oneself when facing a similar situation. Intelligence staffs and policymakers believed that, because they had concluded the losses Japan was likely to incur from a war against the Allies outweighed the costs, the Japanese leadership thought likewise. Without definite indications that the Japanese would resort to seemingly irrational moves, British assessments were unlikely to predict the outbreak of war.

The ambiguous nature of Japan's strategy meant the British could not provide firm answers whether further conquests were impending. Evidence of efforts towards increased economic and political influence in Southeast Asia did not indicate plans aside from the acquisition of French Indochina and Thailand. Assessments of Japanese expansion only spelled out the threats posed by the actions they undertook or were likely to execute. For example, when Japan occupied southern Indochina, the Admiralty simply warned that Japanese forces were in a favourable position for further advances. The FECB went as far as to state, 'the primary objective . . . was to ensure that Japan obtains all of the resources from Indochina', the acquisition of bases for southward expansion being secondary. The growth of Japanese influence in Thailand posed the greatest menace to Britain's colonies. The increasing Japanese–Thai military cooperation, in the form of Thai base concessions in exchange for Japanese arms shipments, entailed the possible establishment of a direct land link with Malaya. In early August 1941, after the occupation of southern Indochina, the JIC concluded that troop movements and dispositions suggested Thailand was Japan's next objective, and a logical precursor to an advance against Malaya and the Dutch East Indies. While the scope of Japan's strategy was calculated correctly, the JIC could not forecast the timeframe in which the Japanese were likely to carry out their conquests. The fall of Holland led Japan to lure the Dutch East Indies into its orbit. However, Tokyo's designs did not signify plans for occupation, and only revealed efforts to obtain access to the archipelago's raw materials through economic penetration and diplomatic coercion. BJ decrypts showed the government's desires to secure guarantees for imports of petroleum and strategic metals, and to ensure that the islands did not fall under US or British control. The IJN's concentration of its main units in the Mandated Islands did not indicate an impending occupation. Godfrey, the Director of Naval Intelligence (DNI), and the Admiralty concluded that the manoeuvres were designed to compel Batavia to offer concessions. British assessments of Japan's strategy were affected by factors aside from uncertainty. The ambiguity was compounded by indications of its questionable ability to confront the Allied powers. The available intelligence also suggested that Tokyo was hesitant to antagonize the United States and Britain. The cumulative effect was a sense of reassurance that Japan's awareness of its own weaknesses would restrain any decision to advance southward. The British believed that, despite Japan's ability to deploy numerically superior forces, its objectives were limited to a piecemeal conquest of Southeast Asia. Such a strategy provided the only way of avoiding a war in which Japan stood to be defeated by an Anglo-American coalition, possibly supported by the USSR.

In retrospect, Japan's lightning conquest of Southeast Asia vindicates the contention that the British were complacent. However, Japan was in fact at two minds about taking risks. Tokyo's attitude concerning the Tripartite Pact, signed in September 1940 with Germany and Italy, indicated the undecided state of its policies. On paper, the pact obliged the signatories to aid each other if any of them became embroiled in a war against the United States. In reality, Japan's actions continued to be dictated by its own strategic considerations. A BJ decrypt on 31 July revealed how an imperial policy conference had decided that military support for Germany's campaign against the USSR hinged upon Japan's policy requirements rather than any obligations to its Axis partners. The evidence pointing to Japan's undecided strategy was reinforced by signs that fear of intervention by the offstage superpowers, namely the USSR and US, was limiting its willingness, as well as ability to advance southward. The Russo-Japanese border clashes at Changkufeng in 1938, and Nomonhan in 1939, brought home to Tokyo that the Soviets remained a threat. As long as war in Siberia remained probable, the IJA needed to keep a large portion of its forces on reserve in Manchuria. Nor did the nonaggression pact with Moscow in April 1941 eliminate the prospect of hostilities. Germany's invasion of Russia in June raised the possibility of the USSR collapsing, in which case Japan's armies needed to be ready to advance into Siberia, so as to share the spoils. On 16 July, the War Office disseminated the contents of a BJ decrypt which revealed how a policy conference held earlier in the month concluded that intervention in *Barbarossa* was not ruled out.

As late as autumn 1941, the overall consensus within the FECB and Whitehall was that Japan needed to protect its position *vis-à-vis* the USSR; hence, the retention of forces on the Manchukuo border precluded an expedition against Malaya or the Dutch East Indies. According to the FECB, aircraft movements suggested that Japan's air forces had been withdrawn from Indochina for operations in the north. The JIC concluded that troop concentrations along the Soviet border pointed to offensive action, and an attack on Malaya was not feasible without a substantial reduction of Soviet strengths in the Far East. Japan also had to consider the probability of US intervention. An invasion of British and Dutch territories in Asia entailed the danger of the Americans aiding their European allies. From late 1940, the Roosevelt administration steadily departed from its isolationist policies and began to actively support Britain. The 'destroyers for bases' deal and Lend-Lease agreement committed the Americans to providing material help to their trans-Atlantic ally. In December, the United States and Britain commenced negotiations for naval cooperation, and in March 1941, the ABC-1 agreement called for the two powers to coordinate their action in the event the United States entered the war. When Japan occupied Indochina during 1940–1941, Washington initiated the imposition of economic sanctions. In August 1941, Churchill and Roosevelt signed the Atlantic Charter, which formed the basis for Allied war aims to rid the world of fascist aggression and secure national selfdetermination in the postwar world.

With the United States taking a more vigorous role in world affairs, Japan was considered more likely to shun the military power the Americans could put up. While the FECB acknowledged that Japan viewed Britain's preoccupation with Europe as an ideal opportunity, its intelligence summaries invariably closed with the reassurance that the possibility of provoking US naval action against its vulnerable lines of communication between the home islands and Southeast Asia was likely to limit its expansion. As late as August 1941, the War Office concluded that the fear of US retaliation precluded an attack on Malaya and the East Indies. Ten days before Pearl Harbor, the JIC reiterated the conclusion it had reached back in January 1941, namely, that fear of a US attack on the home islands would prevent the IJN from dispatching sufficient capital ships to support an amphibious operation against Malaya. In the light of evidence which suggested that Japan faced difficulties in confronting the Allied powers, assessments were likely to assume caution.

The British also held erroneous views of the state of Japanese–American relations. In September 1941, in an attempt to secure a lifting of the economic sanctions, Tokyo ordered its ambassador in Washington, Nomura Kichisaburo, to commence negotiations with US Secretary of State Cordell Hull. The latter made it clear that the minimum price for rapprochement was a withdrawal from China. After five years of waging a costly war, the Japanese government was bound to reject such terms. While the British were aware that the talks were not proceeding well, they were largely unaware of how the US and Japanese positions were so incompatible as to rule out any conciliation. As late as November, when the newly arrived hard-line government of Tojo Hideki was finalizing Japan's war plans, the prevailing view was that confrontation in the Far East could be avoided. GHQ India explained how, if Japan had to choose between commencing hostilities or sitting on the fence to await a favourable solution, past experience gave good reason to believe that Japan would take the peaceful option. Aside from strategic complications, Japan's economic situation suggested that its ambitions were limited by the desire to avoid the consequences of sanctions. Japan's dependence on imported raw materials could only be taken as evidence that Western embargoes were bound to cripple its warmaking capacity.

The possibility that sanctions might induce Japan to solve its problems by occupying new sources of raw materials in Southeast Asia was examined, but invariably dismissed, since such moves were fraught with risks. An oil embargo potentially had the gravest effect. In May 1941, the MEW, the service departments and the Shell Oil Company concluded that if the United States and Britain ceased their exports, unless Japan obtained control over the Dutch East Indies, its stocks would be exhausted in less than a year. The cumulative product of the intelligence pointing to Japan's economic vulnerability was the notion that the prospect of strangulation was likely to hold back its activities. In April 1941, the Axis Planning Section (APS) predicted that fear of reprisals was likely to limit Japan's actions to the peaceful annexation of new supplies of resources in areas beyond British and US control, i.e. Indochina, Thailand and Dutch Borneo.

In August, the Joint Planning Subcommittee concluded that although the oil embargo and freezing orders may have increased the possibility of war, fears over the effects of continued restrictions were more likely to 'make Japan pause and count the cost before taking another step forward'. On the eve of Pearl Harbor, the MEW suggested that unless Japan made sufficient concessions, it faced the prospect of suffering 'an economic situation as to render her ultimately unable to wage war, and reduce her to the status of second rate power'. Although the Dutch East Indies were the only territories which could provide the required petroleum, the islands were not necessarily considered part of Japan's immediate objectives. In light of the strategic difficulties which a southward expedition was perceived to entail, it was logical for British intelligence to surmise that the only realistic means to avoid economic collapse was through negotiations, and to conclude that the continued effects of the sanctions would deter, rather than goad, military action.

For the purpose of strategic planning, the notion that the threat of Allied opposition could contain Japan led Britain to adopt a policy of relying on bluff. Policymakers believed that they could compensate for their inadequate strengths in the Far East by taking a firm stand, and dissuade Japan from further expansion. In July 1940, Japan seized the opportunity to exploit Britain's preoccupation with the German onslaught, by demanding a closure of the Burma Road, which provided one of the main arteries for channelling supplies to China. The COS recommended the Cabinet to agree to a temporary shutdown. The incident marked one of the few occasions when acquiescence was advocated. Nevertheless, the decision was based on the premise that the interim period be used to secure a Japanese agreement to abstain from aggression. Similarly, the recommendation to reopen the Road in October, following Japan's occupation of northern Indochina, was based on the belief that a show of strength was necessary to keep Japan in check.

During 1941, the policy of deterrence gained further credibility, with the unfolding of events which suggested that the Japanese tended to back down in the face of confrontation. In February, concentrations of Japanese transports in the Gulf of Siam pointed to a possible invasion of Thailand. Although the war scare proved false, the Japanese government's abstention from further territorial acquisitions involving the use of force, following Ambassador Craigie's warning to Foreign Minister Matsuoka, was taken as an indication that when pushed to the brink, Tokyo preferred to avoid trouble. The occupation of southern Indochina in July 1941 did little to raise doubts that war with Japan could be avoided. The accepted belief was that so long as Britain synchronized its policy with the United States, and followed suit in imposing economic restrictions and hinting at further repercussions, the situation in the Far East could be stabilized. During the last week of November, Churchill made recommendations to Roosevelt for a joint Anglo- American declaration, on the belief that conquests could be prevented so long as Japan knew clearly that such moves entailed hostilities. Diplomatic and economic measures were not the only weapons for containing Japan.

By late 1941, the prevailing belief within Whitehall and Malaya Command was that if Britain undertook nominal improvements in its military position, Japan would lose confidence in the chances of conducting a successful invasion. Despite Britain's inability to dispatch a fleet to Singapore, the reorganization of Malaya's ground forces was viewed as a viable panacea. In April 1941, following months of plea-bargaining, the COS accepted a proposal by Air Chief Marshal Sir Robert Brooke-Popham, Commander-in-Chief Far East, that Singapore's defence perimeter be extended to northern Malaya, and approved preparations for a pre-emptive occupation of the Kra isthmus (codename *Matador*). The plan involved a slight increase in strengths, and Churchill consented on the con dition that it did not entail a reduction of forces in the Middle East, which was treated as second priority following the home islands. By October, when preparations for *Matador* were approaching completion, British commanders became confident that Japan would not invade, as illustrated by a meeting at GHQ Malaya. The proceedings were described by B.H. Ashmore, a senior commander on Percival's staff, who recalled that the FECB representative 'painted a fairly indecisive picture', and was unable to provide much information whether the occupation of Indochina portended further moves. Although the presence of enemy forces within proximity of Malaya raised worries, the upshot of the meeting was that the Japanese high command would refrain from an invasion after realizing that British beach defences and air opposition posed complications.

The notion that the presence of Allied forces in Southeast Asia and the Pacific could deter the Japanese also pervaded Whitehall. In July 1941, responding to the COS's suggestion to re-examine the possibility of further reinforcements for Malaya, Churchill reiterated his view that the Japanese were unlikely to go to war if the Americans intervened. Unable to present a strong counterargument, the COS gave in. The decision to dispatch the capital ships HMS *Repulse* and *Prince of Wales* to Singapore in October was the result of Churchill's conviction that a token British fleet in Southeast Asia, alongside a US fleet in the Pacific, was sufficient to negate whatever optimism Japan had in its capacity to advance southward.

The COS's agreement to Brooke-Popham's proposal, for dispatching Canadian battalions to Hong Kong, was based on a similar assumption that token reinforcements provided a valuable deterrent. The defence establishment's adherence to its illusionary faith, that Japan could be discouraged by the prospect of opposition, was further underlined by Pound's letter to the British Admiralty Delegation (BAD) at Washington, which suggested that the arrival of the capital ships at Singapore may well have made the Japanese hesitate. Given that war was bound to result in an ultimate defeat for Japan, combined with indications that its actions were being limited by apprehensions over confronting the Allies, the British were most likely to believe that they could avert war. Under the circumstances, it was logical to give minimal consideration for any substantial enhancement of Britain's defensive capabilities in the Far

East. Only the speed and scale of Japan's victories in Southeast Asia convinced the British that their adversary could not be deterred.

As late as the first week of December 1941, when the available intelligence clearly revealed Japan's plans to declare war on Britain and the United States, the defence establishment maintained that such moves did not entail an invasion of Malaya. US and Japanese attempts to reach an understanding had reached an impasse. During the last week of October, port watchers in China reported that landing craft were being constructed in Shanghai. On 2 December, an intercepted telegram between the *Gaimusho* and the embassy in Berlin showed that Japan anticipated hostilities with the United States and Britain. Yet, the precise location of the attacks remained unclear. On 3 December, a BJ decrypt revealed that the Thai government had requested the Japanese to launch a landing at Kota Baru on the Kra isthmus, thereby compelling the British to counterattack via Thailand, giving the latter a valid pretext for joining forces with Tokyo. Even then, there were no clear indications whether Tokyo had agreed. Only the arrival of longrange bomber and fighter aircraft in Indochina, along with observations of Japanese ship movements, provided strong signs that Malaya was a potential target.

The historiography suggests that British commanders in the Far East, as well as the planning staffs in London, became convinced that Japan would not undertake risky ventures, to the point of treating any indications of an impending attack with scepticism. The prevailing view was that Japan held apprehensions about war against the Allies, and would therefore avoid engaging their main forces in Asia; therefore the thrust of Japan's operations was most likely to be directed against Thailand. The reasons for denying the truth are difficult to explain because the available documentation does not describe the thoughts of the people in question. The most plausible cause was a refusal to depart from ingrained beliefs, or a phenomenon which scholars have termed 'cognitive rigidity', or 'cognitive dissonance'. Indications of an attack were explained away because the British were accustomed to believing that such scenarios were improbable, or they felt that to acknowledge the dangers would disrupt their peace of mind. The most reliable intelligence was unlikely to alter the beliefs of Britain's defence planners, at least until the Japanese had landed in Malaya. In his history of the campaign, S.W. Kirby revealed that Brooke-Popham downplayed the FECB's warnings that the convoys detected in the South China Sea were probably destined for the Kra isthmus and northern Malaya. According to Louis Allen, as late as the evening of 7 December, when British reconnaissance aircraft had been fired upon, the C-in-C Far East refused to acknowledge that hostilities were imminent. Recent works by O.C. Chung, Peter Elphick and Richard Aldrich have convincingly explained how Brooke-Popham and his staff ignored the signals pointing to a Japanese invasion. Attention has focused on intercepted ciphers between Tokyo and its embassies in London and Washington, ordering the destruction of confidential papers and encoding machines upon receipt of messages indicating an impending declaration of war. Equally important were the signals between Tokyo and its consul-generals in Bangkok and Singapore, revealing that by late November, fifth-columnists in Malaya had laid the groundwork for invasion. Concentrations of troops and aircraft in Indochina also indicated numbers well over those required for an invasion of Thailand. Yet, as late as 5 December, Brooke-Popham declined to order the pre-emptive occupation of landing sites on the Kra isthmus, on the grounds that no firm evidence existed that the convoy in the Gulf of Thailand was headed in his direction. Even on 7 December, when the convoy's proximity to Singora rendered a landing most likely, the C-in-C Far East maintained that the force was possibly a Japanese ruse to induce Britain to breach Thailand's neutrality, a move that could burden Britain with the blame for provoking hostilities. Brooke-Popham was not alone in discounting the imminence of a Japanese attack. The COS were equally unable to determine whether the convoy was heading for the Kra isthmus or Bangkok.

BRITISH INTELLIGENCE ON JAPANESE MILITARY EFFICIENCY PRIOR TO DECEMBER 1941

While intelligence on Japan's strategic problems provided convincing reasons to downplay the threat it could pose, the available information on its military capabilities did not raise concern. The problem stemmed from the lack of reliable intelligence. The absence of prior experience in engaging Japan's armed forces also meant the British did not have a reliable yardstick for calculating the outcome of an Anglo–Japanese confrontation. By comparison, in the European theatres, defence establishments could draw upon the experiences of the First World War, which provided ominous indications of how the conduct of future conflicts could be affected by modern technologies such as aircraft, armour and naval power. Even then, the British could only speculate how the use of such weapons might affect the performance of their most likely enemy, Nazi Germany.

British efforts to assess Germany were hindered by the rapid pace and secretive nature of its rearmament programme, as well as the shortage of resources and qualified intelligence personnel. Assessments were based on conjecture, and 'untested preconceptions were too often interwoven with hard facts'. Among the most noteworthy of these presumptions was that Britain would face horrific casualties if it attempted to stand up to its enemies. The defeatist attitude was common among British policymakers and military officials throughout the interwar period, and stemmed from the losses suffered during the Great War. The lack of reliable information meant that German capabilities were overrated during the 1930s, and the exaggeration played a profound role in leading the British to take an indecisive stand against Hitler's expansionist moves.

Warfare against the Japanese in East Asia was an even more uncertain venture. There had been few opportunities to observe Japan's armed forces in action since the Russo-Japanese War of 1904–1905. Japanese operations during the Great War consisted of small-scale landings against German outposts in China and the Pacific. Intelligence collection during the interwar period was complicated by military secrets laws which shrouded Japan's rearmament programme. The abrogation of the Anglo–Japanese alliance curtailed opportunities for collecting material through attachments to Japanese units. Without access to reliable intelligence, the British tended to base their judgments on precon ceptions which dictated that Japan could not construct a military machine to match the West. The conclusion that Japan's forces were second rate gained further credibility after July 1937, when the IJA and the air services faced visible difficulties in overcoming Chinese resistance. Finally, despite the Japanese navy's numerical superiority, along with the army and air services possessing the additional advantage of having gained years of experience, Japan's forces had only confronted weak Chinese opponents. As a result, assessments on the feasibility of an expedition against Malaya concluded with the view that British forces would prevail.

Recent works on British prewar assessments of Japanese capabilities have explained how misperceptions were partly due to racist biases which deprecated the martial qualities of non-Western forces. Indeed, comments on the IJN and IJA often demonstrated myopic judgments. The Naval Attaché in Tokyo, Captain Vivian, reported in 1935 that the Japanese 'have peculiarly slow brains', and were therefore unlikely to effect any sort of surprise moves. Naval officers concluded that because of their slit eyes, Japanese pilots could not shoot straight. Remarks on the IJA's performance were equally degrading. In December 1937, following a tour of northern China, Captain Marr-Johnson, a Royal Artillery officer, noted 'various slight indications' that the Japanese soldier's morale was excellent while he was winning, but his fighting spirit tended to break down when 'faced with a nasty situation'. When forwarding the report to MI2, the General Staff at the War Office minuted, 'after all, the Japanese are Orientals!'. Such statements suggest that racial contempt was widespread.

At the same time, racism was one of a myriad of influences, and its role cannot be properly understood without examining the obstacles which prevented a more informed verdict. Assessments of the IJN were based on racial stereotyping because the lack of reliable information precluded a knowledgeable judgment. In regard to the IJA and the air services, the available intelligence appeared to confirm the British disdain for Japan's armed forces. The IJN was the branch which remained the greatest mystery. Not only did military secrets laws prohibit visits to naval bases and shipyards; the collection of intelligence was further complicated because the IJN played only a minor role in China. Efforts to obtain information on Japan's naval services remained unproductive. For example, during spring 1939, the Naval Attaché admitted that he had little information with which to ascertain the types of vessels the IJN was planning to construct with the funds it procured through the Japanese Diet's annual budget. Signals intelligence revealed that the Navy Ministry was requesting its attachés in Europe to secure contracts for badly needed imports of steel, ammunition, and radio equipment. While information on production difficulties correctly signified that the IJN was struggling to meet its construction targets, it tended to obscure the successes it had achieved in constructing a fleet capable of challenging its US and British counterparts.

The shortage of raw intelligence on the IJN had two detrimental effects, the first of which was a lack of knowledge about the size and armament of Japanese capital ships. The Admiralty was aware that the IJN was constructing vessels with tonnages exceeding the Washington naval arms quotas, especially after Japan openly denounced the limits in 1934, and withdrew from the London Conference two years later.

However, the extent of the breaches was never certain. In regard to the possible construction of ships with 18-inch guns and displacements exceeding 40,000 tons, the DNI simply stated that the possibility could not be ignored. In fact, British intelligence was unaware of the existence of the superbattleships *Yamato* and *Musashi* until 1942. The second damaging result of poor intelligence was a tendency to base assessments on dubious sources. The most basic aspects, such as the number and types of ships under construction, were left to guesswork. Calculations by the NID were premised on what the Japanese could produce with their limited resources. Information on armaments manufacture was left wanting. In January 1939, the DNI admitted that, although Kure Naval Dockyard was the only known site for building armour plate, his minute was based on a vernacular newspaper article obtained back in November 1937. In addition to the problems arising from lack of accuracy, production figures could never substitute qualitative information on Japan's fleet. In light of the difficulties in obtaining dependable information, it was only a short step to a situation where the Admiralty relied on racial stereotyping. As Arthur Marder has illustrated, the estimate that the IJN's efficiency was 80 per cent in comparison to the Royal Navy was arbitrary, and based on the presumption that the Japanese could never develop a fleet that was on par with its Western rivals. British efforts to assess the IJA faced obstacles of a similar nature to those which plagued naval intelligence. As with the IJN, information on the IJA was fragmentary, owing to security arrangements. The collection of information on crucial matters such as equipment, training and tactical doctrine was difficult. The available material tended to highlight the troubles facing the IJA. In particular, army commanders appeared slow to depart from their traditional practice of fighting set piece battles, and unable to develop methods for conducting a mobile war which required the proper use of mechanized forces. In 1937, MI2c reported to Inskip, the Minister for the Coordination of Defence, that despite massive increases in expenditure, the effectiveness of the IJA's weapons and training in their use could not be compared with first-rate armies. Suggestions of inherent Japanese deficiencies turned out to be largely correct, particularly regarding the use of modern weapons.

The IJA's progress in this field did not merit praise, as was revealed in its confrontations against the Chinese and more importantly, the Soviets. In 1940, the War Office noted how the use of artillery at the Nomonhan border clashes was poor, with infantry units requesting fire to be delivered against targets well outside the range of guns. Antitank guns were also sited in a manner which disclosed their positions, 'with the result that Soviet tanks were able to knock them out at the start of the attack'. The prospects of improvement appeared unpromising. In a report on an imperial ordinance calling for a rigorous effort to equip units with tanks and mechanized infantry, B.R. Mullaly, the Military Attaché, commented that the Japanese 'lack of experience and the handicaps imposed by national characteristics' were likely to 'restrict the effective use of such formations'. As Alvin Coox has illustrated, the IJA high command realized in the aftermath of Nomonhan that the reverses against the Red Army were due to the shortage of heavy equipment, coupled with poor tactical skill. However, the IJA's ineptitude in operating armour and artillery was bound to hamper its efforts to mechanize. Consequently, Japanese tactics centred on the infantry for the duration of the Pacific War, and the IJA never achieved anything similar to Western standards in the employment of mechanized forces.

At the same time, reports which emphasized the IJA's backwardness demonstrated how the available intelligence obscured one of its key strengths, namely, the efficiency of its infantry units. Their ability to advance long distances without relying upon transport or fixed communications, and overcome enemy defences with light weaponry, proved fatal for Allied forces in Southeast Asia during the opening stages of the war.

The creation of an accurate image of the IJA was further hampered by its failure to achieve a decisive victory during the Sino-Japanese War, which in turn, reinforced the view that its capabilities need not be taken seriously. Assessments of the IJA's performance in China revealed a misunderstanding of how it was confronting a number of unique obstacles, none of which was encountered later in Southeast Asia. First, the geographical expanse of the Chinese theatre meant that the IJA was more likely to contend with enemy counterattacks and logistical difficulties than in a battleground as compact as Malaya. Second, because Chinese armies were fighting on home territory and could draw upon an endless supply of reserves, they were more capable of effective resistance than a Western army operating thousands of miles from home base. Third, and most importantly, Chinese guerrillas, as well as regular troops, possessed a significantly higher standard of training than the British empire forces which defended Malaya.

The British therefore faced difficulties in gauging the implications of Japanese weaknesses and strengths. Its misperceptions stemmed from a mistaken notion that the IJA's problems in China were indisputable proof of its inability to challenge its Western rivals. Field reports illustrated in painstaking detail how guerrilla resistance had forced significant resources to be devoted towards 'pacification duties'. The IJA's difficulties in coping with this type of opposition gave rise to suggestions that the Japanese were hard pressed to defeat the most poorly equipped foes. Appraisals of Japanese morale provided another key example of a prevalent habit, within the British intelligence community and army establishment in general, to overestimate how the IJA's troubles affected its worthiness.

Events in China revealed that the morale of Japanese soldiers, which the IJA viewed as its most valuable asset, was liable to deteriorate in the face of prolonged conflict. Impressions of the IJA's exceptionally high morale were largely a holdover from its performance during the Russo-Japanese war. However, from the earliest stages of the Sino-Japanese conflict, field reports noted how the majority of the IJA's troops were conscripts who openly expressed disapproval of the war effort and regularly demonstrated apathy. Tours of battle areas carried out by British observers, such as Grimsdale and Captain Boxer, head of the intelligence branch in Hong Kong, revealed that unexpected reverses frequently caused a breakdown of discipline.

By the eve of the Pacific War, the British correctly surmised that the Japanese soldier's tendency to lose confidence in unforeseen situations rendered him vulnerable. In March 1941, Major Chapman, head of MI2c, minuted that a spate of Japanese defeats against the British or the Americans might burst the bubble of an ever-advancing army, with the effect being 'so severe as to induce panic'. Nevertheless, allegations concerning the effects of Japanese shortcomings hinged on the optimistic prediction that the Allies would benefit from the opportunity to achieve a decisive victory at the initial stages of the war.

In spite of the analytical faults which plagued British appraisals, one needs to take account of the fact that the only source of tangible intelligence was the IJA's operations in China, which often laid the grounds for negative images. Grimsdale recalled that the reverse at Taierchwang in April 1938 formed the basis of Western beliefs that, given adequate equipment, the Chinese could defeat the Japanese. The corollary to this notion, that since the Chinese army was hopelessly inefficient, it followed that the IJA was also in a poor state, gained wide acceptance. Brooke-Popham's conviction, that the IJA could not be viewed as a formidable enemy, was based on observations of Japanese frontier guards while on a tour of Hong Kong in late 1940. As postmortems on the Malaya campaign invariably admitted, the bulk of Japanese troops in China were second-rate conscript soldiers who did not fully represent the IJA's capabilities. Britain's underestimation therefore can be attributed to the lack of access to information on the training and efficiency of the armies which its forces were to encounter in Southeast Asia. Without a direct confrontation which could provide a full picture of the IJA's capa-bilities, evidence of incompetence was taken at face value.

The numerous indications pointing to the IJA's questionable performance meant that assessments were rarely able to provide straightforward acknowledgements of its prowess. Consequently, no audience in the War Office and the British army was ever likely to take a serious view. As Ferris has illustrated, MI2 was the only section within the War Office which acknowledged how, owing to its experience in China, the IJA was a difficult foe if confronted in the battlefields of Asia. However, even MI2 never explicitly conceded that the IJA was capable of defeating its Western counterparts.

For example, in May 1940, and again in December 1941, a few days following the outbreak of war, MI2 disseminated ambivalent accounts which closed with a warning that the IJA was 'trained for and only required to fight in the Far East, where it will have inherent advantages'. However, before delivering such a discomforting observation, both papers stated that as a general conclusion, 'the Japanese army [had] not yet reached the standards of western armies'. In addition, they contained a number of sharp criticisms concerning poor infantry–artillery cooperation and a tendency to downplay enemy strengths. Such statements were more likely to dilute any worries.

A lecture delivered by Colonel Wards, the assistant military attaché in Tokyo, to a gathering of British officers at Singapore during 1941 which warned of the IJA's efficiency, was not only discredited as a result of dismissive comments by Bond, the then GOC Malaya. More importantly, Wards recalled that the audience began to show doubts of his statements when he was at a loss for ways to explain the poor physique of Japanese POWs in China.

The creation of negative images regarding the IJA was further propelled by the fact that it had conducted most of its operations against poorly equipped Chinese forces, and had yet to face its supposedly more advanced Western rivals. When evaluating the IJA's performance in the event that it advanced into Southeast Asia, the British surmised that the Japanese were unlikely to enjoy the same fortunes. Assessments of Japanese capabilities in amphibious landings and jungle warfare highlighted this dilemma. Combined operations in China were conducted with sophistication. Landings took place with little warning, and advances against inland targets were launched before the defenders could counterattack.

However, because the landings met minimal air and naval opposition, similar operations against well-entrenched forces were deemed to face less favourable results. Likewise, operations in southern China and Indochina gave the IJA invaluable experience conducting operations in undeveloped terrain.

Its forces were able to advance rapidly through heavily wooded and mountainous country, where poor communications and difficulties in transporting heavy equipment required the efficient deployment of infantry units. However, because the Japanese had only confronted guerrillas who did not put up organized resistance, the accepted view was that they could not make significant progress against British forces in Malaya.

The problem stemmed not so much from an inability to understand the IJA's capabilities, as from a widespread ethnocentric view which blindly credited the efficacy of Western armies. The corollary to this belief was the assumption that British forces in Malaya were first rate and in good order. Japanese methods did suffer a number of weaknesses. For example, while amphibious forces had developed exceptional skill in landing on undefended coastlines, their capabilities against fortified positions were negligible.

The first wave of landings in Malaya suffered heavy casualties caused by air interference, and the operations succeeded mainly because the invading troops persisted with their advance in spite of the losses.

The IJA's jungle warfare capabilities were at a similar stage of infancy. The majority of troops embarking for Malaya were given virtually no training for warfare in tropical conditions. Japanese equipment was not made to withstand heat and humidity, and medical provision for malaria was rudi mentary. As Edward Drea has illustrated, 'for the Japanese army, the war in the South Pacific was one against an unknown enemy'.

The successes in Malaya were in many ways attributable to the grossly unprepared state of British troops, coupled with good fortune. The IJA's shortage of mechanized units meant that tactical doctrine focused upon the infantry, who were to rely upon speed and surprise to outflank enemy defences. Such tactics proved effective in Malaya, where the British did not have enough armour and artillery to cover their flanks.

However, in the Philippines, the Japanese were often held up by better-equipped US forces. Thus, Japanese methods succeeded only against weaker opponents.

British misperceptions resulted from a mistaken notion that Western forces would prevail in all circumstances. Yet, while reservations concerning the IJA's efficacy suggest a certain naivety, an equally important factor was the lack of precedents for gauging the British army's strengths against the Japanese. Under the circumstances, the British naturally evaluated the IJA in light of the fact it had yet to overcome the challenges it faced in Southeast Asia.

Appraisals of Japanese amphibious warfare capabilities demonstrated a presumption that the IJA's inexperience in operating against strong shore defences and air power entailed a risk of heavy losses and possibly failure. In his minutes to a report on the landings in the Yangtse Delta area during autumn 1937, the DNI noted, 'the Japanese are gaining experience in combined operations and have shown originality in their preparation and construction of special craft'. However, he closed with a downplaying comment, that the absence of defending aircraft had probably inspired a false sense of confidence among Japanese commanders. The minimizing of the threat posed by Japanese amphibious tactics had a profound effect on assessments of the dangers facing British forces in Malaya. In April 1940, Bond warned that the Japanese development of special landing craft, along with their ability to carry out landings in adverse weather conditions, and in areas which were a considerable distance away from their home base, necessitated an improvement of the peninsula's seaward defences.

The General Staff at the War Office rebuffed, 'regarding the Japanese ability to land on coasts anywhere, this is agreed with . . . although [their] ability to maintain forces like this against European troops and aircraft is questionable'. By winter 1941, the threat posed by Japan's ability to land troops on the Kra isthmus was mitigated by the conception of *Matador*, which envisaged a forestalling of Japanese invasion by occupying the key beachheads and aerodromes.

Major-General Playfair, the chief of staff for GHQ Far East, went as far as to suggest that so long as *Matador* was executed immediately after the Japanese attacked, a protracted land battle was highly unlikely. Assessments concerning the IJA's jungle warfare capabilities were based on similar conjectures which professed British superiority.

The prospects of an advance through the Malay peninsula towards Singapore was considered impossible, because the Japanese armies were doomed to face problems in advancing beyond their beachheads. Churchill was a prime supporter of this contention, as revealed in his minute to the COS in September 1940, suggesting that the 'plight of the invaders, cut off from home base while installing themselves in the swamps and jungle would be all the more forlorn'. As late as the last week of November, the JIC contended that an overland expedition required the prior development of adequate communications, and a Japanese occupation of the Kra isthmus did not necessarily entail an immediate attack on Malaya.

British commanders in the Far East demonstrated a similar level of laxness, and an inability to grasp the need to prepare their forces. In order to hold out against enemy advances in the jungle, infantry units had to conduct a mobile defence, since the poor communications did not permit the use of tanks in large numbers.

Yet, as late as December 1941, only one unit, the 1st battalion of the Argyll and Sutherland Highlanders, had any real training in the jungle. The prevailing attitude was one of complacency. During summer 1941, Grimsdale overheard three senior officers, including a major-general, laughing at the efforts being made to improve existing methods, suggesting that the whole unit would 'go sick from exposure or strike from overwork'.

Command Headquarters, which based its conclusions on information supplied by the FECB, regularly told the troops how the Japanese would not be jungle trained. Intelligence staffs in Malaya played their part in promoting misinformed images, in spite of their occasional efforts to warn that Japanese methods necessitated proper training.

For example, in March 1941, the FECB issued a pamphlet describing how the IJA had demonstrated its proficiency in advancing through undeveloped country, and provided comprehensive accounts of its skill in executing river crossings, enveloping movements and reconnaissance of enemy positions. The document has been cited as an instance when intelligence staffs propagated indisputable evidence of Japanese prowess, only to be dismissed by commanders.

However, the report was prefaced with a disclaimer that Japanese operations were carried out against an inferior opponent, where the IJA 'was able to take risks with her communications . . . which would have proved fatal against a more enterprising enemy'. Thus, the conclusions were to be treated with reserve. Dismissive evaluations of the JAF were based on similar factors that led to the discrediting of the IJA, namely, a lack of intelligence on overall capabilities, coupled with tangible evidence of incompetence.

In a similar fashion to the army and navy, the collection of accurate air intelligence faced the handicap posed by restrictions on visits to Japanese regiments. Assessments by the Air Attaché in

Tokyo were admittedly based on slim evidence. As was the case with the army, the main sources of information were observations of developments in China. The material provided credible indications of inefficiency, while at the same time obscuring the fact that Japan's air services, particularly those attached to the IJN, were able to inflict crippling losses.

Observations of the JAF's performance in China frequently gave rise to suggestions that its pilots and equipment possessed a relatively low standard of efficiency.

Japanese bombing attacks, which were mainly conducted by the naval air services, were noted for their inaccuracy and high losses suffered by aircrews. Attacks against railway lines revealed a failure to hit vital targets such as main junctions and to halt the flow of traffic, leading one British observer to conclude that the Japanese did not use their air power to achieve 'any but minor results'.

By 1940, the Air Ministry provided frequent accounts of the JAF's difficulties in inflicting permanent damage. In spite of numerous attacks on factories, most of which had not met substantial opposition, the effect on industrial production was negligible, leading to suggestions that Japanese bombing techniques were poor. The Japanese fighter force received equally disparaging remarks.

The use of barrage fire, a tactic that had been considered outdated in the West, gave rise to the view that the JAF's methods were backward. Evidence of efficiency was overshadowed by the fact that successes had been achieved against minimal opposition. Although the Zero fighter proved highly effective owing to its speed and manoeuvrability, the Air Ministry merely praised the new type of aircraft for its ability to inflict attrition on the Chinese, whose equipment consisted primarily of obsolete Soviet aircraft. In reality, the JAF's problems were not unique, and were due to a number of common notions held by air staffs around the world during the interwar period.

The Japanese services were no less guilty than their European counterparts in taking for granted the all-powerful might of the bomber, and neglecting the need to develop fighter aircraft to protect their formations from enemy interception. Nor were they alone in failing to understand that the destruction of targets required accurate aiming, and the necessary technology had yet to be developed.

Yet, accounts of operations in China treated the JAF's weaknesses as ones that were prevalent only among the Japanese. The most notable example of this trait was the JIC report on the lessons of air warfare in China, which described how bombing operations failed to hit any significant targets. Instead of attempting to surmise how the experiences could be used to improve the RAF's operational capabilities, the report obscured its findings with a dismissive preface, 'caution must be exercised in drawing conclusions which may have little or no application to a war between first class powers'. The gross underestimation of the JAF's capabilities eventually spread to the highest levels of the Air Ministry. By 1941, the consensus was that the JAF stood on a par with the Italian *Regia Aeronautica*. British assessments also reflected a nearly complete oversight of how operations in China had provided the JAF with invaluable training in conducting long-range air strikes. True, the Japanese derived some faulty lessons which had fatal consequences on their air doctrine against the Allies. The most notable was a false confidence that the tactics and equipment which had succeeded in China would achieve similar results against the Americans, whose air services possessed vastly superior resources and technology.

However, during the opening stages of the Pacific War, these weaknesses were not apparent, mainly because the JAF possessed a number of decisive advantages. The heavy losses suffered during bombing raids in China led the Japanese to provide their aircraft with more adequate protection. As the Sino-Japanese conflict progressed, attacks against lines of communication also achieved enhanced accuracy, and the JAF managed to curtail a significant portion of the traffic on major railways and roads. Attacks against urban areas laid waste to a significant portion of China's infrastructure.

Of equal importance, while British intelligence correctly identified some of the JAF's problems, it had little access to information on the Japanese naval air services' development of tactics against Allied shipping targets.

The Admiralty's *Naval War Memorandum* for the Far East, prepared in winter 1939, surmised that, while total British and Dominion air strengths were inferior, there was little reason to fear Japanese combat capabilities. Owing to their inexperience dealing with antiaircraft fire, and lack of training in the functions of torpedo bombing, overseas reconnaissance and target spotting, the Japanese were judged to be inferior in these fields. As events were to show, by the outbreak of the Pacific War, the efficiency of the Japanese naval air services ranked first among the maritime powers.

The effective employment of torpedo bombing and horizontal bombing tactics resulted in the destruction of the bulk of the British and US fleets during the opening stages of the conflict. Yet, British naval commanders had no compelling reason to believe their adversaries could perform advanced manoeuvres unless visible evidence of Japanese air capabilities was available. The decision to dispatch the *Repulse* and *Prince of Wales* on their fateful mission was based on misleading intelligence on what the Japanese air services could achieve. In January 1942, Pound admitted that prior to the sinking of the *Repulse* and *Prince of Wales*, war experience did not suggest that torpedo attacks could be carried out at extended ranges. In his recollections of the Far Eastern conflict, Hillgarth, who served as the Chief of Naval Intelligence in the SEAC theatres, admitted that the gravest miscalculation regarding the force attacking Malaya was not on its strength and location, but the quality of the bomber convoy.

In addition to technical shortcomings, the JAF was considered likely to face logistical problems in supporting long-range operations across the expanses of ocean in Southeast Asia. In their appreciation of the forces which the Japanese could bring to bear against Malaya prepared in January 1941, the JIC reassured that even in the event of a Japanese occupation of bases in southern Indochina, Singapore was only within range of heavy bombers, while light bomber attacks required the establishment of bases in the Kra isthmus. Correspondence between Brooke-Popham and the COS suggested that fears of the possible scale of air attack were confined to local commanders, whose warnings were dismissed as unduly alarmist.

British assessments of the JAF's logistical capabilities reflected the lack of information on the extent to which the naval air services had made painstaking preparations to ensure that the convoys destined for Southeast Asia were fully protected by land-based air support, and planned their operations with a view to neutralizing Allied air power in the Philippines and Malaya at the earliest opportunity.

Japan's air services also had yet to prove their ability to provide support for operations conducted thousands of miles away from advanced bases. The difficulties involved in supporting operations across the South China Sea led the Air Ministry to predict that in addition to shortages of aircraft with adequate ranges, maintenance difficulties and wastage resulting from operations over large stretches of water were likely to limit the scale of attack. Without visible indications that Japan's air services were a serious threat, the British were not going to raise unfounded concerns.

CONCLUSION

The series of Japanese victories in Southeast Asia following the outbreak of war on 8 December 1941 (Malaya time; 7 December, London time), which culminated with the total elimination of Allied military power in the region, could only have arrived as testimony that the British misjudged their adversary. However, poor intelligence cannot be blamed for Britain's failure to defend Singapore. British grand strategy was shaped primarily by its shortage of surplus resources, and the need to concentrate its efforts on containing Germany's threat to the home islands. The second major concern was to protect Britain's lifelines in the Atlantic and Mediterranean, as well as its vital Middle Eastern oil supplies. The defence of Malaya and Singapore was lowest in the list of priorities. A study of prewar intelligence on Japan therefore does not significantly affect the validity of existing arguments regarding Britain's motives for pursuing the strategy that it did.

One must also be judicious in condemning the British defence establishment for not understanding the situation they faced *vis-à-vis* Japan. In order to comprehend the reasons for Britain's complacency, an examination of the circumstances which prevailed prior to December 1941 is crucial. Intelligence on Japan's strategy failed to show any indications that an attack on Singapore was imminent. Developments following the outbreak of the Sino-Japanese conflict showed that Japan's preoccupation with its objective of defeating China prevented it from taking on additional commitments which entailed a further drain on its resources. Despite evidence of Japan's ability to extend its operations into Southeast Asia following the spring of 1940, its actions did not suggest any concrete objectives beyond the acquisition of greater political influence and increased access to the raw materials of the region.

A military confrontation against the Western Powers was considered illogical, because such moves entailed strategic and economic risks which Japan was ill-prepared to afford. Most importantly, observations of Japan's actions prior to the outbreak of war revealed that its leaders were hesitant to embark on moves which entailed war against the United States and Britain. The inaccuracy of British predictions does not negate the fact that evidence which suggested caution among Japanese leaders was accurate, and that firm indications of plans to seize control of Southeast Asia were lacking. The evidence pointing to Japan's awareness of its own weaknesses, in turn, led Britain to conclude that Tokyo would act prudently. British policymakers and defence planners believed that the combined threat of economic restrictions and Allied military intervention would be sufficient to discourage Japan from encroaching upon Western interests in Southeast Asia. Only the total elimination of Allied military power from the Far East during the opening stages of the conflict could convince Britain that Japan could not be deterred.

The available intelligence on Japan's armed forces also failed to provide reliable indications that their capabilities posed a threat. Because military secrets laws shrouded developments within the Japanese army and navy, the main source of information became observations of their operations in China, which confirmed the belief that their performance was second rate.

Although the available intelligence suggested that Japan's forces enjoyed certain strengths, they also had yet to prove their capacity to defeat their Western rivals. In the absence of firsthand encounters, images of Japan's military capabilities were more likely to be based upon false assumptions, and a mistaken belief regarding the ability of British forces to forestall their adversaries.

Only a major setback could persuade Britain to discard the notion that Japanese forces were unable to defeat their Western counterparts. In the final analysis, Britain's unreadiness in the face of the Japanese onslaught can be attributed to the lack of credible danger signals.

Recent studies on the factors that determined the effectiveness of military preparations during the interwar period have argued that aside from adequate resources, a crucial ingredient for success was the presence of an identifiable threat against which a concrete plan could be drawn. Equally important were defence planners who possessed the intellect and imagination to predict the situation their forces were likely to face, and the ability to innovate new methods accordingly.

Britain's war plans in the Far East enjoyed neither of these benefits. Under the circumstances, the possibility of a Japanese attack on Pearl Harbor and Singapore, or that such an operation would succeed, was unthinkable. Hence, Britain's defence planners adhered to their notion that a total war in the Far East could be avoided, and did not consider the need to enhance the capabilities of their forces.

The fall of Singapore and the elimination of Allied military power in Southeast Asia was essential to compel a more accurate appreciation. As events during the Far Eastern conflict were to reveal, no amount of military intelligence could substitute combat experience as a means to gauge the implications of enemy strengths and weaknesses.

7

Aftermath of the War

The Allies' experiences of defeat and limited victories during 1942 highlighted the challenges which Britain was to face during the Pacific War, in three respects. First, Japan's victories in Southeast Asia provided undeniable signs that its armed forces were able to inflict devastating losses. Second, the turning tide of the war after summer 1942, following the IJN's defeats at Midway, dismantled the view that Japan's forces were invincible, and proved that the Allies could defeat their opponent, given adequate resources and methods of use. Third, and most importantly, while Japan's inferior industrial production precluded its prospects of winning the conflict in the long run, its army and navy were fully capable of fighting a protracted war of attrition. Allied operations in the South Pacific and Burma during the latter part of 1942 and early 1943 provided ominous indications of Japan's capacity to put up tough resistance, as well as the substantial amount of time, effort and resources required to defeat the enemy. However, the British had yet to achieve significant successes, and did not have many helpful precedents for determining the most effective methods of defeating the Japanese. As late as the beginning of 1943, the appropriate strategies and tactics could be developed only through trial and error.

TRANSFORMATIONS IN METHODS OF ASSESSMENT

The aftermath of Britain's setbacks at Singapore and in Burma saw a shift in service culture, insofar as the means of gauging Japanese strategy and military capabilities were concerned. As illustrated previously, prior to the outbreak of hostilities, the British did not have a great deal of reliable intelligence concerning Japan's ability to wage war against the Allies. As a result, it was common practice to rely on racist views which downplayed the quality of non-Western powers, and the ethnocentric notion that British forces were likely to prevail.

Following the fall of Singapore, the defence establishment felt compelled to take a less cavalier attitude, and realized the extent to which they had underestimated their enemy. Japan's war effort did reveal a number of shortcomings, the most notable of which was the lack of resources to defeat the Allies. Nevertheless, the most important fact to bear in mind was that British forces in the Far East suffered a number of shortcomings which had to be repaired before they could overcome their opponent.

The British thus conducted a careful re-evaluation of their own forces, and concluded that drastic reforms were required. At the strategic and tactical levels, the British army, Royal Navy and RAF demonstrated an acute need for improvements in their strength and efficiency. The Japanese military also held an exceptional level of morale, providing further reasons to conclude that British forces had yet to match their opponent. Economic intelligence revealed that the Allies had to undertake a substantial effort in order to bring about any serious depletion of Japan's war resources.

The shift in service culture did not mean that the British completely discarded their reliance on racial images. Assessments of the Japanese began to focus on the features which rendered them a difficult challenge. Insofar as Japanese strategy was concerned, the IJN and IJA demonstrated their propensity to undertake bold ventures and thereby endanger the Allies' position, even if it entailed equally grave risks for Japan. Thus, in assessing Japanese strategy, the most important factor was the enemy's capabilities rather than its intentions. Intelligence on the quality and performance of Japan's armed forces revealed that discipline and tenacity were common traits. The British acknowledged the characteristics of the Japanese and the challenges they posed, and made an earnest effort to formulate a balanced picture.

At the same time, proper account was taken of the fact that Britain was fighting an unfamiliar enemy. Intelligence staffs were careful not to reach conclusions that Japan's forces would operate along definite patterns. The British were aware that they needed to be flexible in their methods, and to innovate in accordance with situations as they arose. The development of war plans took place on the understanding that mistakes were bound to happen. The British accepted the fact that they had to surmount a steep learning curve before they could engage their opponent in a proper manner.

JAPANESE STRATEGY

The magnitude of Japan's advance into Southeast Asia convinced the British to adopt a more vigilant outlook. Prior to the outbreak of war, the accepted assumption was that, although Japan possessed the strength to conquer Malaya and the Dutch East Indies, its fear of provoking Allied retaliation would compel the IJN and IJA to conduct a piecemeal conquest of Southeast Asia in an effort to sound out British and US reactions. Thus, the Allies could take advantage of a breathing spell that would allow them to bolster their defences. Following Japan's lightning conquests, the British based their forecasts on the expectation that the loss of Britain's territories in Southeast Asia was a foregone conclusion.

By March 1942, the Japanese had established bases within striking range of the Indian Ocean, thereby raising the possibility of operations against areas hitherto considered beyond their reach. In early April, the IJN launched a carrier-based sortie against the Royal Navy's base at Ceylon, highlighting the vulnerability of Britain's position.

The situation was desperate because commitments in Europe and North Africa continued to limit the forces available for operations against Japan. Consequently, for the first half of 1942, the British resigned to the probability that any large-scale Japanese expedition would deal a devastating blow. Nevertheless, while Japan's forces reigned supreme, as early as February, they began to face overstretch, and by June, the consequences became clear. The IJN stumbled from one unsuccessful operation to the next, first at Coral Sea and then at Midway, where the IJN lost its predominance over the US Navy.

Yet, the Japanese continued to possess ample strengths to forestall Allied counteroffensives, and the situation warned against any underestimation of the strength that had to be built up before the Allies could liberate their lost territories. At the same time, inaction entailed the risk of enabling the Japanese to consolidate and render Allied operations more difficult. The cumulative result was the development of a strategy aimed to inflict attrition against weak spots on Japan's outer perimeter. The strategy of limited offensives manifested itself in the decision to launch the disastrous Arakan campaign of winter 1942–1943.

The speed of Japan's advance convinced the defence establishment that Britain's position in Southeast Asia was untenable. By mid January, Japanese troops completed their advance through the Malay peninsula and conquered the southernmost province of Johore, thereby gaining an opportune position for besieging Singapore. The COS discarded their notion that Britain's bastion in the Far East could hold out against the Japanese. In response to Churchill's question about the wisdom of sending reinforcements, Alanbrooke, the CIGS, replied, 'the defence of Singapore is part of a delaying action'. The plan was to play for time while withdrawing to rear positions in the East Indies.

The Allies faced equally poor chances of retaining their positions in other parts of Southeast Asia. Given the weak state of Allied defences, Japan was most likely to secure its conquests by establishing a defensive barrier stretching from the eastern frontier of India to the southwest Pacific, destroying all remnants of resistance. In January 1942, the JIC concluded that the conquest of the Malay barrier not only provided vital supplies of raw materials. From a strategic viewpoint, it also served to push the Allies to their rear bases in India and Australia, securing the outer perimeter of Japan's empire.

Any hopes of holding the Malay barrier were contingent upon last-ditch forestalling actions. In mid February, during the battle of the Java Sea, the British and Dutch fleets failed to intercept the Japanese convoy headed for the East Indies. Pownall, along with and Wavell, who had been appointed the C-in-C Southwest Pacific, concluded that the Allies simply did not have enough strengths to forestall a landing. While British intelligence deduced the scope of Japan's ambitions in Southeast Asia, the possibility of operations beyond the Malay barrier remained open to conjecture. The available evidence was replete of information on Japan's long-term strategy. The structure of intelligence collection and analysis did not undergo major changes at the start of the conflict. The GCCS continued to intercept diplomatic signals intelligence, which simply pointed to strategies that were under consideration.

To illustrate a few examples, as late as the end of 1942, information on the possibility of Soviet–Japanese hostilities was contradictory and did not firmly indicate whether Japan intended to invade Siberia. Neither the JIC nor COS were able to produce conclusions. Signals intelligence also revealed that Japan was seeking ways to secure the Congress Party's cooperation in establishing a pro-Axis government in India. The information came at a time when the political situation in the Indian subcontinent was precarious. The colonial government faced increasing difficulties in stemming the nationalists' demands for full independence, and the circumstances seemed ideal for an Axis campaign of subversion. Nevertheless, information on Japanese intentions did not indicate whether a concrete strategy was likely to materialize, and the material simply exacerbated British fears of impending operations against India. Naval signals intelligence proved equally unreliable. When the fall of Singapore became imminent, FECB headquarters was relocated to Colombo in Ceylon. After March 1942, with the cooperation of the US Navy's sigint unit, OP-20-G, British cryptanalysts deciphered the IJN's JN-25 code. However, naval intercepts provided little apart from warnings of impending attacks. Prior to the Japanese attacks on Ceylon in early April, naval sigint alerted Admiral Sir James Somerville, C-in-C Eastern Fleet, who was able to evacuate his ships. The Japanese were prevented from launching another Pearl Harbor style air raid. Yet, long-term forecasts remained impossible, and defence plans had to be formulated on the understanding that enemy attacks could take place at short notice.

The truth of the matter is that until April 1942, Allied efforts to predict Japanese strategy were complicated by the fact that the IJN and IJA had not decided what they were to do after their operations in Southeast Asia were completed. Japan's leaders did not face an entirely favourable situation. The navy and army were stretched to their limit, and the China venture remained unresolved. The high command needed to make difficult decisions whether to consolidate or pursue further conquests. To complicate matters, no course of action held high promises of a decisive victory. An invasion of the Hawaiian islands was out of the question, given the state of alert the Americans were on after Pearl Harbor. An invasion of Australia was also difficult, because the IJA did not possess the strength to overcome the islands' defences, nor the logistics to support such a complex operation. An occupation of Ceylon and outlying British bases in the Indian Ocean would have provided a springboard for invading the Middle East, and in turn enabled the IJA to link up with Rommel's *Afrika Korps*. This move could have dealt a serious blow to the British Empire. Even then, Japan's eastern flank would have remained open to US incursions.

At the same time, consolidation was an equally questionable strategy, for Japan had yet to fulfil one of its main objectives, namely to neutralize US naval power in the Pacific. The failure to sink the carrier fleet at Pearl Harbor confronted Japan's leaders with a situation they had not anticipated.

To complicate matters, disagreements between the IJN and IJA commands hindered a decision. The navy wished to secure Japan's conquests by occupying Hawaii or Australia and preventing their use as bases for an Allied counteroffensive. The IJA, on the other hand, maintained that Japan's ultimate objective remained to conclude the war in China and prepare for action in Siberia. The army thus argued that its resources were insufficient strengths for large-scale offensives in the Pacific, and proposed to consolidate its southern conquests at the earliest opportunity. The IJA general staff premised its policies on the assumption that the Americans would be incapable of striking back for at least the first two years of the conflict, and hence a pre-emptive attack was unnecessary. The question of how to secure Japan's empire in Southeast Asia had not been seriously considered. Within Yamamoto's naval staff, there were disagreements as to whether Japan's key to victory lay in a main fleet action against the United States or the elimination of British positions in the Indian Ocean. Finally, while the possibility of bringing India into Japan's orbit was discussed at the high command level, the plan never transpired beyond a distant pipedream. At an imperial liaison conference held in January 1942, Japan's leaders issued a document stating, 'the Imperial Government has no hesitation in making wholehearted efforts to help the independence movement irrespective of whether inside or outside India'. Yet, the Japanese government did not have any direct contacts with Indian political parties, and was reluctant to support anti-British movements unless the Axis powers were willing to simultaneously send forces to the Indian subcontinent. Because neither Germany or Italy were ready to undertake operations east of Suez, a concrete strategy was unlikely to materialize.

The difficulties Japan faced in making a decision meant that war plans were formulated *ad hoc.* The Combined Fleet did not order the expedition against Ceylon until the third week of March, when the buildup of the Eastern Fleet at Trincomalee convinced Yamamoto's staff that British naval power in the Indian Ocean had to be neutralized. Only in late April did naval leaders decide to direct the IJN's main thrust against the US Fleet in the Central Pacific, after the Doolittle air raids on the home islands had revealed how the Americans could bring carriers within proximity of Japan. The IJA's plan to occupy Port Moresby was not drawn until mid spring, when mopping-up operations in Southeast Asia were approaching completion. Under the circumstances, no matter how thoroughly British intelligence tracked Japanese strategy, the evidence was bound to remain contradictory. The absence of conclusive intelligence required British forces to guard against attacks at all possible points. In assessing Japanese strategy, the British looked at the overall situation in the Asia–Pacific theatres, but tended to focus the larger part of their attention on the Indian Ocean areas. This was because the Pacific theatre, including Australia, was a US sphere of responsibility. The loss of Singapore severed Britain's links with the Dominions, and the latter requested US military support in forestalling a Japanese invasion. Roosevelt accepted the request, and on 9 March 1942, Churchill agreed to the US proposal that the Dominions be placed under General MacArthur's Southwest Pacific Command. Thereafter, the British entrusted the defence of Australia to the Americans, and were more concerned about the possibility of Japanese incursions against their imperial possessions in the Indian Ocean.

British appreciations of Japan's strategy reflected a growing realization that efforts to predict enemy strategy were futile. The most important factor to be considered was the enemy's capabilities rather than intentions. The lack of indications of plans for an invasion was not taken to mean that such scenarios would not materialize. While an expedition against areas to the west of the Malay barrier entailed exposing Japan's eastern flank, its forces still possessed ample strengths for operations against British positions in the Indian Ocean, and stood to reap tangible benefits through such actions. In February, the JIC warned that Japan could muster the necessary troops for an invasion of Ceylon at any time, and its naval power and shipping resources were more than adequate. On the question over the probability of such operations, the committee admitted that no data was available for making a definite forecast. However, the Japanese were likely to realize that the loss of Ceylon would deprive Britain of its main base in the Indian Ocean. The uncertainty which plagued efforts to predict Japan's war plans, along with evidence of sufficient forces for further offensives, meant that the only way to ensure security was vigilance.

The increasing likelihood of Japanese expeditions against the Indian Ocean necessitated a closer examination of the strategic balance, and the upshot was that the British were not in a favourable situation. The *R* Class battleships used to reinforce Somerville's Eastern Fleet were relics of the Great War, and did little to help. The carriers *Indomitable* and *Formidable* were equipped with limited complements of aircraft whose performance did not match their

Japanese counterparts. Nor was the garrison at Ceylon able to forestall a landing.

To complicate matters, the war against Germany remained Britain's top priority. Shortly after the United States entered the war in December 1941, the British and Americans held their first summit meeting (*Arcadia*) at Washington. Churchill insisted that the Allies needed to concentrate on Germany. The US representatives, in particular Admiral Harold Stark, the chief of the naval operations, argued that offensive operations against Japan should commence immediately. However, Roosevelt accepted Churchill's view that Germany posed a greater threat.

Nevertheless, the 'Germany First' strategy meant that Britain could not substantially strengthen its position against Japan until operations in Europe and North Africa had progressed sufficiently. Under the circumstances, no amount of intelligence could remedy the fact that British defences in the Indian Ocean were precarious, and the prospect of improvement in the near future were minimal. By March, the British conceded that few alternatives existed apart from accepting the consequences which could arise from a Japanese invasion, namely the loss of control over the territories adjacent to the Indian Ocean, and severance of the sea communications to the Middle East. Within India Command and the Eastern Fleet, the prevailing view was that Ceylon could not be defended without adequate air and naval reinforcements. In February, shortly after his appointment as C-in-C India, Wavell warned, 'to attempt to provide against a large scale invasion [by strengthening Ceylon's ground defences] would involve locking up troops which could be better used in offensive operations elsewhere'. The garrison in Ceylon was of little use if the Japanese gained control of the surrounding ocean and airspace, and the Eastern Fleet could not repel a Japanese foray until sufficient numbers of carriers and their accompanying aircraft could be deployed. However, the Joint Planning Section (JPS), COS and Churchill maintained that until Allied forces had neutralized Germany's threat to the Middle East, and U-boat attacks in the Atlantic had ebbed, Britain could not provide the necessary forces for the larger part of 1942. The IJN's sortie into the Bay of Bengal in April highlighted the vulnerability of British territories in the Indian Ocean. The ease with which the Japanese brought a fleet within striking distance of Ceylon reinforced the conclusions reached previously. Sir Richard Peirse, commander of Air Headquarters India, and Wavell repeated their warnings that Ceylon and the east coast of India were defenceless without substantially increased air strengths. The COS concluded that if the Japanese pressed westward, India would be placed in great danger, and the Middle East and essential supply lines via the Indian Ocean placed under threat.

At the same time, the difficulties involved in strengthening Britain's position were acknowledged, and its strategy continued to be influenced by its global commitments. While Wavell insisted the defence of Ceylon be treated as a matter of the utmost urgency, the COS and Churchill replied that operations in the Middle East were more important, and hence the protection of sea communications with that theatre take priority. The Indian Ocean was to be secured by occupying Madagascar. As the official history on the war against Japan has pointed out, 'Wavell's difference of opinion with the COS was natural'. Churchill and his staff had to view the problem from the broader angle. The security of the UK had to take precedence, and the needs of India related to those of the Middle East.

Churchill and the COS realized that Britain's only hope of protecting the Indian Ocean, in the absence of an adequate Eastern Fleet, was to obtain US cooperation. Urgent requests were made for the US Pacific Fleet to either launch naval offensives on Japan's eastern flank, or send warships to join Somerville's fleet. Naturally, the Americans, who were reluctant to commit their limited strengths to defend the British Empire, made it clear that Britain's proposals were out of the question. The visible indications of Ceylon's vulnerability, and the difficulties involved in bolstering its defences, gave rise to a strategy of withdrawing major British units from the enemy's striking range and minimizing potential losses. The Eastern Fleet was moved to East Africa on the premise that until adequate capital ships and carriers could be deployed in the Indian Ocean, its presence was more likely to lure further attacks. FECB headquarters was relocated to Kilindini on the assumption that the raids may have heralded an invasion. In reality, Japan had no plans for further incursions into the Indian Ocean. However, only after Japan's defeats at Coral Sea and Midway had depleted the IJN's surplus of naval and air forces, could the British conclude that the enemy was unlikely to muster the strengths needed to support large-scale invasions. The possibility of Japanese offensive operations could be dismissed only by evidence which pointed to a diminution of its capabilities. During May and June 1942, Japanese naval losses provided reasonable grounds to conclude that the peril of a seaborne landing on India and Ceylon had passed. Churchill minuted to Pound that the loss of four Japanese carriers at Midway had improved Britain's position in the Indian Ocean and Bay of Bengal, and that a 'severe restraint [was] imposed upon the Japanese' by their need to husband their extensive naval requirements. Pound responded that the position had improved 'inasmuch as the Japanese are less likely to stick their head into [the Indian Ocean]'. Assessments of Japan's strategy also emphasized how its forces had lost the initiative. In September, the JIC suggested that to win the war, the IJN and IJA had to 'resist whatever counteroffensive Allies may put up', and 'build up her military machine' in the hope that 'the exhaustion of [Allied] resources would force the latter to sue for a negotiated peace'. The shifting balance of power in the Pacific, along with Japan's shortage of surplus forces, meant that its strategy had shifted to one aimed to consolidate its outer perimeter. Nevertheless, Japan's waning capabilities did not obscure the scale of effort required. The turning tide of the conflict, accompanied by evidence that Japan was turning to the defensive, meant that the Allies could begin contemplating a strategy for liberating the western Pacific and Southeast Asia. The IJN and IJA continued to possess ample forces to defend Japan's conquests. While naval sigint began to provide comprehensive information on the IJN's strengths and dispositions, information on the IJA remained patchy for much of 1942 and the early part of 1943, because the army employed a more complicated code system. This created continued difficulties for Allied cryptographers and intelligence staffs. However, the British could deduce that the Japanese armies which had successfully ejected the Allies from the Malay barrier remained unscathed, while British strengths in the Far East had not undergone any substantial increase. The scenario supported the contention that an attempt to dislodge the enemy from its conquests was premature.

The situation was further complicated by the Allies' adherence to the 'Germany First' strategy, which relegated operations against Japan to secondary importance in terms of resource allocations. The COS maintained that the Allies did not possess sufficient strengths for simultaneous operations against both Germany and Japan. Whereas Germany could become invincible if it was allowed to recuperate, the same did not hold true for Japan. The Allies thus needed to focus their efforts on a decisive German defeat, while diverting only the minimum force necessary to hold Japan. The argument that operations against Germany necessitated a limited commitment in the Far East was employed at the highest levels of Allied planning. At the January 1943 Casablanca Conference (*Symbol*), Admiral King, chief of naval operations, argued that while Germany was the prime enemy, the Allies should be prepared to move against Japan after the European war had been won. King suggested that the Allies double the quota for force allocations in the Asia–Pacific theatres from 15 to 30 per cent. Alanbrooke agreed, strictly on the condition that the effort against Germany would not be prejudiced. The decision to continue allocating priority to the European and North African theatres meant that British forces in the Far East were bound to suffer neglect and correspondingly limited capabilities. British appreciations concerning the practicability of large-scale counteroffensives warned that until numerically superior forces could be deployed, Japan's defensive position was virtually impregnable. On 11 July 1942, the COS met with General Harold Alexander, the commander of British army on the India–Burma front, to discuss Wavell's plans for recapturing Burma during the winter 1942–1943 campaigning season (*Anakim*). The plan called for an assault across the Assam border, accompanied by landings on the west coast. Wavell had already expressed concerns over the lack of air power and the shortage of aerodromes and communications. Without a clear British numerical superiority, defence planners tended to focus on the problems created by the substantial forces which the Japanese could put up. Alexander was not confident that a landing on the Burma coast was feasible since the British did not possess the resources for such a laborious process. The COS feared the plan committed British forces to extended operations supported by unreliable communications, while the Japanese could easily bring reinforcements from the southern regions. Although Churchill criticized his advisors for basing their assessments on worst-case scenarios, on 12 July, after extensive debates, he conceded, 'unless the Japanese air forces available' are 'cut down below the present level and their military forces cannot be reinforced, we need not commit ourselves to *Anakim*'. At the same time, inaction could only allow Japanese forces to consolidate.

In June 1942, the JPS warned that the defeat of Japan would become progressively more difficult if left too late. Its armed forces would have the opportunity to strengthen the defences of the conquered territories. The most economical strategy was to 'concentrate sufficient force in one area to threaten Japan's vital interests', and attacks on sea communications were the best means to achieve this objective. The COS warned that it was important to seek measures to maintain pressure and thereby prevent the IJN and IJA from developing threats against Allied forward bases. The Allies also had to deal with the possibility of minor offensives against the Southwest Pacific and Indian Ocean areas, as part of a Japanese attempt to disrupt Allied preparations for counterattacks, even though Japan's offensive capabilities had faded. In August, the IJN and IJA staged a landing on the South Pacific island of Guadalcanal. The aim was to secure a base for conducting attacks on the lifeline between the US west coast and Australia, thereby hindering the Allies' ability to use Australia as a base. The ensuing contest was not a guaranteed victory for the US Navy, which was unable to put up a numerically superior fleet. The IJN also demonstrated a high level of skill at conducting raids during hours of darkness, while US forces remained inept at conducting night engagements. The deadlock was not broken until mid November. Back in London, the

JPS estimated the Americans would not achieve parity with the IJN until 1943. Without carrier support, the US Fleet had to remain on the defensive.

On the India–Burma front, the Congress Party passed the 'Quit India' Resolution in August 1942, sparking civil unrest and threatening Britain's hold on its main base for operations against Japan. The prospect of revolution rekindled concerns over the possibility of an invasion, and while Japan had no clear ideas how to exploit the 'Quit India' movement, the unrest came at a time when Congress leader Bose was in Berlin, courting Axis support. Germany never made a firm commitment to the campaign; however, Bose's efforts created the impression that the European Axis powers were seeking to undermine Britain's hold on India, and wished to see Japan attack in the near future. The JIC and India Command warned that Japan possessed sufficient forces for a landing in the Bengal regions, and the operation was most likely to coincide with local disturbances. Although there were no indications that the Japanese considered the prospects of success to be high, it was important to monitor the situation. Evidence of Japan's capabilities for further offensives thus continued to warn that British forces needed to take the necessary precautions.

The twin dilemmas of the shortage of forces for large-scale offensives, and the inherent dangers of staying on the defensive, led the British to conduct limited advances against Japan's outer perimeter. While the strategy of steady attrition reflected a realization of the need to take all possible measures to gradually weaken Japan's defences, it also signified an overestimation of how limited operations could affect the enemy's war effort. In November, the COS decided to dispatch the carrier HMS *Victorious* to the Southwest Pacific Area (SWPA). The move was based on the grounds that the Eastern Fleet's strengths were insufficient to counter a Japanese incursion into the Bay of Bengal, and the carriers could be pu' to better use if they joined the US counteroffensive in the Pacific. While the US fleet achieved significant progress in pushing back Japan's forces, by the end of 1942, the IJN's defeats at Guadalcanal resulted in a depletion of its strengths, to the point where the *Victorious*' presence was superfluous. Incidentally, the *Victorious* did not engage the Japanese fleet during its entire tour of duty.

Decisions concerning operations on the Burma front revealed a similar lack of vision. In autumn 1942, Wavell concocted a plan to reconquer Japanese outposts in the Arakan regions. The plan stemmed from an oversight of the fact that Japanese armies in the region were well entrenched, and supported by a line of communication that enabled them to bring reinforcements from rear areas at short notice. Against such opponents, limited offensives were unlikely to yield favourable results.

Operational ineptitude played an equally significant role in laying the grounds for Wavell's decision. Prior to the Pacific War, Britain's military involvement in the Far East was confined to policing actions in its colonies. British forces had not conducted campaigns in Southeast Asia which required the provision of substantial forces and logistics. In the expansive jungles of the region, mobility was restricted due to rugged terrain and poor communications. In close country warfare where movement was slow, attacks needed to be conducted on a wide front and accompanied by diversionary moves. Such measures were necessary to prevent the enemy from consolidating, and also to guard against interference with the attacker's communications. Although Wavell realized the inherent dangers, his plan was based on the hope that a rapid advance could secure his objectives. In late August, he informed the COS that he planned an overland advance against Akyab, aimed to bring the Japanese air services into battle and inflicting losses. In addition to depleting enemy air strengths and thereby helping Allied operations in other theatres, the operation also appeared to hold prospects of preparing the way for further operations into Burma, and lessening the threat to India.

In mid September, Wavell justified the operation on the grounds that Japanese army strengths in the frontier regions of Burma were weak, and the IJA was too tied down in the SWPA and China to provide any reinforcements. Although the COS replied that air requirements could not be met, Wavell maintained that risks had to be accepted. Despite their objections that British positions were likely to be untenable, the COS acquiesced. The operations faced further difficulties when diversionary attacks in the form of amphibious landings and long-range penetration operations behind the enemy's positions were scrapped owing to shortages of landing craft and manpower. Thus, the attack was confined to a narrow axis on which British forces faced the risk of being held up and outflanked. The campaign was nonetheless launched on the belief that the attackers could prevail with their preponderance of strength.

While the first Arakan offensive ranked as one of Britain's greatest blunders during the Far Eastern conflict, the decision has to be viewed in light of the fact that adequate precedents for determining the effort required to deal with Japanese defences were lacking. British planning for counteroffensives during the opening year of the conflict reflected the fundamental dilemma which its military planners faced. In short, estimates of the strategic situation only permitted broad conclusions concerning the challenges faced by the Allies. The most effective methods for overcoming enemy opposition could be determined only with the help of adequate firsthand combat experience.

TACTICAL AND TECHNOLOGICAL CAPABILITIES OF JAPAN'S ARMED FORCES

The efficiency demonstrated by Japan's forces during their invasion of Southeast Asia convinced the British to acknowledge their opponent's tactical skill. The failure to hold out against the IJA, IJN and Japanese air services also highlighted how British forces needed to undergo extensive improvements in order to overcome their opponent. As far as the British army in the Far East was concerned, the prevailing opinion was that its tactical skill and discipline were no match for the IJA. In regard to the Royal Navy and RAF the British realized that they could not fight properly without significant steps towards re-equipment and modernization.

Although Japan's reverses during the latter half of 1942 dispelled the contention that its armed forces were invincible, they continued to demonstrate a high level of proficiency. Assessments on Japanese capabilities urged that a considerable level of caution be exercised when engaging the enemy. Most importantly, Allied successes had been entirely in the form of limited advances by US and Australian forces in the South Pacific. Britain's forces in Southeast Asia, on the other hand, remained idle and lacked firsthand experience defeating their adversary. Consequently, while the opening year of the conflict provided reliable indications of the challenges which the British were likely to face at the battlefield level, even at the start of 1943, there remained a great deal of misunderstanding over the tactics and equipment that were needed to overcome the obstacles.

Bureaucratic obstacles also continued to hinder the intelligence machinery. The FECB was forced to relinquish responsibility for handling material on Japanese tactics and technology as its headquarters at Singapore was forced to relocate in the face of invasion, and its activities fell into disarray. The British navy, air force and army began to set up their own intelligence services in the Far East, but their development was slow. The problem stemmed from the absence of an effective staff which could fully utilize the lessons which the British had learned from their defeats. This was especially true within the army. The intelligence directorate at General Headquarters in India had focused its attention on the possibility of a German invasion via the Middle East, and did not acquire a team of Japanese specialists until autumn 1942. Whitehall carried out the bulk of the analysis and dissemination, and its staffs were removed from the front lines. As a result, Japanese capabilities were often exaggerated and weaknesses not fully appreciated.

At the level of dissemination, the more seasoned British staff officers in the Far East found it difficult to educate their subordinates on the lessons they learned, mainly because the rank and file lacked the experience needed to properly apply the information on the battlefield. True, a large number of British and Commonwealth officers who fought in Malaya and Burma ended up in captivity and were unable to share their stories. At the same time, a number of senior personnel, including Wavell and Pownall, did manage to escape. Drawing upon the information compiled from their field officers, they produced a fair number of critical accounts concerning the lessons to be learned. However, for much of 1942, the middle and lower ranks of Britain's armed forces consisted of raw recruits who had little idea of the threat which the Japanese posed, nor could they fully grasp the proper countermeasures they needed to employ. The lack of battle experience meant that the British needed to climb a difficult learning curve before they could develop the capacity to overcome their opponents.

Despite the difficulties, the aftermath of Singapore and Burma saw intelligence staffs and defence planners adopting a more judicious view of Japanese tactics. Due heed was paid to the fact that the Japanese possessed strengths which the British were yet incapable of coping with. For example, the Allies' failure to halt the Japanese amphibious landings in Southeast Asia convinced the British that their enemy exerted a threat which was not to be ignored. B.H. Ashmore, a senior commander on Percival's staff, noted how the Japanese amphibious forces at Kota Baru conducted their landings with little concern for losses, and commenced their inland advance without awaiting reinforcements. The efficiency demonstrated by Japanese amphibious methods was also acknowledged by intelligence staffs as well as the highest sections of the defence establishment. On one hand, the Japanese continued to carry out their landings against minimal resistance, and enjoyed complete security of sea communications, along with naval and air superiority. Because beach defences in Southeast Asia were often nonexistent, the IJA and IJN did not need to conduct opposed operations.

However, as far as the British were concerned, the most noteworthy fact was that Japanese forces were fully capable of achieving their objectives with remarkable efficiency. In March 1942, the War Office propagated the conclusion, 'the suitability of the Japanese landing equipment and the thoroughness of their preparations . . . largely account for the rapid attainment of the objective with small loss'. Japanese landing parties were likely to prevail in weakly protected areas, no matter how tenaciously the defenders fought. A report on the experience of American forces in the Far East in March received an 'A' grading, as it provided an accurate account of how Japanese landing operations were preceded by thorough reconnaissance of the beaches and hinterland, enabling amphibious parties to exploit weak spots while bypassing strong-points. Japanese army tactics on land forced similar reassessments. Although the IJA had not been particularly trained for operations in the jungles of Southeast Asia, its unimpeded advances proved that its infantry troops were capable of achieving a high level of mobility in undeveloped terrain. More importantly, the failure to hold out against the Japanese onslaught spawned a general consensus that British and Commonwealth armies possessed a lamentable standard of efficiency.

Experiences in Malaya and Burma proved beyond doubt the IJA's ability to outmanoeuvre British positions. In December, the War Office warned that enemy troops were capable of overcoming any natural obstacle. Scenarios of this nature quickly broke the myth that the jungle acted as a reliable barrier. The aspect which posed the greatest challenge was the IJA's practice of outflanking Allied forces by circumventing the main roads. Ten days following the Japanese landing, Brooke-Popham conceded that in light of the Japanese army's skilful manoeuvring, British forces had few choices apart from withdrawing and consolidating themselves in more tenable positions in southern Malaya. The IJA's tactical skill entailed equally slim hopes for defending Burma. Poor communications had not deterred the Japanese from launching invasions. Hutton, the GOC, concluded that given the IJA's practice of enveloping its opponents and their ability to live on the country without proper maintenance facilities, it was reasonable to assume that the enemy would 'deploy the greatest possible strength' on 'as many approaches as possible'.

Postmortems on the British defeats in Southeast Asia invariably attributed the IJA's successes to its high level of training, and credited the Japanese army as a top-rate force. Wavell cited the Japanese army's practice of fully utilizing 'the primary infantry virtues of marching and fighting', which placed 'minimum reliance on mechanized transport', as one of its key assets. H.P. Thomas, an OBE (Order of the British Empire) from the Indian Army, acknowledged, 'as an Asiatic power, maintaining European standards of efficiency, and at same time operating on Asiatic soil, the Japanese had a great initial advantage'.

The most important lesson drawn from the defeats in Malaya and Burma, however, was that the combat effectiveness of British armies was substandard. The IJA did suffer a number of weaknesses, including a lack of concern for providing reinforcements, and a tendency to underestimate enemy opposition. However, the experiences of defeat forced the British to admit that their own forces faced problems, and had yet to develop the skills needed to exploit their opponent's disadvantages. In contrast to prewar assessments which suggested that the IJA's weaknesses undermined its ability to engage its Western rivals, appraisals following the setbacks in Southeast Asia signified a realization that poorly trained armies were not a match for the IJA. For instance, the British army's traditional method of employing fixed defences was unlikely to work if the positions could be outflanked and were not held with adequate strength. The Japanese success in carrying out infiltration movements showed how the defenders needed to conduct an aggressive patrol of their surroundings, and in situations where poor communications restricted mobility, the proper use of infantry was vital. Jungle warfare was a 'matter for feet rather than wheels', and Japanese troops clearly demonstrated their skill. They wore rubber belts which could be inflated for use as river transport, and used captured bicycles for transport.

British troops, on the other hand, depended on motor transport, and hesitated to march through the jungle by foot. This characteristic rendered them incapable of countering the IJA's rapid movements. Major-General H.G. Bennett, commander of the Australian forces, alleged that British empire commanders suffered a 'retreat complex'. As a result, the slightest Japanese attack was enough to compel defenders to abandon their positions. The development of adequate countermeasures against the Japanese not only entailed an alteration of methods. Equally important was to reassess the quality of troop training within the British army. Commanders in the Far East conceded that their failures were due to a prevailing lack of discipline. Pownall pondered upon the British soldier's dependence on creature comforts and aversion to strenuous work, both of which gave rise to a situation where training was conducted without preparing troops for battle conditions. Brooke-Popham acknowledged that a key feature which enhanced the IJA's efficiency was the way in which its indoctrination programme aimed to instil sentiments of hatred for the enemy, whereas British troops were not exposed to such types of instruction.

British army commanders made urgent demands for measures to instil a more aggressive attitude among soldiers. Reflecting upon lessons drawn from encounters with the IJA, Wavell warned that British soldiers needed to overcome their fears of long periods of isolation in the jungle and the disorientation caused by the enemy's deception methods. Field commanders in the Far East insisted that troops needed to develop individual initiative. Upon taking command of the 15th Corps in autumn 1942, Slim set up a programme at his headquarters in Ranchi to train infantry units to hold their ground in the face of the enemy's encirclement and surprise tactics. The IJN's establishment of superiority in Southeast Asia and the western Pacific led to reassessments similar to those which took place regarding the IJA. Encounters in Southeast Asia provided visible proof that the technology onboard Japanese capital ships and auxiliary vessels was top quality, while training among naval crews was high.

Japanese capital ships were proficient at delivering fire over extended distances and outranging their Allied opponents. This achievement owed itself largely to the fact that for much of the interwar period, the IJN's doctrine was fixated on securing its decisive victory by fighting a surface action along the lines of Tsushima. The Gunnery and Antiaircraft Warfare Division was aware of the extensive efforts which the IJN had made to equip its fleet with improved guns and stressed that, although there was no information regarding recent progress, there was 'no reason why they [the Japanese] should not be superior' in long-range direct fire and medium-range blind fire. In light of the IJN's effective performance, the Admiralty was compelled to acknowledge the strong possibility that British vessels needed extensive modernization before they could stand up to their opponents. Capital ships had to be refitted with radio direction-finding equipment and longer-range guns if they were to possess adequate firepower and accuracy. Objections against the operation of the battleship *Malaya* with Somerville's main fleet for the defence of waters adjacent to Ceylon were based on the grounds that it possessed low endurance and limited gun range, and only the most modern ships could engage a concentration of Japanese vessels.

Naval operations also had to be undertaken by crews with adequate training. In February 1942, Somerville minuted to Pound that operations in the Far East needed to be commanded by flag officers who were well informed on gunnery matters. Assessments of Japan's air services also revealed how combat experiences provided the British with unquestionable signs that the enemy's performance posed a formidable contest. Japanese fighter aircraft demonstrated a high standard of manoeuvrability and an ability to undertake both coordinated and independent attacks against ground targets. The Air Ministry's praise for enemy fighters was clearly reflected in a report on the Zero, titled 'a formidable fighter'. The comment was based on inspections of downed aircraft, which revealed a high engine output and fuel capacity. Findings of this nature quickly dispelled the notion that the Japanese were unable to produce aircraft that could match their Western rivals.

The failure to provide adequate defences against the JAF led both intelligence staffs and air commanders to reconsider whether their opponent's weaknesses justified complacency. The Air Ministry continued to emphasize shortcomings by noting how the Japanese used a number of obsolete aircraft in Malaya. British commanders in the Far East took a less condescending view, and realized that and Allies were defenceless unless they remedied their own weaknesses, namely numerical inferiority and poor efficiency in the air. Wavell concluded that the JAF's successes in Southeast Asia were largely due to its establishment of local air superiority. While Japanese fighter aircraft raised concern, British reactions to the IJN's air arm was one of alarm. The sinking of the *Repulse* and *Prince of Wales* demonstrated the exceptional skill of Japanese torpedo bombers. Within a week after the capital ships were lost, the Air Ministry observed, 'recent spectacular results . . . indicate that intensive training and practice have been carried out'. The aircraft involved was the Mitsubishi T-96, whose aiming was described as 'very accurate'. The accuracy of Japanese attacks against naval targets also highlighted the necessity of bolstering the antiaircraft (AA) defences onboard British vessels. During the interwar period, the Admiralty did not fully grasp the extent to which aircraft could develop the range and striking power to attack capital ships in the high seas. The result was a misperception regarding the types of vessels the Royal Navy would have to operate when confronting the Japanese. Because Britain's war plans in the Far East before December 1941 had been based on the assumption that the main fleet would operate under the cover of aircraft based in the Malay peninsula, the Admiralty adhered to its belief that the battleship was the centrepiece of its strategy. As a result, little attention was paid to the need to develop carrier tactics. Experiments during the interwar period also revealed that fighters were incapable of providing full protection. Naval officers concluded that AA cover provided the most reliable defence, with supporting aircraft filling the gaps. When adequate fighter cover was unavailable, ships were vulnerable against determined attacks.

The Royal Navy's AA capabilities were further handicapped by its lack of the resources and technology needed to develop accurate fire control systems. The devastation inflicted on Force Z gave rise to a dramatic rethinking about the threat which air attacks could pose. The incident demonstrated not only that aircraft had become a highly effective naval weapon, but that the Japanese had developed it beyond all expectations. The terms of reference for the enquiry into the sinking of the *Repulse* and *Prince of Wales* explicitly stated that the main objective was to review the circumstances attending the loss of capital ships since the beginning of the war. In order to do so, it was of the utmost importance to consider the measures to be investigated or pursued, with 'the intent to improve the defense of British warships against existing or anticipated enemy weapons'. During the IJN's attacks on Ceylon in April 1942, its air arm managed to sink a number of British vessels, including the light carrier HMS *Hermes*, as well as the heavy cruisers *Dorsetshire* and *Cornwall*. The encounter reinforced British views that Japanese pilots and aircraft possessed a high standard of efficiency, while acting as a reminder that British vessels needed to be equipped with the most up-to-date radar and AA guns. Naval commanders in the Eastern Fleet were overawed by the force and precision of Japanese naval aircraft. The captain of the *Dorsetshire* was impressed with the way in which enemy pilots overcame British AA defences by exploiting blind spots. The captain of the *Hermes* commented that the attack on his ship was carried out 'perfectly, relentlessly and quite fearlessly . . . '. Within the Admiralty, opinions did not show the same level of trepidation; however, the incident reinforced the view that Japanese methods and technology were commendable. The Director of the Naval Air Division (DNAD) commented that the degree of accuracy achieved by the Japanese 'could only be obtained by highly trained personnel'. The Director of Gunnery and AA Fire (DGF) noted how ships possessing inadequate armament and lacking proper radio direction finding and gunnery ranging sets had 'little chance of survival against massed air attack'. All ships destined for the Far East had to be equipped with the most updated material before setting off.

At the same time, efforts to provide adequate protection for seagoing vessels were complicated because British fighters such as the *Seafire* were too heavy for carrier-based operations, while the performance of aircraft with lighter designs such as the *Hurricane* could not compete with the Zero. The production of the *Barracuda* fighter, which had the right combination of speed, manoeuvrability and weight, had faced delays. Upon realizing that the British did not possess adequate fighters, Churchill lodged urgent requests to Roosevelt for the loan of suitable American aircraft. The JAF's demonstration of its capabilities was not only taken as a reason to reassess the enemy. More importantly, the British realized that their forces were in need of extensive improvement.

The turn of the tide against Japan's armed forces during the latter half of 1942 dispelled apprehensions insofar as to prove that the enemy could be defeated at the tactical level. The IJA, IJN and air services continued to demonstrate skills that urged wariness. In addition, because the Allies had yet to acquire sufficient experience, precedents for gauging the effort required for success were patchy. To further complicate matters, British forces in Southeast Asia remained largely inactive for the latter part of 1942. Intelligence was thus mainly derived from reports on US and Australian operations in the Pacific theatres. The information did not permit accurate appraisals as to whether the British had developed the capabilities necessary to confront their opponent. Assessments on the matter revealed continued unease as well as a lack of understanding of the appropriate methods for defeating the Japanese.

On the ground, the Allied successes in New Guinea and the Solomons during autumn 1942 proved that the IJA was not invincible. However, in both offensive and defensive operations, its performance continued to reveal competence. Accounts of US and Australian encounters in the South Pacific urged due caution.

In the South Pacific, the IJA continued to demonstrate their proficiency, while US ground forces were 'poorly prepared for what they had to face'. American soldiers, while high in morale, were not trained to conduct the battles of attrition they faced at Guadalcanal and New Guinea. Although Australian soldiers were trained by officers who had battlefield experience from the 1914–1918 conflict, their performance showed room for improvement.

The Japanese army's offensive operations continued to demonstrate their expertise at surprise moves. Engagements on the Kokoda Trail in New Guinea showed the enemy's adeptness at deploying infiltrators to encircle Allied positions, often using jungle cover to conceal their presence so that the defenders could not notice. At the same time, Allied troops proved highly adaptable, and displayed ingenuity. The Americans and Australians managed to repel their attackers with increased frequency. Intelligence bulletins and field manuals thereafter highlighted a number of Japanese weaknesses that could be exploited. The War Office concluded that although enemy soldiers were skilful at conducting surprise moves, their success depended on catching opponents off guard. A chapter in the *Handbook of the Japanese Army* (*HJA*) in December 1942 pointed out that the tenacity with which the Japanese conducted their envelopment tactics frequently gave false impressions of their strength, and enabled the attackers to overcome considerably larger forces than their own. Combat experience also revealed that so long as the defending forces undertook a number of basic countermeasures, Japanese assaults could be repelled. A meticulous reconnaissance of the environs was important. At Milne Bay, US marines deployed scouts against enemy night attacks. The parties prepared to meet the Japanese onslaught, and the ensuing encounter often threw the enemy off balance. Such developments dispelled the view that Japanese forces were formidable in the attack.

However, British forces had yet to prove their capabilities, and needed to practice due caution against the obstacles likely to be encountered. A chapter in the *HJA*, based on observations in New Guinea and Guadalcanal, summed up the situation: 'Defense against Japanese attacks must be principally against infiltration. It must be organized with strong points properly adapted to terrain features. If possible, they should [provide] all round defense'.

Positions had to be protected with barbed wire and landmines, while intervals were to be covered by strong automatic fire. Most importantly, defending troops needed to fight without becoming panic stricken by enemy attacks. Evidence of the IJA's weaknesses therefore did not obscure the arduous effort required to defeat it.

Intelligence on the IJA's defensive capabilities gave equally few reasons to alleviate images of a resilient opponent. Allied encounters during the Solomons campaign quickly disproved the preconception that the IJA's lack of experience rendered its defensive operations ineffective. Experiences in the SWPA gave rise to the conclusion that the Japanese army was capable of inflicting significant delay and attrition on its attackers. Positions were made to provide all-round fields of fire and maximum protection from bombardment. Defences were laid out so as to create systems of mutually supporting bunkers, using whatever materials were available. The War Office disseminated an account of enemy fortifications at Buna and Sanananda in New Guinea, describing them as 'simple, but effective'. Significantly enough, without visible indications of deficiencies open to exploitation, assessments focused on the obstacles arising from the IJA's proficiency. For example, JIC appreciations and intelligence bulletins reinforced the contention that the IJA was a difficult adversary, regardless of whether the Allies achieved numerical superiority.

A section in the *Handbook of the Japanese Army* in February 1943 exhaustively described how experiences in the Pacific had highlighted the need for thorough preparations against camouflage, surprise methods, counterattacks and defences prepared in depth. For British field commanders, the absence of sufficient combat experience tended to result in a misperception of how to surmount the challenges, in spite of their awareness that Japanese defences were difficult to reduce. After the Eastern Army was established in autumn 1942, field officers attempted to learn how to overcome the IJA, but their efforts encountered a number of initial setbacks. The problem stemmed from a habit which prevailed within the British Army, namely an undue dependence upon overwhelming firepower to neutralize enemy forces. The practice was a byproduct of the carnage suffered in the trenches on the Western Front during the Great War, which gave rise to an accepted belief that assaults against prepared positions could only result in mass casualties.

While the doctrine of relying upon heavy weaponry aimed to avoid excessive losses, it had the unfortunate result of rendering British commanders slow to grasp the need to fight a combined arms battle, which was crucial when engaging a well-entrenched opponent. Enemy defences needed to be neutralized through a combination of artillery fire, aerial bombardment and armoured attacks, while ground troops mopped up the remnants of enemy resistance. The Eastern Army was certainly not alone in facing difficulties in scaling the tactical learning curve. Following the defeat at Dunkirk, British field officers in the home army and North Africa upheld the belief that heavy weaponry alone could overcome the Germans, and the misunderstanding resulted in further setbacks during the early phases of the desert campaign. Indeed, one of the British Army's greatest shortcomings during its campaigns against the *Wehrmacht* was the absence of a uniform doctrine for combined arms tactics. Infantry units suffered excessive casualties because they were not trained to manoeuvre against enemy positions unless the defending forces had been completely neutralized.

Although British forces in the Far East eventually achieved a higher standard of efficiency than their counterparts in Europe and

North Africa, the Eastern Army's experience during the opening stages of the Burma campaign reveals parallels. While the defeats in Malaya and Burma exposed the deficiencies British armies had suffered in defensive operations, precedents for planning counteroffensives against the IJA were nonexistent.

The Japanese invasion of Malaya and Burma clearly highlighted how the skilful use of infantry often had a decisive effect on the outcome of battles in jungle conditions, where poor communications and the prevalence of natural obstacles restricted the use of heavy weapons. However, appreciations on the lessons to be drawn from the Allied setbacks were prepared at a time when Britain's immediate objective was to forestall further Japanese advances. Even in the autumn of 1942, when British forces began to recover from the shock brought about by their defeats, commanders had not had enough time to come to grips with the lessons to be drawn from the IJA's operations.

The situation was further complicated by a lack of experience involving operations in jungle terrain, which in turn created difficulties in grasping the methods which the British needed to employ. Throughout the interwar period, the garrison in India remained committed to its traditional role of acting as a police force against local disturbances in areas such as the Northwest Frontier. Training was focused on mountain warfare against weakly defended guerrilla forces. Insofar as foreign invasions were concerned, the scenarios which raised the most concern were a German or Soviet advance via Afghanistan and Persia. Consequently, minimal efforts were made to prepare troops for operations in the jungles of Burma. British field officers were thus forced to concoct tactics for unfamiliar battlefield conditions. Any lessons which staff officers did learn from the early phases of the war were not enforced upon troops. The Directorate of Military Training did not commence creating a uniform doctrine in its manuals until autumn 1942. The absence of communication between the SWPA and India regarding the lessons that had been obtained during operations in New Guinea and the Solomons also negated the prospects of obtaining the necessary information.

The tactics employed during the first Arakan campaign of winter 1942– 1943 illustrated the dilemmas facing the British. While army commanders were aware of the dangers posed by the IJA's resilience, they did not comprehend the necessary countermeasures. The Eastern Army's decision to advance down the Mayu Peninsula in November 1942 was made on the assumption that the Japanese soldier's tenacity could be overcome by artillery fire and tank support. The stalling of the advance at Donbaik and Rathedaung during early January 1943 revealed how Japanese bunkers were impervious to bombardment. Following this, Wavell ordered Noel Irwin, the GOC of the Eastern Army, to launch a second attack on the peninsula, on the assumption that with a fresh British brigade and improved covering fire, enemy defences could be neutralized. Irwin and Lloyd, the GOC 14th Indian Division, executed the operation on the same conjecture.

That British commanders based their plans on a faulty understanding of the tactics necessary to defeat the IJA, rather than an ignorance of the challenges their troops faced, is also illustrated by documentary evidence. In their correspondence between January and March 1943, Wavell and Irwin clearly stated that one of the main purposes of the operation was to acquire valuable experience of Japanese methods, which could allow for future successes. Reminiscing upon the first Arakan campaign, Wavell admitted that while the difficulties of launching the operations without properly trained troops had been realized, he miscalculated how numerical superiority and a rapid advance could help his forces attain their objectives. The decisions leading up to the first Arakan offensive therefore illuminate how evidence pointing to the IJA's strengths could rarely provide accurate information on how to defeat the enemy. In the absence of combat experience, the evidence was open to various interpretations. The development of appropriate methods could take place only through experimentation.

In regard to the IJN, the shortage of information, compounded by the Eastern Fleet's lack of engagements, rendered accurate assessments virtually impossible. Naval intelligence continued to be a grey area. As late as December 1942, evidence was obtained primarily from US sources, which provided little beyond rough figures on Japan's naval construction. The shortage of reliable intelligence precluded accurate estimates. For example, when Churchill ordered an enquiry into the reasons why Japanese carriers were able to hold more aircraft than their British counterparts, Pound was unable to go further than to suggest that the actual tonnage was probably greater than disclosed. The situation was further complicated because of the continued shortage of firsthand encounters between the Royal Navy and the IJN. An example of this dilemma arose in June, when the Admiralty disseminated possible methods of countering enemy submarines. The recommendations were accompanied by what amounted to a disclaimer that the report represented only the opinion of US commanders. In the absence of combat experience, the available intelligence could not provide a clear picture of the IJN's capabilities against its British counterpart. Naval intelligence staffs hesitated to suggest that Japanese vessels possessed shortcomings open to exploitation, and were more likely to highlight evidence of the IJN's proficiency.

In the air, as late as the end of 1942, the available intelligence was thin on signs of weaknesses likely to hamper the JAF's ability to challenge its British counterparts. Owing to the RAF's relative inactivity following the defeats in Southeast Asia, information was primarily derived from accounts of Allied operations in the Pacific. Accurate evaluations continued to be hindered by the lack of data. Information on crucial aspects, such as the production of new prototypes, was scanty. Optimism was further precluded by continued indications that Japanese pilots and aircraft were capable of putting up a serious challenge. Commenting on the Battle of Midway, the DNAD noted how American fighters were particularly vulnerable owing to their practice of conducting individual attacks on enemy bombers. This practice enabled the Zero pilots to take advantage of their aircraft's manoeuvrability, and pursue planes flying out of formation.

When the Allies began to bolster their airpower in the South Pacific during autumn 1942, they did not immediately establish air superiority. According to Eric Bergerud, 'for most of the time between spring 1942 and winter 1943–1944, neither side was completely dominant'.

Because the topof- the-line US fighters were dispatched to Europe and North Africa, Allied air forces in the Pacific consisted mainly of P-39s, whose manoeuvrability, range and speed were inferior to the Zero. Only when the more advanced fighters of the US air fleet, such as the F4F *Wildcat*, P-51 *Mustang*, P-47 *Thunderbolt* and *Corsair*, were dispatched to the South Pacific in large numbers during late 1942, did the balance begin to gradually shift against the Japanese. The situation demanded due caution in assessing enemy capabilities. In December, the Air Ministry propagated an account of US encounters in Guadalcanal. US aircraft 'could not stay with [the Zero] at all and dog fight at any altitude'. Japanese pilots were highly trained, and aircraft output had kept pace with losses. The only source of comfort was that intensified battles were likely to take a heavier toll on the enemy.

The RAF's ability to confront its Japanese counterpart was also questionable. In the absence of significant successes, the most notable feature was likely to be the high level of efficiency the enemy had demonstrated during the onset of the conflict. Pilots arriving in the Far East were inducted with tales by veterans who had confronted the JAF in the skies over Malaya, Burma and Ceylon. They almost invariably emphasized how enemy aircraft were manoeuvrable, and described Japanese tactics as 'excellent'. Any indications of the JAF's weaknesses had to be viewed alongside the fact that British pilots and aircraft in the Far Eastern theatres had yet to equal their opponent.

MORALE AND MATERIEL

The available intelligence on the morale and economic strengths of Japan's war machine was replete of indications that the enemy suffered deficiencies that would hinder its effort, at least for the first half of 1942. On the contrary, intelligence on the Japanese soldiers' fighting spirit revealed their exceptional dedication and stamina. Economic intelligence showed how Japan's conquest of Southeast Asia provided ample supplies of raw materials.

The situation was further complicated because the enemy's morale and war economy did not permit easy exploitation. Although Allied encounters in the Pacific theatres during late 1942 revealed that the Japanese soldier's morale tended to deteriorate in the face of adversity, his will to continue fighting remained unbroken in the absence of overwhelming defeats. Japan's difficulties in maintaining adequate production did not negate the fact that its war economy was unscathed without substantial attacks on its infrastructure. Most importantly, the Allies did not have precedents for assessing the possible effects of psychological and economic warfare against the Japanese. The only certain conclusion was that strategies such as the use of propaganda to erode military morale, and launching attacks against the enemy's economic infrastructure, were unlikely to suffice in defeating the enemy. The Allies could win only by destroying Japan's armed forces, and psychological and economic warfare had to complement rather than substitute operations on the battlefield.

The performance of Japanese troops during their campaigns in Southeast Asia demonstrated their exceptional endurance. Whereas prewar assessments focused on indications of the IJA's poor discipline during its operations in China, the tenacity which enemy soldiers showed in Southeast Asia eliminated all disdain. By the middle of 1942, the British already began producing a more objective picture of Japanese army morale. If assessments were distorted in any way, it was mainly because they tended to overlook the fact that the Japanese soldier's psyche possessed shortcomings. This was natural in light of the overwhelming efficiency which the Japanese had demonstrated. The IJA's operations in Southeast Asia during early 1942 highlighted a number of its characteristics. Action reports from Malaya and Burma conceded that, while the Japanese army's successes in Southeast Asia could be attributed to skilled planning and tactical skill, the morale of its soldiers was a key factor which upheld the momentum of their advance. The Japanese soldier's fighting spirit derived largely from his high discipline.

This feature, in turn, was deeply embedded in Japanese traditions which demanded respect for one's duty to his nation and people. Wavell concluded that while the ragged attire of Japanese troops and their thuggish behaviour towards civilians were definite indications of sloppiness, their respect for authority was commendable. Wavell's admiration for these aspects was illustrated by his observation:

> . . . customary behavior such as saluting between superiors and subordinates is still rigidly maintained. Inter-unit rivalry and any other manifestations of competitive spirit is discouraged and virtually nonexistent. A strong army tradition, based on loyalty towards the Emperor, and an offensive spirit exists, and is the basis of morale. No inducements such as high pay and good food is ever offered, and . . . hard living is enforced as good for morale and discipline.

The Japanese soldier's willingness to maintain the offensive against all obstacles also rendered him a formidable opponent. Hutton noted that the cause for the IJA's victory lay not only in its skill in jungle warfare. The fundamental cause was the extent to which the enemy had been imbued with the offensive spirit. The middle- and lower-ranking officers in the British army, who bore the brunt of the fighting, tended to pay attention to the contrasting levels of fighting spirit between Japanese and British Empire troops, the latter who held a passive attitude towards their enemy. As the campaigns in Malaya and Burma progressed and the Japanese achieved a spate of unbroken advances, the British were overtaken by defeatism.

The gap in morale grew wider, thereby adding to the advantages already enjoyed by the IJA. Colonel Stewart of the Argyll and Sutherland Highlanders conceded, 'emotional coldness made British troops slow and cautious against an eager enemy who were aggressive and fast'. An officer who participated in the Malaya campaign, from the time of the landings at Kota Baru to the fall of Singapore, noted that one of the fatal flaws of British and Commonwealth troops was their tendency to panic when faced with heavy bombardment. The image of the Japanese soldier's exceptional level of morale was upheld by the tide of the war, which clearly stood in Japan's favour during the first half of 1942. This meant that the enemy's will to continue fighting was likely to remain intact. Under the circumstances, it was difficult to depart from the view that the IJA's morale rendered it a formidable opponent. Observations of the Allied counteroffensives in the Pacific theatres in autumn 1942 revealed how the IJA's morale was liable to certain levels of deterioration in the face of setbacks. The material dispelled the widespread notion that the Japanese soldier's threshold of pain knew no limits. At the same time, the available intelligence did not provide signs that the enemy suffered peculiar weaknesses. For example, Japanese troops demonstrated their tendency to suffer depression when faced with food shortages. The Allied attacks on Japanese convoys during the Guadalcanal campaign prevented the IJA from obtaining supplies, and on a number of occasions, its performance was affected. Captured diaries revealed that many Japanese units were subsisting on jungle vegetation. In November 1942, the SIS, basing its findings on an article written by the IJA's board on military education, reported that as early as July, supply shortages had caused malnutrition and with it, anxiety. In some cases, unit cohesion had deteriorated, with troops disobeying orders. However, the evidence was not treated as a sign that the IJA was suffering war-weariness. Commenting on the SIS findings, MI2 warned that similar pieces of evidence had been received, but these symptoms were 'local and of no consequence'. The evidence went no further than to suggest that the IJA's morale was suffering the same damage as any army facing similar situations.

Intelligence obtained from Guadalcanal also revealed that Japanese troops who had faced defeat against Allied forces had suffered demoralization. Captured diaries revealed how the IJN's failure to provide naval and air support after November, when the Allies gained control of the surrounding waters and airspace, had led troops to lose their will to advance against the US marines, and created a suspicion that the navy had abandoned the army. The increasing strength of the Allied garrison also led Japanese troops to abandon some of their operations. In January 1943, the War Office noted how a second lieutenant at Guadalcanal had resisted orders to stage a night attack, and commented, 'it is heartening to see that Japanese disobedience of orders is being successfully carried out'. However, the evidence simply demonstrated that the enemy was not invincible, and was not treated as an indication that the morale of Japanese soldiers was prone to abnormal levels of demoralization.

The Japanese soldier's vulnerabilities also had to be assessed while bearing in mind that even the most overwhelming odds were unlikely to compel him to surrender. The IJA's tenacity created images of an enemy whose morale immeasurably enhanced its defensive capabilities. In December, the War Office warned that, while the IJA was materially inferior to its Western opponents, 'the core of [Japanese] military strength is unquestionably [its] high morale and plentiful supply of tough and hardy soldiers'. The JIC concluded that the Japanese soldier's aptitude in jungle and amphibious warfare, combined with their offensive spirit, meant that in conditions of its own choosing in Southeast Asia, the Japanese army was 'the most formidable in the world'. Combat experience in the Pacific theatres revealed an aspect which entailed one of the greatest challenges for the Allies, namely, the IJA's institutionalized belief that surrender entailed social ostracization. The first implication of this attitude was that operations against Japanese armies were likely to see the enemy fighting to the last man and round, thereby requiring British and US forces to conduct laborious mopping-up operations. The second implication was that POWs were likely to be rare, and as a result, opportunities to obtain information from this source were low. While the IJA's reverses proved that it was not the undefeatable enemy portrayed during the opening stages of the conflict, due attention was be paid to the fact that the Japanese soldier's psychological strengths entailed additional obstacles for any Allied campaign.

While the opening year of the conflict highlighted the strengths and weaknesses of the IJA's morale, assessments on the potential means to exploit the Japanese soldier's vulnerabilities through propaganda and psychological warfare (psywar) remained a matter for conjecture. Until the Far Eastern conflict broke out, British propaganda operations had been concentrated on Germany, and the possibility of waging psywar against Japan received minimal consideration. The organization responsible for planning and executing psywar operations was the Political Warfare Executive (PWE), which had been set up under the Foreign Office's auspices in August 1941. The executive was an amalgamation of the overseas propaganda sections of the SOE and the Ministry of Information (MOI), and worked under the Foreign Office's supervision. The PWE also maintained liaisons with the service ministries and Cabinet to ensure that its activities accorded with British policy.

The main problem concerning psywar operations against Japan's armed forces was the absence of precedents for gauging the potential effects. The only certain conclusion was that weaknesses in the IJA's morale provided opportunities for exploitation. For example, in May, the MOI suggested that as the tide of the war turned in Asia and the Pacific, enemy troops would become vulnerable. Among the themes that could be played upon were the overstretching of Japan's armies, and its inability to match Allied industrial production. However, the paper did not venture to forecast the way in which propaganda could damage the IJA's fighting capabilities. Similarly, the PWE could only conclude that one of the Japanese soldier's key weaknesses was his dependence on orders from higher authority and inability to act on his own initiative. British intelligence staffs and propaganda organizations were reluctant to arrive at conclusions that were not based on factual evidence. The tide of the war had to turn significantly further against Japan before the potential damage could be knowledgeably calculated.

Economic intelligence did not provide reasons to expect a deterioration in Japan's war capabilities during the opening year of the conflict. Although accurate information was scarce, Japan's acquisition of new resources in Southeast Asia laid reasonable grounds for concluding that its war economy had achieved self-sufficiency in most categories of vital raw materials. The JIC appreciation on Axis strengths prepared in February warned that while the extension of its scope of operations had forced Japan to draw upon its stockpiles, its conquests in Southeast Asia had 'materially improved her position in respect of many important commodities'. Most importantly, material shortages were not a solid indication that Japan's war effort was likely to suffer in the immediate future. The only certain conclusion was that the enemy could not outproduce the Allies in the long run. In May 1942, the MEW conceded that while Japan's capacity for steel production was relatively low, there was 'no reason to assume that [Japan's] industry [was incapable] of maintaining and perhaps slightly expanding its potential'.

Evidence of economic weaknesses also did not permit exact calculations of the extent to which Japan's industries were struggling to meet its requirements. For example, intelligence on shipping shortages did not provide accurate figures concerning Japan's ability to obtain adequate raw materials. Signals intelligence simply indicated that the shipbuilding industry was facing difficulties in keeping pace with demand, and the government was expressing anxieties. Assessments on the situation could rarely go further than to state that Japan's war production hinged upon its ability to maintain its lifeline between the home islands and Southeast Asia. The MEW concluded that because the bulk of the oil obtained in the Dutch East Indies had to be transported back to Japan to be properly refined, extensive tanker sinkings were likely to result in a corresponding decline of stocks. In summer 1944, the JIC prepared an assessment in conjunction with the MEW, admittedly based on 'temporary estimates'.

The evidence pointing to the deficiencies of Japan's productive plant was equally replete of reliable data. Japan's aircraft industry was an aspect which attracted the most attention. The available information only revealed that productivity was low by Western standards. During summer 1942, the Air Ministry went no further than to suggest that wastage was in excess of production. To provide a key example of the extent to which estimates were based on guesswork, in April, the MEW and Air Ministry conducted a joint effort to examine a list of figures on Japanese aircraft production which had been received by the *Manchester Guardian*, suggesting that the industries had increased output by up to 260 per cent between 1938 and 1941. The MEW and Air Ministry agreed that the figures were excessive, and that Japan's industries were incapable of such production increases. However, at the same time, Portal admitted that evidence was 'too scanty to allow an accurate estimate', and provided a wide margin of 5,400 to 7,800 aircraft per annum. In the absence of accurate intelligence, assessments on Japan's war production capabilities were unlikely to predict whether output was likely to increase or to slow down. Assessments of Japan's economic situation also had to take into account the fact that the Allies were unable to exploit the enemy's difficulties for the time being. Until adequate forces and bases could be developed, efforts to inflict damage on Japan's productive capacity were unlikely to succeed. The Future Planning Section (FPS) concluded that Japan's economy possessed vulnerable targets in the form of compact areas in the home islands in which a disproportionately high percentage of its industrial production was concentrated.

In addition, the bulk of Japan's raw materials travelled along extended sea communications that were exposed to interdiction. However, before attempting to sever the links between Japan and the East Indian archipelago, the Allies had to acquire submarine bases in the western Pacific. Evidence of Japan's vulnerability to economic warfare was therefore of limited value unless the Allies possessed sufficient forces with which to capitalize on the situation.

In addition, the absence of adequate precedents meant that the effects of economic warfare remained a matter for speculation. The failure of the Allied bombing effort to disrupt Germany's war production, as well as the failure of the U-boat offensive to cripple Britain's lifelines, provided grounds for predicting that economic warfare was unlikely to yield any substantial results when employed against Japan. In their comments on the JPS's evaluation of the war against Japan, MO1a went as far as to conclude, 'it is not now accepted that [the bombing of industrial targets] alone can prevent Germany from continuing the war, and it seems illogical to think that it can work against Japan'. In the absence of tangible evidence that economic warfare had caused serious damage to the enemy's war effort, its potential value in the war against Japan was open to doubt.

BIBLIOGRAPHY

Arend, A.: *International Law and the Use of Force*, London, Routledge, 1993.

Bellamy, C.: *Knights in White Armour: The New Art of War and Peace*, London, Random House, 1997.

Chandra, R.: *Judicial System in Mechanical Warfare*, Lucknow, Print House (India), 1992.

Davies .A.: *Telecommunications and Politics*. The Secentralised Alternative, London, Pinter, 1994.

Friedman, G.: *The Future of War: Power, Technology and Western Military*, N.Y., Random House, 1996.

Heimanson, Rudolph: *Dictionary of Military*, N.Y.: Oceana Publications, 1967.

Huntington, S.P.: *The Soldier and the State*, N.Y., Vintage Books, 1964.

Jones, W.H.: *Politics of Military*, London, Hutchinson, 1971.

Mary, W.: *Military Space Force: the Cultural Dimensions of Authority*, Cambridge, Belknap Press, 1985.

Posen, B.R.: *The Sources of Military Doctrine*, Ithaca, 1984, Cornell Univ. Press.

Peterson, B.R.: *The Sources of Military Space Force*, Cornell Univ. Press.

Rosen, P.: *Societies and Military Power: India and its Armies*, Ithaca, Cornell University Press, 1996.

Simon, D. : *Societies and Military Power*, Ithaca, Cornell University Press, 1996.

Index

□□□